Not Going Gently

Yvonne Wright

Further Thought Publishing
Inkpen, Berkshire

First published in Great Britain 2018 by Further Thought Publishing

© Yvonne Wright

The moral right of the author has been asserted.

ISBN 978-0-951-8771-8-0

British Library Cataloguing in Publication Data – a catalogue record for this book is available from The British Library.

For 'The Captain'

Who through all the difficulties in his life has continued to be an adventurous, humorous and well-loved companion during our many years together.

4

Introduction

This book is not a diary: the story of Humph is taken from the log we kept of our journey, and the stories of Mr Bean and Koopman Welvaren V are taken from letters I wrote to friends about our experiences on the canals of France, Belgium and Holland. The book is not an accurate geographical record; for me, it is not where we are that is important: I am interested in making a record of our reactions to events as we perceive them at the time. In my work as a psychiatric nurse I have always been interested in how a client's perception of a situation affects their behaviour and where the origin of that perception lies.

Our first boat, Humph, had been a tug in the port of Hull in the distant past. The second boat, Mr Bean, was a standard narrow boat that had been built for the previous owners. Koopman Welvaren V had started his boating life carrying milk, calves and cheese from the farms around Amsterdam into the city markets. Koopman was small for a Dutch boat but seemed large to us when we bought him. Usually boats are feminine but all our boats have had male names, so I refer to them as "he".

I was surprised that most of my friends had kept the letters, some of them for years, and as the time approached for me to retire "properly", unbeknown to each other, many of them gave me the letters back, urging me to "put them in a book".

The period the letters covered was ten years and three boats, from raw novices based on the South Yorkshire Navigation Canal, to experienced boaters. Looking back, it is difficult for me to believe that we were so ill informed before we set off, both in England and on the Continent. I, for example, did not realise how low and dark the canal tunnels were. In England, by the time electric light had become available the canals were already in commercial decline, so canal boaters were left in the dark. Colin, my husband, handyman, engine mariniser and Captain, lost a stone and a half on our first trip, as he was not aware for most of the voyage how shallow the canals outside our region were. Colin has a "wooden" leg, a result of a road traffic accident twenty years ago, and he told me he was secretly dreading having to swim for the bank. My husband was amazed when talking to a passing swimmer on the Oxford Canal: the man stood up and the water only came up to his waist. I was equally amazed – at Colin's lack of knowledge: even I knew most canals were very shallow; that's why we have flat-bottomed boats.

Almost as important as the events and what, according to my friends, made the letters amusing was what was going on in our heads at the time. As well as reprinting some of my letters verbatim, there will be some scene-setting in terms of our expectations and reactions to the reality of the position we were in. Furthermore, on all our voyages we met people who have experienced similar joys and disasters, and with whom we have spent many a happy hour reminiscing over cups of tea or, as in France, a glass of wine, so I have no hesitation in including in these memoirs a colourful cast of characters besides our family, the boats and the two dogs.

I'm very grateful to Doug Lawrence for the cartoons which beautifully capture the spirit of our times on the water and to Roger Titford who has attempted editorially to knock this ship into shape.

Yvonne Wright, January 2018

CONTENTS

BOOK ONE – HUMPH

BOOK TWO – Mr BEAN

BOOK THREE – FRANCE AGAIN

BOOK FOUR – KOOPMAN WELVAREN V

BOOK FIVE – BELGIUM AND HOLLAND

BOOK ONE - HUMPH

Chapter 1

Enter the dream

I'm going to run away on one of them
Not without me

On a bright spring morning in 1980, my husband Colin and I sat on the canal bank at Thorne, in retreat from yet another family crisis: it was my fortieth birthday. We sat there idly watching the boats go by while our teenage boys caused angst, as all teenagers do. "I feel like running away on one of those boats," I said. "Not without me you're not," Colin replied. "It's teenagers who are supposed to do the home leaving," I pointed out. "Our lot are too well fed for that," their disenchanted father grumbled. Reluctantly we made our way home.

Colin and I have now been married for over fifty years. We are both strong-willed and stubborn and it never ceases to amaze me that we have stayed together for so long. Perhaps part of the secret is that for many years we had different interests and work.

We also had six children: five boys – Steve, David, Iain, Andrew and Peter – and one girl, Sally. Sally, the eldest, was ten when the youngest, Peter, was born. For many years I stayed at home and looked after our family while Colin worked in the power industry and on our three-quarter-acre garden plot growing vegetables and soft fruit. Colin also bred and reared chickens and goats, although despite repeated attempts, he never managed to kill a chicken for the pot. I lost count of the number of times we had beans on toast for Sunday dinner as a cockerel lived to crow another day. As the children grew up I "discovered my brain" and went back to school to get the necessary qualifications to get a "proper" job. That first job was as a part-time doctor's receptionist. During my first week, Colin was knocked off his motorbike and was in hospital for the next six months. The result of the accident was that, after many months of trying to save his foot, he had a below-right-knee amputation. Colin also sustained permanent injury to his right arm, which was now fixed at a right angle, the result of the elbow joint being knocked off by the car as it hit him. The rotational movement in his right arm is only about forty degrees.

Thus, in 1980 my husband was medically retired and I started full-time work, in effect swapping roles. (For two "Andy Capps", this was very difficult, and to my disappointment Colin proved adept at looking after us all.)

My second job was in newspaper office, as a Classified Advertising Supervisor. In this world, I found it hard to accept the sex discrimination which meant I was earning a third of what the men were for more responsibility; I also found that the men I worked with treated the women with a lot less respect than I was used to. Hence, in 1983 I decided to change direction and began training to be a psychiatric nurse. I would like to say I had a vocation but the truth was that first and foremost I needed equal respect and equal money. After I qualified in 1986 I continued training and eventually became a play therapist, working with behaviourally and emotionally disturbed children. I became very successful in my career but at heart neither I nor Colin could quite accept our changed roles. Often our children would be called in to referee heated debates, as I told him how to look after the family and he told me how to cope with the world of work.

In 1983, just as I started my nurse's training, we moved away from the house with the large garden and rescued an elegant but decrepit old house, complete with workshops, on the main road in the next village. Although Colin's movements were restricted, he had adapted to his disability and was able to do many of the activities he had done before. He and the boys were kept very busy rescuing the house, and as soon as it was finished, our daughter and her family came home from South Africa, so that for a while there were fifteen of us living there. Gradually, though, the house emptied, and the pressure on Colin to feed the family lessened. And it was then that I saw the advertisement for the boat, and, as I thought, another rescue project for him.

We both remembered that day in Thorne when we had felt like running away. Now, in 1983, the worst of our children's adolescent problems were over, and hence buying a boat didn't mean we were running away from our problems: by restoring and then sailing on Humph we were simply embarking on an adventure. What we did not realise at the time was that our expectations of the adventure were in many respects very different. I imagined sailing away into the sunset, whereas for the handyman sailing anywhere was a long way off. First there was the excitement of restoring the boat to its former self.

I realise now, how the experience of the restoration and the eventual cruising on all three boats highlighted the differences in our personalities and brought a whole different dimension to our relationship. Alongside the adventures we had with the boat, we had the adventure of coming to terms with a new relationship between two people who had known each other for most of their adult lives. When eventually we did set sail, we had been married forty years, and thought we knew each other.

For Colin, messing about on the river meant memories of building log rafts on the River Don, and walking underwater with a straw in his mouth, attempting to be invisible. He also remembered slapping mud all over his body, letting it dry, and then scaring passers-by, approaching them with the gait of Frankenstein's monster. All this fun was had at a time when the River Don was one of the most polluted rivers in the world. As well as messing about in the river as a child, Colin also firmly believed he could fly, having escaped unscathed after jumping out of Hodgeson's oak tree, arms akimbo, landing up to his waist in a very old and well-nigh decomposed potato pie. Being scrubbed clean of the stinking slime in an old tin bath by his mother in the yard did not lessen his pride in his achievement. Even the motorcycle accident did not dent Colin's belief in his own invincibility, and in my opinion, even with one leg he is more agile than most men I know. Two weeks after the amputation, Colin was out of hospital. A week after that, he was found by the works nurse on a home visit up a ladder dismantling the greenhouse.

My own childhood was very different, although we were both children of elderly parents. Even as an adult my parents would only fill my teacup halfway, "in case you drop it", and if I ever as a child attempted to climb a wall, the grown-ups would react with panic. Consequently, I have become quite clumsy and fearful. On top of all this, the good fairy gifted me with an over-active "we are doomed" type of imagination. As a girl I did not laugh at Hancock: I knew where he was coming from. In my family there was only a younger brother and myself. My father was a totally impractical office worker, my mother the DIY expert, seamstress and homemaker. There were eight children in Colin's family, and all five boys were very practical and skilled at engineering and carpentry. Colin was not brought up to be the tender plant I was; emotionally, he is much tougher. Mistakes, for him, if they don't kill you, are something to be learned from and not a disaster.

When we first saw Humph, he was in a field, resting on six oil drums, behind a small council estate. The boat was half full of water. The chap who was selling Humph told Colin that the boat had travelled more miles on the road than on the water having been owned by four men who were "gunners": great at dismantling but no idea how to make the boat canal-worthy. Colin felt sorry for Humph, and determined to put him back together (I was not aware of these thoughts until much later, and I now realise that Colin "feeling sorry" for engines spells trouble . . .).

"I can do great things with that..."
" Well if you say so..." (thank God it's only £1000)

13

What *I* saw was the perfect little narrow boat; just a quick reassembly job and off we could go into the sunset. My eagerness to have the boat caused me so much anxiety that I could not bear to be part of the buying process: Colin is known for driving a hard bargain, and I felt that, at eleven hundred pounds, the boat was very cheap – we had thought the price a misprint for eleven *thousand*. I felt we should give the man the money and go before he realised his mistake. From a distance I could hear Colin's voice as he haggled. Eventually he came and told me he had bought Humph for a thousand pounds. I was ecstatic, thinking that we would be sailing away in a month or so.

But my dreams were shattered as Colin began to dismantle the boat, now on oil drums at the top of the gently sloping drive beside our house. (The garage owner over the road lived in constant fear that, as result of all the banging and grinding, the boat would sail across the main road and into his premises one day.) Altogether, it was eight years, two houses and three retirements before I finally pushed Colin into committing himself to a cruise. Colin imagined sailing down the canal for a few miles and back, just to give the engine a bit of excitement, but I had other ideas. I had waited long enough, and booked us in for the Inland Waterways boat rally at Henley.

Humph became a flight of Colin the handyman's imagination. Originally a tug boat in the port of Hull, Humph was 24ft long and 6ft 6in wide. When we bought him he had a leaky fibreglass top and a load of spare parts, and to me looked fantastic and very "boaty". Over the years, Colin stripped the fibreglass and ground the metal until only the hull and propeller shaft were left of the original boat. In place of the fibreglass top, Colin built sides of cedar wood planks with sliding mahogany windows, two on each side, and a larger one at the bow that could be used as an escape route. The roof was curved wood covered in green sealed canvas. We later realised that Colin had unconsciously got the idea for the superstructure from an old wooden road-worker's caravan abandoned in a farmer's field that we used to pass every day. A special feature of the boat was the internal wall on which were the height markers and ages of our grandchildren; Richard, who was to accompany us on part of our first voyage, had just started walking when the first mark was made. On the back deck, Colin constructed a beautiful mahogany banister rail with turned pillars to support the rail, the idea of which owed a lot to the design of the Spanish galleon. Despite his rather odd appearance, Humph had a beautiful swim and attracted a lot of fans on our journeys, and even made an appearance on the TV programme Boat Show, sandwiched between two million-pound boats – but more of that anon . . .

The engine was a two cylinder Lister diesel, which, in a previous life, had driven a road-laying machine. Colin was very proud of his bargain: he had bought the engine for £400. He reassembled it on the floor of the workshop at home, and all the family gathered for the first turn of the reconstructed power plant. The scones had been baked (cheese being my speciality) and the big pot filled with tea for the celebration. Despite much sweat, many "bloody hells" and much cajoling, the engine stubbornly refused to start.

"Come here, Dad, let me do it." First one son then the other impatiently yanked at the starting handle. There were red faces all round from the effort – not a splutter from the engine. No one said anything; we all felt sorry for Colin, so proud of his handiwork (the engine represented hours of work largely in the dark, as there was no instruction book). But to the indomitable engine restorer, this was merely another challenge, a setback, not a disaster: he would make the engine work. His more realistic family were very deflated, especially our sons, who were already beginning to think their dad was past it and should stick to safer things, like breeding birds. We all trooped miserably into the kitchen for the non-celebratory tea.

The next day Colin consulted an expert from the boat club, who came down to give the engine "a coat of looking at".

"You daft bugger, you're turning it the wrong way," said the expert as he turned the starting handle. "On this model you turn the handle backwards."

And lo and behold, the engine burst into life, pothering out smoke and emitting the familiar 'thump thump' sound characteristic of Lister engines. Colin, relieved that he had not wasted £400 and that the engine actually worked, fell about laughing at himself; but the episode was the beginning of his unfair reputation at the club as a bit of a Mr Bean.

The design of the inside was a masterpiece of how to fit a lot into a small space. We had a flushing pump-out toilet (I could not cope with a thing called a *porta potti*), a shower, cooking facilities, a bed/table and a pot-bellied stove. The inside woodwork was a rich rose coloured cherry wood, set off by white curtains decorated with multicoloured stars. To us, Humph looked a pretty comfortable cottage on the water; but how would she perform when she was finally launched?

In 1996 the boat was finally ready to return to his natural environment after 20-odd years of being stranded on the bank. A trailer towed by a Land Rover arrived on a sunny morning to take Humph to the boat club at Strawberry Island. Roger, the driver, had already moved Humph six times in fifteen years, and never once had the boat's bottom touched water. For a short while it looked as though yet again Humph's bottom was to be denied lubrication: the trailer with the boat on it was too wide to get past the front doorstep by about an inch. Fortunately, through, a liberal application of Fairy Liquid to the tyres of the trailer the problem was solved. As trailer and boat moved out of the gate I could see the amazed faces of the passengers of a bus, which had to stop to let Humph sail past, en route for the canal.

A few days later, a large group of invited friends and all the family, including in-laws gathered at the boat club for the big launch. Peter, the "resident Fred Dibnah", manoeuvred the boat off the oil drums and onto the mobile hoist/trailer, to be towed by tractor the short distance to the launch pad. In the past, Peter had built the hoist to launch club members' boats, and despite being partially sighted, he was regarded by all as the expert boat-launcher. (No one in those pre-health and safety days considered it odd that Peter would get under the boats to feel if the lifting slings were in place.)

Before the hoist backed down the slipway, I smashed a bottle of Asti Spumante on to Humph's bow, wishing all who sailed on him God speed. Slowly the boat was pushed into the canal and began to float on the water. I felt like crying: all those years of waiting, all those remarks from friends about the "yard boat", were about to come to an end. Colin, David our middle son, and assorted grandchildren clambered aboard, the engine fired up, and they were off, parading up and down the cut. We were all waving at each other in triumph, except Peter, our youngest, who suddenly clasped his head and fell to the floor screaming, "The earth's moving! Help me! Help me!"

I was suddenly very angry: trust hypochondriac Peter to spoil one of the biggest moments of my life. Sally, kinder than me, said, "Mam, he's really ill." Reluctantly, I turned to Peter, who by now was laid out face down on the bank, moaning and clutching the earth. I asked him to describe his symptoms, and realised he was having an attack of vertigo. "There's nothing to be done. It will pass, Peter, someone will take you home in a minute." I'm afraid there was not much sympathy in my voice.

As the boat returned to its mooring, and someone in the crowd hollered that it seemed to be going down at the back and up at the front. "Oh, that's cos there's too many bodies on it," replied Colin nonchalantly. "Tomorrow we will do the maiden voyage."

Leaving Peter on the floor, we all invaded the buffet, eating our fill before leaving Humph, at home in the water at last. In the car on the way home we all grumbled that Peter's dramatics had spoiled the big event. Poor Peter: vertigo is horrible and we should have had more sympathy, but as a family we don't do sympathy very well. In our defence, Peter had in the past been just as dramatic when faced with nothing more than another hill out hiking in the Dales, falling to his knees on the floor and yelling, "Mum, I can't go on!" (He was, however, ten years old at the time . . .)

There were enormous gaps in our knowledge of boating. We knew about the dangers of water – we had lifejackets and anchors – but our knowledge of canals was confined to the fact that boaters drove on the right-hand side. A week before the launch we were asked by a fellow club member if we had any maps. Colin asked his friend, "What maps? I didn't think you could get lost on a canal, you can only go up and down." I made a phone call to Waterstones but could not remember what we needed, so I bought the lot. We now had maps in abundance but before we could use them we had to have a test run of the boat. The aforementioned club member, a very large, jolly ex-chef, and his wife, who was nearly as large and jolly, offered to be passengers on the voyage to and through the nearest lock. My brother, who was in the merchant navy, once told me that all ships' captains and chefs were mad, but chefs were more dangerous as they had access to knives and brandy.

It was a lovely May morning as the four of us and Bob, our dog, friend and companion, set off the mile or so to the lock at Doncaster. Bob was a blonde, long-haired golden retriever who was really owned by our eldest son, Steven – and Bob was female. Exactly why Steve had called a female dog by a boy's name is unclear, but he refused to change it. I believe Bob's confused sexuality led him to be the most neurotic animal ever. He was frightened of everything physical – a plastic bag blowing in a hedgerow was enough to ruin her day. In contrast, Bob's people skills were second to none: she knew how to work an audience like a professional; she could tremble and gibber for England, paw-shake like a queen and convince anyone she would really be better off living with them. Another talent of Bob's was her recognition of conflict and danger vibes (long before a row happened or we had recognised "that sinking feeling"). As soon as she felt the vibes, Bob left the danger area – with the result she often landed in even more danger. On numerous occasions when travelling on our boats we thought we had lost Bob, only to find she had inveigled her way onto another boat and was contentedly eating or sleeping in front of her "new owners'" fire or sitting beside their table. Food was

Bob's main tranquiliser, and warmth her second option – especially human warmth.

On board Humph for the maiden voyage, Dave and his wife leant on the balustrade and I fussed about making our first underway cup of tea and buttering scones. I was very nervous: Dave and his wife were proper boaters with years of boating under their belt, as well as Dave being a chef. The voyage started well, with both passengers leaning back admiring the swim, seemingly thrilled to bits to be on such a unique boat. Later, though, Colin told me that almost as soon as we set sail he began to see that the "line" of the boat against the bank was showing that the back was down and the front up. After half a mile, he popped down to see if the gearbox was getting hot. As he lifted the lid he exclaimed, "God we're sinking! There's all water round the gearbox!"

"How much water do you mean?" I called down from the galley.

"A *lot*," he replied as he hopped up the steps.

Trying not to panic, I stopped buttering the scones. Imagining that we were in imminent danger of sinking, I wondered whether I could make it to the bank towing both the dog and the Captain, or whether we would drown in front of the parish church. I followed the Captain up onto the deck, where Dave and his wife were chatting away, seemingly unaware that the bow of the boat was now 20 degrees higher than the back.

"I think we're sinking," Colin told them, and, after a moment's hesitation (he told me later he was trying to be tactful), he asked them if they wouldn't mind going and sitting at the front. The Captain thought the problem was due to the uneven distribution of the ballast.

"Put your bilge pump on," said Dave, still cheerful, as he and his wife manoeuvred through the narrow opening and down the steps. The command was passed on to me.

A row of switches confronted me. "Which one is it?" I shouted.

An impatient "harumph", and then, "The first one . . . I think," shouted He Who Must Be Obeyed, "and look over the side see if the water's coming out."

"Where should it come out?"

"Bloody hell, Yvonne, look over the side towards the back."

"I can't see anything," I said, thinking to myself, "Why should I feel stupid"?

"It's not my job to know about bloody pipes I do the scones".

"Try another switch," Colin yelled.

By this time I was thoroughly embarrassed by the Captain, who, in my opinion, was acting like a lunatic in front of our astonished and soon to be drowned friends. This scenario was repeated three times, me running up and down the stairs to the switches, tripping over the dog every time I changed direction to complete each task. Down the steps to move a switch; back up again to look over each side. I had no idea really where the water should spurt from. In between my dashes back and forth, the dog would resume her efforts to lie on the Captain's feet and across the top of the steps.

It was after three trips that Colin realised the row of switches he had installed at various times throughout the eight years had not been labelled, and he had no idea what I was doing. "Switch the bloody lot on," he decreed. I did, and miraculously water appeared from a spout on the outside of the boat.

By now we had abandoned the idea of the lock and were heading back to the moorings, listing after a sluggish turn. Dave and his wife continued to watch in silence; it was obvious the bilge pump was having no effect at all. The boat had come up 10deg when Dave and his wife first sat at the front, but it was now back to a 20deg front to back list, increasing by the second. Also, the water was very close and coming closer.

We hurtled into the mooring, cut the engine and tied up; it was then we heard a noise of running water. Investigation revealed that the noise was from the shower; further checks of another unusual noise revealed that the water pump was running. The gushing pipe I had seen was emptying the shower, not the bilge. All the lights were on too, including the outside spot. The only thing *not* working was the bilge pump.

Much later, Colin found that the bilge switch had been installed upside-down. The pump had been working but I had switched it off in the panic. Our present search revealed that the cause of the water intake was from an unscrewed weed hatch.

"What's a weed hatch?" I asked.

"It's a plate over a hole in the bottom of the boat; you can lift it to get obstructions off the propeller, things like dead cows," Dave said, his normally ruddy colour coming back.

What's he mean "dead cows"? I wondered.

"Yes, and its years since I checked it, so it wasn't tightened up," Colin added.

Unknowingly, the Captain had added another Mr Bean episode to his reputation. Like almost everything else on Humph the switches had been reclaimed from a wrecker's; Colin thought he had put it in the right way up, but somewhere along the way in the eight years it had taken to reclaim Humph, one or two wires had got crossed. All this discomfiture was too much for Dave, who, full of relief and mischievous gossip, hurried back to the boat club to regale the members with tales of his near-death experience.

We were not aware of Dave's mischievous gossip until months later when we found out that boat club members were running a book on how far we would get on our maiden voyage: the furthest projection was ten miles and four locks. At a farewell night out in the club, the Commodore approached Colin and hesitantly suggested that it might be a better idea to travel to Henley via the Leeds and Liverpool canal and not on the Trent, our intended route. Tactfully, the Commodore pointed out the beauty of the new route; at no point did he express his doubts as to our and the boat's fitness to travel on the Trent. Years later, I wonder if he had been delegated this task by the rest of the committee; nevertheless, after our conversation with him we did indeed change our route.

The doubters were so nearly proved right when we set off for real a few days later. We had gone four miles and passed through one lock when the Captain heard what was either a passing tractor or a bird in pain. Colin often hears engine-in-pain noises that other human ears cannot hear. He is very sensitive that way (though he is not so in tune with humans. On a cycling holiday in Brittany after too much wine for lunch, I once fell off my bike while Colin cycled on, oblivious to my shouts. To make him, my husband and so-called partner, feel guilty, I deliberately left the blood running down my leg until he was goaded into noticing when eventually I caught up with him). No longer able to stand the Captain's twittering, and unable to see either tractor or bird, I offered to drive while he went in down into the saloon to lift the engine cover.

"It's the belt drive that's slack," he shouted up the stairs.

"Is that important?"

"Well, if we don't fix it we won't be going anywhere soon."

I didn't believe him, but didn't know enough to argue.

"We'll have to go home and get a tension pulley," he continued.

Masking my irritation I offered an alternative plan. "Let's phone Andrew, he'll bring us one." I wasn't going to let him get off that boat, as I believed that once off he would abandon the trip to nurse the engine.

"Good idea, we'll use the mobile phone," the Captain replied.

We had bought our first mobile phone ready for the trip. Colin had not been convinced of its worth and had absolutely refused to buy a 12-volt charger, which meant that for the whole of the trip we had to go into pubs to charge the phone secretly while we made one drink last an hour or so.

It took us ten minutes to work out how to use the phone. The Captain stood on the bank, his Dennis Healey eyebrows furrowed in concentration as he waved a stubby finger over the keys while I shouted out the number. We finally managed to contact Andrew, and a jockey pulley was soon on its way; after all, we were less than five miles from home.

Andrew and grandson Richard stayed for a cup of tea, and then worked the lock while we stayed on the boat. We were on our way again: three miles to the next lock. At this lock there was a frantic search for the BW lock key – to no avail. The strain of canal boating was beginning to tell, and we had a huge marital, each of us blaming the other, and the dog a mass of shaking hairs. After half an hour's searching the boat like rampaging burglars, we suddenly remembered that Andrew had used the key to open the lock, and as it could not be removed until the process of going through the lock was complete, he must have the key. And so, at last, after another visit from the family, the dog stopped shivering and we were all smiles: we were on our way again.

Soon it was raining cats and dogs. Bob was trying Colin's patience: when she was not trying to abandon ship, she was insisting on lying on his good foot, severely hampering his jumping up and down. The Captain's brain works faster than either of our legs and jumping up and down seems to be a coping strategy. It is a habit, but one that drives me nuts and gives Bob paralysis of the brain. The habit is guaranteed to make the heat of any situation combust into full-on flames.

Fearing dog-murder, I lectured the Captain. "She's picking up your panic, so calm down and shut up shouting."

"I'm not shouting, I'm thinking fast and encouraging you. I'm not in a panic. The bloody dog's stupid, carrying on like that just cos of the siren," the Captain continued. At some of the locks we had passed so far, there had been a road bridge, and as the barriers dropped across the road the sirens would sound an alarm. The sound provoked the dog into attempting to abandon ship just as the Captain was moving the boat into the middle of the canal to pass under the rising bridge. As Colin has only one fully useful arm, he had to choose between hanging onto the dog or steering. Bob had added another neurosis to an already long list, and her newfound fear of water did not stop her from trying to jump off. What it did mean, though, was that when she did jump she was too frightened to swim, and without outside help she was too heavy for us to lift out.

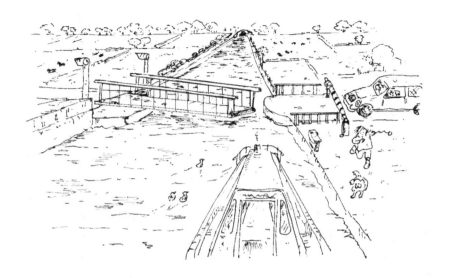

At the next lock I said I would take Bob and show her there was nothing to be frightened of. All went well until the siren sounded. Bob reared up, slipped her lead, and hared off into the distance. All thoughts of the Captain and the boat disappeared from my mind as I chased after her. I had no chance of catching her though, I was too unfit.

I was devastated. I felt we had lost Bob forever. We were miles from anywhere with no means of transport to go looking for her. As I went back to the lock, a few cars were waiting for the bridge to go up. I was oblivious to the car drivers' dilemma: I just wanted to find Bob. I stopped beside the first car and told my tale to the driver, and after listening to me, she must have decided she would be going nowhere until I had found my dog.

"Get in," she said as she turned her car round.

After a mile or so, we saw something grey and thin in the distance: Bob. As we got closer, I could see and smell that she was covered in grey pig slurry. I gave her a cuddle, but as I looked back towards the car driver in thankful relief I saw her wary look. "Thank you! Thank you, but I think we will walk back."

Relief flooded the woman's face. "I'll tell them you are coming" she said.

By the time I got back, there was quite a traffic jam, and Colin could not make up his mind whether to be glad or mad. "Bloody stupid dog," was all he said.

We had to stop again after traversing the lock, this time to bath the stinking Bob with a bucket, my shampoo and canal water. It was raining even harder as we continued boating for half an hour to prove we could, and we decided to moor up for the night at Pollington, which was a completely deserted village; not even a pub. We put our socks on the engine to dry and had strawberries and cream for tea. We were exhausted but not downhearted, and went to bed in good spirits, with Bob lying gently clacking, clean and safe at our side.

Our first day of boating was over.

Chapter 2

Henley or bust

The next day we set off in high spirits; Humph was finally sailing as he should, his engine growling satisfaction. At last he was doing what he was built for: sailing. As we cruised along, Bob, ever vigilant, picked up on our mood and was confident enough to move off the Captain's feet and stretch out at my side. The next two days were uneventful apart receiving a good shaking from the wash of the passing Tom Pudding, a sand barge heading for Goole.

"The bugger did that on purpose," said an amused Colin. "I thought we were going to turn over."

I think, now, the Captain said this for dramatic effect, to impress me with his new skills: when I look back, he did not seem unduly worried, but it sowed a seed in my mind that boats could turn over. We continued on the New Navigation and the Aire and Calder until eventually we arrived in Leeds and excitedly went shopping for things we had not realised we would need: water hose, curling tongs, shoes without holes, and TV wire. The TV wire was very important as I was beginning to experience Coronation Street withdrawals. The lack of a TV was the only cloud on the horizon; we felt like seasoned travellers as we toured Leeds, had a meal in a restaurant where we could charge up the phone, and basked in a heroic glow while each of the kids expressed delight that we had got so far.

After three days' "holiday", we set off for the first lock on the great Leeds and Liverpool Canal. What a shock we were in for: we did not realise that the Leeds and Liverpool had been constructed in the days before electricity and Yale keys.

"There's nowhere to put my key," I shouted to Colin at the first lock that morning.

A crowd had gathered to help me search for the keyhole, and I was beginning to feel foolish.

"Oh, I wonder if that's what this is for," Colin replied, holding up what looked like a starting handle.

At that moment, an official-looking man walked up and asked me what I was doing. Judging by the chap's badge, his name was Dave and he belonged to British Waterways.

"Give me your windlass and I will show you what to do, but before I do, fasten your shoelace and never let me see you on a lock with loose shoelaces again."

My confidence shrank even further, and I determined to be a star pupil in future.

"Now, never open the gate paddles before the ground paddles. Do it all slowly and watch the boat whilst you wind the paddle up, see?"

"Yes, I understand, I said earnestly, pretending I knew the difference between gate and floor paddles or even what a paddle was.

The Captain, with Bob the dog on his left foot, slowly rose in the lock. Dave asked me if I had an anti-vandal key. I gave him a blank look.

"It's a T-shaped thing," Dave said to the Captain helpfully.

Colin had now risen, and he scrabbled around in a cardboard box containing all the "bits" that had been left on the boat. Dave picked out a T-shaped piece of metal with a square socket on the bottom and took me back to the lock gates to demonstrate how the "anti-vandal key" fitted on the bar near the winding sprocket. When the lock was locked it was impossible to wind the paddles up.

"It's to stop bloody kids and idiot boaters leaving paddles up and draining the canal," he said. "But don't lock anything up until you have finished using the lock in case of accidents," he continued, looking at me fiercely.

The advice was wise but inconvenient as it meant going back to lock the paddles after the boat had gone through the locks. The Captain would have to moor up to wait for me to finish. I can honestly say I always obeyed the rule, although some we travelled with did not. A few years later, as a result of locked gate paddles and water entering the boat, several wheelchair-bound children drowned, and the last time I travelled on the Leeds and Liverpool canal the gate paddle winding gears had been completely disabled to prevent further accidents.

Our training session finished just as another boat came through the lock and was about to pass us. "Here, travel with these," Dave said, "they will show you how to go on."

Chastened after our training session, we proceeded to the next lock following the big boat as directed. Colin manoeuvred alongside the boat, staying close to the back of the lock as instructed. The couple driving the boat appeared to be experienced and indicated they wanted to be in charge. Thinking everyone knew more than me, I let them get on with it. I stood at the top of the lock holding the rope and contently watching the man as he attacked the gate paddles with gusto. I thought to myself, I thought you weren't supposed to do that – though maybe I had misunderstood the lock man. The pouring water made a horrendous noise, and I thought, I haven't the energy to argue with this bloke against this racket, so I stood and watched.

Big mistake! The man's boat was sixty foot long and only just able to fit in the lock with hardly any room to go back as the water poured into his bow. I looked on in horror, imagining the boat sinking like a stone. Surprisingly, though, the boat found space to manoeuvre: the back end swung across and behind us (there was a lot of space behind us), but there was no room for the front and the boat attempted to mount Humph. Viewing the impending disaster, I believed I was about to become a widow: I was sure the bigger boat would take our boat and Colin to a watery grave with it.

Due to the rapid movement of our boat as it attempted to move back, the rope I was holding shot from my hands into the water. I was paralysed by fear; I had no means now of rescuing the Captain and Bob. The boats rose rapidly to the surface, bouncing all over the place. The noise of the water was horrendous. I was shouting to the man to shut the paddles, but he could not hear me over the roar of the water. He just stood there – unconcerned, I thought at the time, although now I think he was as paralysed as I was. Colin had unceremoniously kicked Bob off his left foot and I could see that he was shouting, but I could not hear what he was saying. I guessed the Captain wanted me to attack the man and lower the paddles myself to turn the water off. But my legs refused to move until there was no point: the water had risen so quickly as it had rushed in through the openings. Humph's engine was roaring and smoking as Colin tried to maintain some control, fortunately it quickly reached the top of the lock.

We let the big boat go first, and decided to "lose" our companion by unspoken mutual consent. All that was said by me was, "Shall we stop for a cup of tea?" This brought heartfelt agreement from Colin. By this time my neurosis was rivalling the dog. I felt I had suddenly dropped into a nightmare; I am only glad that, at that moment, I did not anticipate the nightmare continuing.

We continued towards Rowley in pouring rain. The swing bridges proved very stiff, necessitating Colin jumping off the boat to give me a hand.

"I remember some old chap telling me cow dung was a good lubricant."

As Colin said this, he picked a huge slop of mud and cow dung, and threw it onto the turning mechanism under the bridge. After a few more hefty shoves the bridge started to move. It was then the Captain turned to nip over the half-opened bridge to move the boat forward.

"Bloody hell, it's taking off!" he yelled.

An inexperienced Captain hadn't thought to tie the boat securely, and in the increasing wind and rain we were astonished to watch Humph take off and turn completely round. I thought it was very funny and fell about laughing. I could tell by Colin's face, though, that he was not amused: he could not imagine getting the boat back.

Fortunately, the wind that had blown Humph round blew him into the same side, although facing the other way. Colin was able to leap on board before the boat took off again. I stood and watched as Colin fandangled about, trying to turn the boat against the wind. Eventually he managed to get the boat the right way round and under the bridge.

It was just as hard to close the bridge as it had been to open it and Bob refused to cross the bridge after me. I tried persuasion, but Colin thought that what Bob needed was discipline, and started shouting, "Come on you stupid bloody dog!"

He started to move off from the bank, shouting to me, "If you don't get on the boat now the bloody wind will turn me round again!"

Fuming, I replied, "Shut up shouting. The poor thing's confused and you're making it worse."

I reassured Bob and persuaded her to cross the bridge and

get on the moving boat. But as soon as I turned my back she was off the boat again sitting po-faced on the bank.

I got off the boat, giving a warning look at an exasperated Colin; I imagined the boat would take off and leave me behind. Well, as long as it took Colin I wasn't bothered.

I manhandled the reluctant dog back on deck, the last point at which we could safely jump. We continued to the next bridge where I decided that Bob and Him Who Must Be Obeyed needed some re-bonding time. I set about getting lunch, during which we had a huge marital while reviewing our boat handling skills, each claiming the other was useless, and me pointing out that at least I was calm in tricky situations. Bob gibbered on the settee. Whatever happened to sitting on the pointy bit, drinking wine and gently moseying along? I asked myself.

I am a quick learner when I think my life depends on it. The Captain deals with his anxiety by shouting at me. By the time we got to Bingley I felt confident enough to tell Colin I was sick of everyone on the cut knowing my name and if he didn't shut up, wooden leg or not he would be shoved in the cut. Shortly after this my confidence took a steep dive as we arrived at the foot of the Bingley Five Rise. I quote from the Ordnance Survey:

> *Bingley Five-Rise Locks. A very famous and impressive feature of the canal system built in 1774 in "staircase" formation, i.e. they are all joined together rather than being separated by ponds of "neutral" water. The top gates of the lowest lock are the bottom gates of the lock above, and so on. This means it is not possible to empty a lock unless the one below is itself empty. The rapid elevation thus resulting is quite daunting . . . The locks may only be used under the supervision of the lock keeper.*

I had not yet learnt the necessity of reading the map. I was about to insert the windlass into the mechanism to wind the paddle when I was accosted by a fast-moving, shouting, tomato-red-faced man in a green overall.

"Don't open those paddles, the top lock's empty. In fact don't touch anything, don't move until I tell you!"

With these instructions the tornado disappeared. I learned later that this was Bingley Lock Barry, known far and wide (although not to us) as the ultimate authority on the Bingley Five Rise. Under his close physical and verbal supervision we went up the locks. I was told what to do and when, Bob did not attempt to abandon ship, and not a peep was heard from the Captain. Emerging from the last lock I commented that it seemed to me there were an awful lot of chiefs on the canals and only one Indian. Colin did not answer my comment. Ever the "Steptoe", he had noticed a beautiful bit of teak floating in the canal.

"Get that bit of wood, it could be very useful," he ordered me.

Hanging off the boat's side at a dangerous angle, I managed to retrieve said bit of wood. It was then that Colin realised the boat was beginning to drop to bits: the piece of teak I had fished from the water was part of Humph's handrail.

By now, with the fraught atmosphere between the two of us, the dog was insisting on travelling laid on both of Colin's feet. I am told Bob was in a submissive pose; well, there was no way I was going to act submissive to a shouting tyrant who cared more about an old engine and a bit of wood than his wife.

A good night at Riddleston restored all our spirits. We had a drink in the local pub and listened to the live jazz band. Regaling locals with tales of our ill-starred voyage encouraged us to laugh at ourselves and, full of bonhomie, we made a fuss of Bob on our return to the boat. We had rediscovered our enthusiasm for boating.

The next morning I cleaned the boat and Colin did things to the engine that men do. We had a leisurely dinner, after which we groomed the dog and, deciding to ignore the gathering storm clouds, set off once again.

Our enthusiasm stayed with us despite our arriving in Skipton in a downpour. Colin, in an attempt to keep me happy, allowed me to buy a new television as our existing one suffered from a mysterious shrinking picture syndrome, and the Captain is a great believer in the efficacy of Coronation Street in improving women's hormonal moods.

Carefully we carried our prize, plus special shelf, back to the boat, only to discover that it too had shrinking picture syndrome. We took the television back to the shop, where it worked perfectly. Back on the boat, though, the picture shrank again. Colin, by this time, had lost interest in making either the television work or me happy. I think the Captain had the idea that the television's malaise had something to do with the boat's wiring – but even my moods were preferable to the work involved in a rewire. To make matters worse, when we set off in high winds the following morning I pulled the boat in too sharply onto a concrete bank in response to an urgent order from Him Who Must Be Obeyed. We heard a loud crash. Shocked, we went hesitantly into the boat to find the source of the noise. The television had fallen off its shelf, bouncing onto the settee on its way to the floor. Among my friends, I am known as a car driver who cannot see a gatepost without making a very close relationship with it, and Colin has never criticised in those circumstances, saying, "It's only a bit of metal, as long as you're

OK." But I learnt on this cruise – and many others – that Colin's softly-softly sympathetic approach only works when it comes to cars and gateposts. A boat and concrete moorings are an entirely different matter.

Despite having given up on ever seeing Coronation Street again, I began to feel much better. I thought I knew what I was doing, Colin had shut up, and the dog was happy working alongside me. The weather was still foul but who cared? I wouldn't leak, I'd got skin, hadn't I?

Soon I began to pick up lame ducks instead of being one. While waiting to use the lock I started talking to two chaps who told me their wives had gone home and would not return to their menfolk until the weather improved. I felt very pleased with myself, and didn't hesitate to tell the Captain the story, hoping he would put two and two together and begin to appreciate what a fine First Lieutenant he had in me. Later we paired up with a solitary man for a while; he stayed on his boat and I worked the lock for both of us. After six locks, still in pouring rain and wind, he let it be known that his wife was in bed: "She had a bad night, you know."

For once Captain and First Lieutenant were united: both of us were speechless. Fearing our disgust was obvious in our faces, I asked sympathetically, "Is she ill?"

"No," was the reply, "the dog howls all night when he is on the boat, we have tried everything, nothing works."

Suddenly we were very grateful to be the owners of our lovely Bob: neurotic as she was, she did at least sleep at night, even if she did clack her teeth. And if you were asleep yourself, a good clack did not bother you.

With no more mishaps, and enjoying the spectacular views, we eventually passed "over the top" and approached the gateway to Lancashire, the Foulridge Tunnel. We had a "lie in" to celebrate our arrival, and then it was into the café for a homemade bread and bacon sandwich. So full of joy were we that we even treated Bob to the same.

Full of love and peace, we set off for the tunnel entrance. As we rounded the corner we saw what appeared to be a large rabbit hole. The light turned to green as we approached, and in no time we were in the dark. The boat's headlight flickered once; it seemed to be nothing serious. The dog sat quietly on my feet as we sailed in. I was surprised at how dark, low and wet it was; I was amazed that in this day and age there were tunnels with no lights.

Half an hour or so later we emerged into the daylight. We had learned a new set of skills: how to steer a boat in the dark. Now we were about to go down the Barrowford Locks. The dog, having just got used to going up again, went to pieces: she jumped off the boat and refused to get back on. We gradually sank from Bob's sight. In a panic, she took off, looking everywhere for us; we could hear her barking, first at one end of the lock and then the other.

We came out of the lock and had to moor up. I jumped off the boat and went back to find her Bob? Can you see her?" I shouted.

"No, she's gone" was my husband's irritated reply.

As soon as we got back to the boat the Captain and I were back to arguing over "the bloody dog". Eventually we found Bob being petted by a couple out for a walk no doubt telling them about her sadistic owners. The Captain's view was that the dog needed discipline, while in reply I shouted, "What the dog needs is for you to shut up!"

What the dog really needed was for us both to shut up. We stopped in Burnley to give us and the dog a rest, bought some essential supplies and continued on our way. By now it was getting late; Colin and I were both tired and not reading the map as we should have been. Unexpectedly, we drifted into the Gannow Tunnel.

Once inside, we switched on the spot light; it worked for a few minutes and then – nothing. Terrified, I searched for the dog, but not a sound could be heard from her; and nor could I feel anything on my hands and knees in the dark.

I said, "Colin, the dog's gone. Stop, go back."

A disembodied voice shouted, "I can't go back, it's not a car you know. Go and find the torch."

As Colin said that, the boat hit the side with a mighty clang and scraped along the side. The noise was horrendous. The metal hull boomed, wood splintered and cracked, and the bells on the bikes tinkled as they scraped the roof of the tunnel.

"The dog's not with me" he replied.

"God, I bet she has abandoned ship," I shouted back, suddenly feeling very sick.

Gingerly, I tried to go down the steps to search for the torch. It was pitch black as I searched, all the while thinking of poor old Bob swimming forever in the dark until she died.

"I can't find it," I shouted above clangs, splintering and bells.

"Bloody hell, have a good look, I can't see a thing," replied Colin.

At that moment, at the top of the steps I felt something soft and furry.

"Oh Bob, you're alive!"

I wept, and lay on top of the dog. I soon I gave up all hope as I believed we were going to be entombed, although not without a lot more noise.

Eventually, though, still banging, splintering and tinkling, we emerged into the light.

"You've got the dog, why didn't you tell me? I thought we were going to have to go back for her into that bloody tunnel," shouted a red faced but obviously shaken Colin.

"I was too frightened to speak," I replied.

By this time we were both crying with relief as we formed a comforting huddle with Bob in the middle. It wasn't until we were talking to our friends in the boat club that we learned we could have put the lights on inside the boat and they would have been enough to steer by. As it was, Colin had to aim the boat for the light of the opening at the end of the tunnel; but the sides of the tunnel although they appeared straight were far from it, and hence the constant banging into them.

We were now desperate to find a mooring for the night, and at last approached a deserted industrial site named in the map book Rose Grove. The boat had started making strange noises; I went down to look in the engine compartment, as I lifted the engine cover I discovered all was not well down there. Colin followed me down into the saloon and looking in the compartment found that the propeller shaft had moved a few inches, throwing the jockey pulley out of line.

Colin said, "We must have hit more than walls in that tunnel." He diagnosed jockey pulley problems and said, "We need a couple of washers this size." He showed me what he meant. "Go and cadge some off some fella with a shed. Chat him up if you have to" he continued

I set off. Everywhere was deserted; it was six o'clock: tea time. I eventually saw a chap coming out of his house, and said to him over the gate, "Have you got a shed?"

He looked at me, puzzled. He was bald and in his mid-fifties. If he had a shed, I knew he would have a couple of washers; I also knew that, because that age group had been brought up to look after damsels in distress I would get what I came for.

The man did indeed have a shed, and after looking through many tins and glass jars he found me two washers. I gave him my best chat-up lines, telling him how wonderful he was to have such a well-stocked shed.

Triumphantly, I returned to the Captain and to Humph. The Captain was pleased but not surprised that I had obtained the spare parts free – I was once told by a very cheeky man that I do a good line in "learned helplessness".

After running repairs, we limped into Hampton Boatyard. Steve, the boatyard owner, came to assess the situation. Steve, I later found out, was a man of few words, and after a lot of thought he said, "My god, what a marvelous piece of engineering – but an engine like that should be in a paddy field in India where it would run and run."

"Tell me honestly, can anything be done? Or shall I set fire to Humph and push him into the cut?" said Colin emotionally.

Steve laughed. "Send it to Valhalla? Oh, I wouldn't do that, the boat's unique, it deserves another chance."

I immediately warmed to this man: he understood what it is to have a dream, even though he had no immediate answers. He was also small dark and handsome, and so struck another chord with one of us. There was some discussion about another engine, but before a decision could be made regarding the boat Colin phoned and asked our son to take us home for a bit of rest and recreation.

David came the next day and said later that he had told his partner: "It must be bad, Dad never asks for help like this." He also told me later that he was shocked at our appearance: both of us seemed to have aged years.

Back in Doncaster, our friends were amazed we had got so far but not surprised we were back. Colin discussed the situation with several of his expert friends, one of whom, Peter, wondered whether Colin had tightened the grub screws (whatever they are). Apparently this was a 'eureka' moment, and in no time at all Colin knew how to give Humph a new heart. Colin had assembled the jockey pulley years previously and couldn't remember tightening the grub screws. Peter was to give us invaluable advice several more times, and we were enormously grateful for his help. Later we would cruise quite a bit with him and his wife, Carol.

We returned to Hampton to continue our journey. The repairs were soon made, and after lunch we set off for Henley again. As we sailed away I turned round to give Steve a wave, and was amazed: I got the distinct impression he would have liked to come with us.

While we had been at home we had visited the vet and he had prescribed some tranquilisers for Bob. As a result, for most of the first two days Bob was looking decidedly shifty, her eyeballs swapping sockets.

"I can't stand it. Poor thing, we have *got* to think of something better than these tablets," said Colin.

We discussed a behaviour modification programme for Bob. We would praise appropriate behaviour, and Colin would stop shouting because immediately he raised his voice Bob's brain scrambled. The tablets were chucked in the cut, a gift for some fisherman or other. The programme had some success, but Bob had extra-sensory perception: she could feel the vibes and respond before we knew *we* had them.

We began to relax, and enjoyed the cruise until we reached the Wigan Flight, also known as "Indian country" among narrow-boaters. We had been warned by people travelling on the waterways to be wary of the children who frequented the locks; the British Waterways men who accompanied the boats down the locks were there to escort you through the locks, not to protect you from these young marauders. Frequently used tactics included jumping on the boat at the bow, running through the boat and out the other end pinching anything movable; another favourite was standing on the bridge over the canal dropping stones, spitting or weeing on the boat crew passing beneath.

As expected, a crowd of kids gathered halfway down the locks, but I was ready for them; I was hot and tired as I faced up to a thin, pale girl attempting to take a ride on the boat. "Touch that boat and I'll run you through," I said, pointing the boat-hook directly at her. She must have thought I meant it (and I probably did at the time), because she immediately went back to the gang who then went into a huddle.

The kids watched us as we travelled through the lock. As we approached the next lock, the kids were all stood on the bridge over the gates. Anticipating a certain form of behaviour, I shouted, "You can forget it, I'm a nurse and I've seen more spit, snot and vomit than you'll see in a lifetime."

"We weren't going to do that," they shouted back.

"Well, I wouldn't show yer little willies if I were you. I've seen plenty of them as well," I yelled back.

We passed under the bridge unscathed. By this time the Captain thought I had completely lost it and was in serious danger of committing a crime. The kids too must have thought I was mad; they cleared off, running along the bank towards the last lock without a backward glance. I suppose, for some males, to cast aspersions on the size of their tackle is enough to put the fear of God into them; I do know that when I was working with aggressive adolescent males, the threat of my ultimate weapon was enough to deflate any stroppy behaviour. What was my threat? A kiss from me! And I never had to carry it out.

I found out that the captain of the boat travelling with us gave the kids a huge block of chocolate to clear off. I also found out later that he was a retired chief of police. We didn't see those kids again, and I could never make up my mind if they had cleared off because they were in fear for their lives, or because they had been bribed.

We moored up for the night at Plank Bridge where thousands of huge flies, despite repeated attacks with a wet flannel and the tea cloth from Colin, decided to spend the night with us.

We spent the next morning repeatedly stopping to clear the weed and other gunge from around the prop. Every time Colin did this he felt nervous, as we had been told that one boater had put his hand through the weed hatch straight into the remains of a dead cow. The Captain's fears were nearly born out: a terrified scream brought me running. "God, there is a cow; I've just grabbed it instead of weed!"

"How do you know it's a cow?"

"Well it's slippy and it moved."

"It's not dead, then, or it wouldn't have moved, and if it's a cow we should be able to see it over the side." I looked over the side of the boat and saw a huge fish on patrol. "I bet it was that big fish," I reassured. Well, *sometimes* two brains are better than one.

As a reward to ourselves and Bob, who was doing well on her programme, we decided to treat ourselves to lunch at the Bridgewater Hotel. Unfortunately there was no bone for Bob but we shared our sausage with her. We chatted to the barmaid about our trip and charged the phone.

"Oh," said the barmaid "I think it's so romantic what you're doing."

Both Colin and I nearly choked on our sausages while images of dead cows floated in our minds.

The following night we moored at Watch House Cruising Club. There were very few customers but the few that were there gave us a very good night. I have vague memories of staggering home with a blind lady and a lady with a bad back, both of whom were keen boaters and intent on giving me some Dutch courage.

At Preston Brook we went through another tunnel, during which more bits of Humph's Spanish galleon back were forcibly removed. I suggested to Colin that maybe we ought to have a bit of a redesign, as it was clear that square backs and rabbit holes were not compatible. On the towpath the carved balustrade supports were taken off and a narrower balustrade fitted within the width of the boat. Then we varnished the wood, repainted the bashed bits, and felt renewed and ready for a fresh start the next day.

It was a lovely day as we set off with our redesigned and repainted boat. This is what we had come for: moseying along just enjoying the fresh air, Bob contentedly lying at my side. As usual I prepared the tea and Colin went down to do things to his engine. Next thing I heard was Colin shouting my name, although by now it was my practice to ignore the Captain's shouts because, unbeknown to him, I had put him on a behaviour programme. Nine times out of ten the shouts were unnecessary and there was no crisis except in the Captain's mind. But the shouts continued, and there was something about their intensity that made me go upstairs. As I emerged at the top, a figure in baggy blue shorts and a floppy white sunhat was hobbling away from me shouting, "The boat's on fire! The boat's on fire!" Then another shout: "Yvonne, the bloody boats on fire, get off the boat! And get the bloody dog off!"

This statement was followed almost immediately by, "Oh god, *I'm* on fire!" By now the Captain was stamping and flapping his feet and arms. "My bloody leg's melting!"

fire ...fire...
get off the bloody boat .. NOW !

Colin began bashing his false leg with his good arm. He bent down and rolled his sock down. The false leg was exposed and we could see there was a large hole in the calf. It appeared that while lying at the side of the engine the Captain's false leg had rested against the manifold and melted. The smell of the melting plastic skin was the same as an electrical fault, hence Colin's dramatic exit from the boat (the saying about women and children first is obviously a myth). The hole in the leg was covered by the largest plaster I had, but as the suction had gone the leg was unreliable, threatening to drop off when Colin was going down stairs. Later, when we got the leg properly repaired, the staff who worked at the Limb Centre were incredulous as Colin explained the damage to his state-of-the-art Icelandic leg. For the time being, when Colin walked he made a noise like an espresso machine.

The war with the youth of England continued as we journeyed through the old industrial parts of the Midlands: bricks and stones dropped from bridges seemed to be the favourite form of attack. Retaliation measures were discussed with fellow boaters; these ideas ranged from bribery to pretending to photograph the culprits while using the mobile. One chap we met was armed with a powerful klaxon horn, a catapult and three pellet guns, though we thought that these measures were likely to escalate the situation. We decided to rely on humour and a hard hat – which must have worked, as we arrived in the Gas Street Basin unscathed.

Gas Street was a real eye opener. We had come through a jungle of weeds and dereliction – what amounted to a war zone – to a mooring in the centre of Birmingham that resembled Venice. Everything about the place – the arena, shops and restaurants – suggested sophistication, and I looked at Colin with new and critical eyes. For a start, the trousers that had fitted him at the start of the journey now hung baggily down his legs, only prevented from falling by enormous decorated braces that emphasized the Captain's lopsided gait. The shirts Colin had brought with him were all splattered with oil, varnish and multi-coloured paint. On top of all this the Captain's naturally curly hair had grown up and out in an Anglo-Saxon version of the Afro. All this, as well as sounding like an espresso machine.

I decided that after doing the washing I would go and have a makeover, and off I went to find a hairdresser. Canal living and beauty care had not been compatible: the perm I had done in

Doncaster was growing out and I had millions of split ends, as well as a bit of grey. I went into the centre of Birmingham with a pocketful of money and a determination to repair the damage. The stylist, in a very modern up-market salon, got to work and I emerged two hours later with short spiky hair and red streaks. More important, I felt feisty and determined that something was going to be done with Robinson Crusoe.

Walking proudly back, I found Colin checking the damage to the boat.

"What do you think?" I said.

"It's very nice." Colin was always a master of understatement. "How much?"

"£45," I replied.

"What! Bloody hell."

Ignoring the shock and horror on his face, I said, "You'll have to have *your* hair done now."

"Not at that bloody price."

As he replied, a family was walking past us. Colin turned and spoke to the young lady. "Can you cut hair?" he asked. The older man turned and said, "Yes, she always cuts mine."

"Will you cut mine?" Colin asked, to my mortification.

The young lady's name was Alison and she agreed to cut the Captain's hair there and then on the towpath. George, who we learned was her father, set up the generator, Colin fetched a stool and in the rain, which was just starting, Alison, watched by her mum, June, her son, plus me and various passers-by, gave Colin a number three haircut.

Not content with getting what in the end was a free haircut, the Captain grumbled loudly that she was pulling his hair out. Alison was a slight, shy young woman in her early thirties and I was surprised at her resolve both to cut Colin's hair and to ignore his dramatic protests. I chatted to her parents to try and cover my embarrassment at what was happening on the towpath: we, or more precisely Colin, had put these people to a lot of trouble and then had the cheek to grumble about it. But I needn't have worried; George and June were the nicest people you could wish to meet. George was a short, stocky man with a grey number three cut of his own, a pronounced Darlington accent and a broad friendly grin; when George laughed, which he did often, his whole face crinkled up. Ever since I have known George he has exhibited the most equable of temperaments. June, his wife, and mother of his five children, was small, wiry and full of energy; although not a strong person she always pushed herself to the limits. June was the kindest of friends and was one of those rare people who mothered me, always calling me in the Geordie way "hon". George and June had sold everything, bought a narrow boat called 'Slocomotion' and were living their dream, continuously cruising the canals of England.

The haircut was the start of a wonderful friendship and the end of the first part of our journey to Henley. We had got further than most of our friends and fellow club members had thought we would, and we had partially redesigned the boat and learnt to manage the locks and the vandals – only coping with the dark tunnels was beyond us. Furthermore, our new friend George promised to show us how to safely pass through them without leaving bits of the boat behind or Bob trying to commit suicide.

Chapter 3

Henley or bust – Part Two

In a very short time Colin, I and Bob the dog were firm friends with George, June and their family. But as so often happens, in the comparative safety of the Gas Street Basin, frictions that had been buried under a solid layer of fear began to surface. I was sick of the Captain's obsession with "lollipops", the mileage indicators on the maps: the minute I told Colin how many lollipops we had done that day he would immediately forget the number and ask again. On the other hand, He who *thought* he *should* be obeyed was sick of my inability to respond to his commands before he had thought of them. I was even daring to argue back and had threatened him on occasions with the boat hook. We were both fed up with Bob's insistence on travelling sitting on both of the leader's feet.

Bob decided to bring all the conflict to an end by moving onto George and June's boat; they returned from a trip to the shops to find Bob stretched out on the rug in front of their stove. Bob had forced a solution, and, sorry for the dog, George and June volunteered to travel with us for a while and to train us to go through the tunnels without losing bits of the boat or the dog.

Our training did not get off to a very good start as we headed towards the Branwood Tunnel. George and June were in front in Slocomotion when a driverless boat travelling at speed met us on a corner. The boat appeared to be heading straight for us. Colin blew the horn and a head suddenly appeared as the boat skimmed by. We realised the driver had been a child. The supervising adult threw up his hands to indicate his apology, but it was too late: we were impaled on a blackberry bush. The dog, in a panic, attempted to abandon ship; but the bush was too dense and she retreated, leaving boat-loads of hair on the branches.

We came out of the bushes and were immediately in the tunnel. Here, the light failed again; but this time I was prepared: I had bought an enormous halogen lamp in Birmingham. The dog managed to get out of her collar (I think she was losing so much hair that her collar was slack) but at least while she was on the captain's feet I knew where she was. As we emerged from the tunnel the bloody light came on; I was beginning to think I was under the spell of a malevolent spirit. But this time the dog was still on board and the boat survived intact.

George and June could not believe our bad luck; they had turned round to look back in the tunnel and found that we were missing. George could not believe how completely we had disappeared for a few moments. As we sat under the trees at Lapworth, he informed us that there was another tunnel but that this time, with his help, we were bound to emerge unscathed. June and I worked the eighteen locks in happy companionship with a now calm and happy dog. This was the life: fresh air, exercise, and most important, good companionship. Not only did the dog feel calm but the Captain and First Mate did as well.

We then came onto the Grand Union Canal and the Shrewley Tunnel, a tunnel with each-way traffic. George and June were again in the lead and went in a few minutes before us with no hesitation. Looking in, we could see an intermittent light, which we interpreted as a signal to proceed. We set off full of confidence; but as we travelled down the tunnel the intermittent light seemed to get nearer and there were sounds of screaming and shadows leaping off the walls. The dog and I thought we were in a horror movie and clung to each other for comfort. As the light got nearer, it was clear that it was intermittent because numerous kids were jumping up and down in front of it. George passed the kids' boat safely, but as we approached, the kids suddenly veered diagonally across our path, the bow crashing into the wall of the tunnel to our right. We could not stop, and banged into the side of their boat.

As the driver had hit the wall, he had put on the revs in an attempt to back off. The tunnel was now full of smoke, jumping yelling kids, the noise of screaming engines, and men shouting. Only the dog and I were silent, both paralysed with fear at the thought of being entombed for life. The dog was shaking violently; if she had lost much more hair she would have ended up bald. Meanwhile, Colin was suddenly catapulted into the "expert" role, and shouted to the other driver to turn off the revs. But hysterical kids were *my* speciality, and suppressing my fear and rage I threatened and cajoled them into pushing their boat off the wall. Eventually we emerged into the daylight unscathed, to find an appalled George and June, who both said they thought we were seriously jinxed.

But the jinx decided to desert us for a while and we began to do normal things like going for walks in the evening. One night we were walking around a small industrial estate when the sound of a beautiful choir drifted on the night air. We expected to find a chapel or church round the next corner; instead, we found that the sound was coming from a small industrial unit. A man in the yard informed us that locally the sound was known as "Top of the Poppadoms". The singing was truly uplifting.

After Itchington Locks, George and June left us. We were sorry to see them go: they had been good fun, and impartial referees. (They have remained our friends, and we were to do another journey with them before they eventually returned to a conventional life in a flat in Darlington.) Someone who missed George and June more than us, however, was Bob the dog, who had gone to them for respite from her warring owners. But Bob sorted out the respite problem: for the rest of her life, whenever she saw a blue boat, she was on it and lying in front of anything that resembled a stove – much to the surprise of various boat owners.

We continued through quiet country with only cows and sheep for company until we reached Cropredy, where we discovered another problem: thunderstorms. Bob was terrified. Unable to find a hole big enough to bury herself in, Bob finally decided that she would get into bed with us. Humph was only 24ft long, and the bed was only 4ft wide. Bob, regardless, got under the covers and shook, clacked her teeth and panted all night. For once I was glad Colin had only one leg, as the extra space stopped me having to sleep on the floor with my head against the chimney.

Our daughter Sally visited us at Banbury, bringing our granddaughter and our son's son, Richard. It was too wet for them to put up their tent, so they decided to sleep in the boat. It's a good job Sally and Jenny are small and that Richard was exceptionally thin – even so, two of them slept leaning against the wood-burning stove.

Richard decided to stay on for a few days after Sally and Jenny went home. It wasn't a planned stay, so we visited a few charity shops to kit him out in clothes for the journey (good job he was not yet of an age where the wearing of second-hand clothes mattered!). I am not sure what he expected, but he certainly had to take some stick from Colin, whose captaincy had not mellowed with his increasing experience.

In the dykes of Somerton, the dog, in a burst of bravado, decided to jump ship and chase a few bullocks. Richard managed to jump off after her and get the lead on before the bullocks saw her; but before he could re-board the boat, the curious bullocks began to gather for a good look at her. Continuing to be unusually brave, the dog barked, some of the bullocks ran off and the dog gave chase. "Oh-ho," thought the rest of the bullocks, "we will show this dog a thing or two," and en masse they turned and faced the dog.

The dog saw the danger before Richard and set off hell for leather in the opposite direction. Colin, mindful of the last episode with bullocks, yelled at Richard. "Don't let go of that lead or we're done for," followed by, "Keep hold of that dog, you big girl's blouse!"

Richard, who was only ten, was fearful of his grandad's wrath, and being called a "big girl's blouse" made him hang on for dear life. Faster and faster ran the dog until the inevitable happened and Richard fell. Bravely, though, he hung on, and through the cow pats he went, leaving plumes of wet cow poo in his wake. No sympathy from Richard's grandad, just further shouts of, "Hang on, lad!"

An added complication was the wind caught the boat and spun us completely around. Colin was beside himself, shouting instructions to all and sundry, dog, grandson and his wife; he was like an erratic machine gun. In response I jumped off the boat on the other side of the canal to Richard and the dog. I meant to catch the rope to halt the boat's voyage back to where we had started at Banbury, but Humph sped on and I had to let go leaving the rope trailing behind the disappearing stern. The Captain was now alone on the boat with no one to issue commands to. I was pleased to see him go, Richard and the dog were lost from sight, but at least they were heading the way we wanted to go, i.e. towards Oxford. The Captain, with no one to shout at, decided he would have to shut up and help himself eventually managing to steer the boat around, pick me up and follow in the direction of the lost dog and boy.

After twenty minutes and many recriminations we were all together again. We decided we had enough for one day and moored up at the edge of the bullock field. After bathing both the dog and Richard in the canal we had a barbecue and cooked beef burgers, a warning to certain parties that we were not to be trifled with.

By now we were getting nervous about sailing on the mighty Thames; every spare moment, Colin was down below checking his engine. We were very impressed by the Heinz variety of boats moored along the canal as we approached Oxford, especially those moored near the Isis Lock. Everyone was different. There were boats that were nothing but barely floating sheds, and boats that had obviously been painted by their owners under the influence of LSD. Some of the more adventurous residents had built tepee extensions on the bank with rings of log seats surrounding evidence of bonfires I thought the site very interesting but have since learned that civilisation and the tax man have caught up with many of the itinerants and they have been moved on many of the boats to skips.

We were sitting under the trees at the side of the canal as our friends Helen and George approached; it was the first time we had seen them since we left Doncaster. We could tell as they came towards us that they were heavily laden, and on inspection it proved that they had hit the Marks & Spencer's food hall big style. (It seems odd now, but at the time it had never occurred to either of us that we were anywhere near such a civilised thing as Marks & Spencer's. We had not only travelled on strange canals, but in our minds we had come to believe we were miles away from any form of civilisation.)

I did not know it, but Colin, used to the commercial canals of home, had believed that all canals were very deep and that he was at serious risk of drowning if he ever went in. While moored in Oxford he saw a chap swimming in the canal, and as Colin spoke to him the man stood up to converse better. Colin was shocked to see that the water only came up to the chap's waist. Colin's fear of drowning was why he had lost a stone and half since we had set out; mind you, his fear hadn't stopped him expecting me to leap six feet from boat to bank at a moment's notice.

It was like Christmas as we set about investigating the bags Helen and George had brought. What a feast! We had wine, cheese, pate, baguettes, tomatoes, crisps, ham and mouth-watering desserts. As we ate we told them of our horrendous adventures and then gradually we all began to laugh hysterically. How could we have been so naïve? Helen told me I had always tended to do things back to front: to have the experience first and learn what I should have done afterwards. An example is having six children and learning about child development when they were all adults . . .

Our fears of the past few weeks drifted away on a sea of good company and wine. Feeling cherished and confident, we began to look forward to the next part of the cruise. I am not sure the same applied to Bob who sat looking at Helen with adoration, a paw resting delicately on her knee. When the time came to say goodbye to Helen and George, Bob had to be restrained from following them up the towpath. Richard had also decided to abandon ship, and went home with them.

Once again on our own, I said to Colin anticipating entering Thames through the lock, "Just think: we are going on the river that carried Elizabeth I."

There was no reply.

"Do you remember the cranes dipping as they carried Winston Churchill on that barge to his funeral?" I continued.

Again there was no reply. But then the Captain said, "I just hope the stupid dog doesn't jump ship, cos the river is really will deep and with my leg I'm bound to float upside down."

On reflection, I suspect the Captain was very nervous about going on the mighty Father Thames. As a girl I had learned in geography lessons the names of the main English rivers parrot fashion, and when I have had too much to drink I can still recite them; and here we were: the River Thames, heart of our country's history and the place where, on our honeymoon, we had spent a wonderful afternoon rowing a boat among the wildlife at Wargrave. The first task was to get a river licence from the dapper, bearded and very fierce-looking lock keeper. He reminded me of Mr Mackay from 'Porridge' in the way he gave his instructions. I listened attentively as the lock keeper explained the penalties for over-staying on the river past the licence expiry date one month hence. Mr Mackay also informed me that I would not be allowed to work the lock myself and we would all have to stay on the boat unless we were sinking.

Suitably chastened, we emerged from the Isis Lock onto the river. Goodbye gypsy boat encampments and the dreaming spires of Oxford; hello historic palaces and houses with sweeping green lawns to personal boathouses. In the event while it was lovely to look at these houses, I began to resent the "No mooring" signs, and it was with difficulty that I restrained my socialist inclinations to claim that the river belonged to all of us by defying the notices and mooring in a "forbidden zone". It had been a sad experience for me, travelling through a once-working environment, now almost all of it given over to middle class tourism; now, wealth on this part of river was very conspicuous and far in excess of anything I had seen on the canals, with huge "gin palaces" passing to and fro at speed, giving us a good roll into the bargain.

We had our lunch at Abingdon, and after eating we decided to take Bob for a walk around the town. Imagine our shock when at the Oxfam shop Bob was refused entry.

I said to Colin, "No dog, no us."

Colin was in a dilemma: non-entry was a big sacrifice for him. Cathedrals and stately homes hold no charms for the Captain: if I insist on doing the touristy things he develops a pronounced limp and heads for the nearest seat. But if car boots, *vide greniers* or charity shops are on the agenda, Colin can walk for miles without rest. One of the big negatives of growing older for the Captain is that he has no use or no room for all the bargains he sees is charity shops and car boots. I would describe Colin as an "early Womble": on one occasion he had spent hours making a gadget that saved him under a pound, and I can remember saying to him, "It would ruin your life if you ever came into money." One of the rare occasions our daughter, Sally, has defied her dad was when he came home with some charity-shop cord trousers. With the comment "Old men leak so you are not wearing them" the offending trousers went straight in the bin . Hence, Abingdon has never been forgiven by either of us for its dog discrimination.

After mooring for the night at Shillingford, we continued downriver. It was very hot and the Captain was twittering about water coming up his rudder tube and the engine sounding "different". In front of us there appeared a very posh hotel with moorings in front of the veranda.

"To hell with the expense, let's treat ourselves." I looked at the Captain pleadingly.

I know from past experience that if I take responsibility for spending exorbitant amounts of money, Colin will really enjoy the experience. So we approached the moorings and were amazed when the chef, complete with hat, emerged to pull us in.

We recounted a brief history of our voyage so far, and the chef and his friend the waiter were very amused by our story – although I think they must have thought we were in need of some TLC. We were shown into the restaurant and treated like royalty on a progress. Bob, as usual, had to stay outside; but she lay contentedly on the veranda in the shade, a bowl of water by her side.

In every restaurant we had visited on our journey, Colin had asked, to no avail, for a bone for Bob. The refusal to accede to his request was usually accompanied by some health and safety reason (I think anthrax was mentioned a few times). By the time we got to this restaurant I was becoming mortally embarrassed by Colin's persistence in begging for bones. And now, undeterred by my dark, threatening frown, Colin said to the waiter, "Have you got a bone for the dog?"

The waiter looked surprised.

"Take no notice of him, he asks everywhere and he knows it's against the rules," I said.

I must have looked as embarrassed and ashamed as I felt. "I'll see what I can do," the waiter replied, before disappearing through the swing doors.

"I wish you would shut up about bloody bones, and this a posh place too!"

"What's wrong with that? Don't posh people have dogs?" was the truculent reply.

At that moment the swing doors parted and the chef, still complete with hat, advanced with a silver platter held high in one hand. He bent towards Colin. On the salver was the largest, whitest shinbone I have ever seen, resting on a delicate white doily.

"Will this do?" said the chef.

"Will it!" replied an astonished Colin. "Bob will think it's her birthday."

Carefully, Colin wrapped the bone in the doily. The service in the restaurant had been so attentive and the food so good that I was unaware of any other customers that day. With many thanks we paid the bill. The chef and his waiter friend pushed us off into the sparkling water of the river. Abingdon was all but forgotten, but memories of that restaurant have abided in that part of the brain that stores special moments.

We carried on downstream with few problems for me, but the poor old Captain again thought water was coming up his rudder tube and that the engine sounded 'funny' and hence that we were in imminent danger of sinking. Consequently, he found my emotional appreciation of the experience of sailing on the Thames irritating to say the least. With the other side of my brain and a woman's logic, I worked out that such a small boat would sink in five minutes, yet we had been on the river a few days and were still afloat. There was nothing to worry about. Bob, ever intuitive where Colin was concerned took an early opportunity to abandon ship and dived straight into the river; not a good idea. It took a complete stranger and me over half an hour to get her up the steep bank and out of the water. Every time we pulled on Bob's collar, her head threatened to come out: weeks of stress had taken its toll on her weight. Finally the stranger put his life at risk by leaning over the bank into the rushing water, putting his arm under the dog's bottom. As the Samaritan pushed up I dragged on her collar, and the sodden dog was eventually landed, panting and frightened on the bank.

After thanking Bob's saviour we resumed our journey. I resolved to buy a dog harness at the next town, and I think it was then that Bob decided to stop the pseudo suicide attempts. Thereafter, she perfected her gibbering technique to let us know how she felt about certain situations.

The next stop was Mapledurham Lock for tea, scones and jam. For me the experience was evocative of the Forsyte Saga (I think I am more a Fleur than Irene, as I've always thought the latter was very smug and not very feisty.) Chatting to the lock keeper I forgot to watch the lock and earned a telling off from the Captain as though I was a five year-old. A huge marital ensued and I ran along the boat roof in an attempt to spear the captain with the boat hook.

listen to me instead of chatting ....

don't you speak to me like that I know what I'm doing

Soon after, we were looking for a mooring at Goring; we had noticed that as we were nearing the rally site mooring opportunities were in increasingly short supply.

Suddenly, we heard a shout: "Eh up, Edna, it's Colin Wright. Bloody hell, we wondered where you'd got to. Come an' breast up against us and tell us all about it."

The voice belonged to John Ecclesfield, a tall large bluff Yorkshireman with wild white hair. Edna, his wife, also tall with grey hair was a much quieter character. They made an imposing couple and were among the well-travelled leaders of the boat club where we were members. While they had spent time with us discussing our plans, I wondered now if they really thought we would make it.

Later we were joined by another couple of members and spent a happy evening telling of our initiation into the world of canal boating. The Captain also learned that his rudder tube required some sealing and that it was normal for the engine to sound "funny" when travelling on very deep water.

The following day we went with our friends to a church fête, where I bought a very appetising-looking cake that turned out to be uncooked in the middle; I hoped this was not a metaphor for our stay in the South.

As we approached Henley, I totaled our canal miles at 389, passing through 256 locks. We had been travelling for 54 days, and had gone from raw novices to competent boaters (or so I believed). We saw the arches of Henley, and as we passed under them I turned to the Captain in joy and wonderment, to find tears streaming down his cheeks.

"God, I never thought we'd do it," he choked.

There were rows of gaily painted boats strung out along the bank, most with bunting from stern to bow. As we emerged from under the bridge, Colin immediately spotted a big 14 painted on the grass bank, and we were delighted to find that our number, 14a, meant that we were alongside this bank. Most of the boats were moored three abreast; after so long being mostly on our own, we were now part of a village; if someone on one of the other boats coughed inside their boat, we could hear them. We would have to go "cold turkey" with the maritals.

In no time at all we had the umbrella up and the chairs out on the bank at the far side of the path across from the side of Humph. People were walking up and down the path viewing and commenting on the boats, and inevitably we began chatting to them. We decided to put a short history of Humph and our voyage on the side of our boat.

On hearing we had arrived, Sally, Andrew and David, our children, and assorted grandchildren, decided to bring a couple of tents and pay us a congratulatory visit. We felt we were truly living the dream: the weather was hot, the river sparkled and there were plenty of things to see and do. For me, the biggest plus was that some of the family had found time to be with us. To celebrate, I bought a very cheap but flattering dress and hat in Henley. I wore the dress for years – not only because it suited me but because it brought back memories of a magical time. The dress also reminded me that bargains can be obtained in the most unexpected places.

Chapter 4

Humph becomes a star

The children arrived, all excited, on the Saturday. Humph became the base they all returned to after looking around the myriad attractions of the rally. Colin got his shorts on and his bike off the boat and went off on his own to enjoy a day of engine talk. I was content to make sure there was enough to eat for the returnees, and to sit on the bank in the sun with a newspaper. An unexpected benefit of sitting on the towpath with Bob was the amount of free post-traumatic stress counselling that was available for both of us: gradually, I was able to re-frame the whole canal and river experience in a more positive and humorous light. Bob refined her paw-shake, combined with a slight tremble, to perfection. Over numerous cups of tea I learned from many other boaters how they had survived similar events to ours; I marvelled at how they had recovered strongly enough to keep boating.

Towards the end of the day, as the stream of passers-by thinned to a trickle, I began chatting to a very handsome stranger. The stranger was an appreciative audience of my by-now-well-embellished story of "A Wright Journey".

"Would you mind if I brought a TV crew to film you, the Captain and Bob the dog for a programme I am making?" the stranger asked at length.

I was, as they say in Yorkshire, gobsmacked. "What programme?"

"Oh, just a programme on boating," the handsome stranger replied.

"Well, yes, that would be OK," I said, in a voice which I hoped sounded slightly indifferent, while inside my head there was a scream: *Yes. Yes. Yes. Fame at last! One in the eye for all the doubters!*

Handsome stranger continued, "I'll be back with a crew about six o' clock." And with that promise, he went on his way.

I had to hold onto my excitement for a full half hour before Colin and Andrew arrived back. I launched straight in at the Captain. "Come on, hurry up, you'll have to get a shave, change that shirt and get out of those shorts

"What for?" the Captain replied.

I could sense rebellion. "A TV crew is coming at six o' clock to film us."

"Who says so?"

Rebellion was turning to disbelief; I could see it in the Captain's face. "I have been talking to a chap and he says he is making a programme about boating and he wants to feature us."

"Oh aye, he's been spinning you a line."

Stung, I replied hotly, "I'm not that daft, he meant it."

"What programme?" said the Captain.

I could see now he was amused at my apparent gullibility. "I don't know, he didn't say," I admitted. "But anyway you can still get a shave now."

I was in recovery: now the Captain would get a shave.

"Well, I am not taking me shorts off."

By now the whole family were back, and without exception I could tell that they all thought granny had been spun a line.

It was half past six when the film crew arrived.

"Thank God you've come," exclaimed Andrew, ever one to deflate my ego, "me mother has been and bought a new hat and we thought she would have to take it back."

There were three people in the crew: the handsome stranger, a man with a muff thing on a long handle, and a bossy girl who began to arrange the poses. Nothing could go right for bossy girl: the inside of the boat was 20ft by 6ft, and in that space was a toilet compartment, kitchen sink, cooker, solid fuel stove and two four-foot-long settees that converted into a double bed. Five adults, the dog and the "muff" meant that posing was impossible. So a rethink was required, whereby it was decided to interview the Captain and me posing on the back deck, with the TV crew and muff on the bank. The handsome stranger also wanted a picture of a suicidal Bob looking out of a window in desperation.

But Bob had other ideas: with all these people interested in her, she was in la la land, all thoughts of suicide abandoned. Retrievers can smile, and Bob was an expert. Laughing all over her face, she insisted on looking through the window – from the *outside*. No amount of persuasion worked, so in the end the TV crew had to accept it. Bossy young lady had met her match.

Until I saw the programme, our problems with Bob were all I could remember and I was full of pride and enthusiasm about our prospective appearance on TV. I wrote to all my friends who promised to record our appearance on what I had found out was a programme about the Boat Show scheduled for the week of the show in January. But oh, what a fall my pride had to take! After all the hassle, who were the stars of the appearance? Not the Captain and me but the boat and the dog.

Several boats were shown before we appeared, all of them expensive "gin palaces"; then it was our turn. Throughout the interview, the background music playing was the "cement mixer" – a reference to my comment (not quite true but I believed it at the time, that the engine was "off a cement mixer"). There I was in my elegant, slightly fitted, long, flowing dress and floppy hat, leaning languorously against the balustrade; Colin wearing his washed out "Eric Morecambe's", mismatched legs and socks, ill-fitting but clean shirt and white floppy sunhat. Excitedly, we spoke into the "muff", answering questions from the unseen handsome stranger about the boat and the journey. Oh my God! I had never realised how strong and awful my South Yorkshire accent was; and if that wasn't bad enough, my tone and intonation rivalled Hilda Ogden's. The Captain, on the other hand, came across as a gentle if slightly gormless boating enthusiast who had managed a real achievement despite having a neurotic harridan as a partner and First Mate.

The real stars were Bob, looking elegant, beautiful and floaty, smiling through the sliding window, and Humph himself, looking brave, graceful and colourful, the wooden superstructure having weathered to a rich golden colour. Tactfully, most of our friends enthused over the dog and boat and played down our appearance, for which I am eternally grateful. The recording of our appearance lies at the back of our cupboard; it has never seen the light of day since January 1998.

Chapter 5

Goodbye to Humph

After all the excitement of the TV appearance and the children's visit, we turned and headed for home in a more reflective mood. We intended to take a different route, which would lead us to the dreaded tidal Trent. The scary moments were fewer now we were more experienced.

There was one amusing moment on the Thames, when we were being buffeted about in the wash of a "gin palace". As we rolled, the mobile phone rang. Thinking the worst, I answered it, moving along the narrow gangway in order to hear the caller. With one hand gripping the top rail and the other holding the phone, I rolled with the boat. "Yvonne Wright."

"Can you do me a massage this afternoon? I'm desperate."

I could not believe what I was hearing.

"What did you say?"

"Can you do me a massage this afternoon? I'm in agony."

To my shame I burst out laughing. "At this moment I'm about to roll into the Thames. I am sorry but I can't fit you in this afternoon."

"Do you know anyone who can give me a massage?"

"I am sorry but you will have to look in the Yellow Pages."

I had to finish the call as another wave hit us.

"I don't believe it, Colin," I told him.

"Somebody's having us on," he replied.

"No, I think it was genuine, but I wonder who gave him my number."

After I had retired from full-time nursing I had retrained as a Therapeutic Masseuse and it was hard work building up a business in the front room; to find I had a customer who sounded as though he really needed me, while I was in the middle of the river, was galling indeed.

Needless to say, despite all the lecturing from Mr Mackay we had overstayed our licence time on the Thames by one day – even less, if reckoned in hours. Despite all my blandishments, Mr Mackay stuck to the letter of the law and we were fined. And so, despite the lovely welcome at the restaurant, I was disappointed overall in the Thames. Those "No Mooring" signs abounded, and mooring places were in short supply. And where we had moored at Henley, three foot from the tow path, there was a fence, and behind this a huge expanse of beautiful green grass. But we were "Not allowed on the grass": it was reserved for the Hooray Henrys of the regatta. The regatta is in June and the rally at the end of August; and surely one of the great characteristics of grass is that it *grows*. Hence, all trace of the rally's participants would have been eradicated by the end of September. But we had enjoyed the rally despite being treated as second class citizens.

well you go and tell the committee they might not want me to pic-nic here...... but I do

Leaving all that behind, we ambled along the canal home. The blackberry season was in full swing and, full of peace and goodwill, I treated the Captain to various blackberry-based puddings and cordials. The nights were drawing in, and during the day we gathered bits of wood for the fire as we travelled. Bob had settled into the routine, apart from the occasion when we had a thunderstorm. As the thunder banged and the lightning flashed, Bob gibbered. Inconsolable, the neurotic mess of flying hair got into bed with us. The Captain is not the most tolerant of people in the middle of the night, and for hours the sound of teeth chattering was interrupted by, "Bloody hell, shut up, Bob!" and "Yvonne, get this dog off me!" I thought this last remark most unfair: despite having parts of his person missing, the Captain has to spread himself about in bed, and between him and Bob they left me hanging onto the side with about six inch of mattress to lie on.

Despite the storm, the journey home was a fantastic and relaxing time. We travelled on the Trent as far as Newark, where we had decided to have Humph lifted out of the water and taken via a lorry to Strawberry Island. I wish now we had attempted the Trent: it would have made a fine end to our adventure; but we still felt like novices, and beholden to take the advice of more experienced boaters.

Through the winter nights, we talked over our adventures. We decided that, while Humph had fulfilled our expectations and more, we wanted more space on a boat to allow family to visit us more easily. We advertised Humph for sale, and luckily found a man to whom we thought we could sell him. And even though we did find Humph a good home, for once the Captain and I are in agreement: we both feel guilty that we abandoned that unique, stout-hearted little boat that was our first love.

BOOK TWO – Mr BEAN

Chapter 1

Yvonne's dream

Our second boat was Mr Bean, so called because the previous owner was taking the boat's existing name with him, and had commented to his wife, who was reluctant to part with the boat, "It's a lot of cans of beans, Margaret."

Somehow, the name seemed so suitable for how I thought of us, I said, "Colin, that's it: we will call the boat Mr Bean, 'cause we are like Mr and Mrs Bean."

My husband looked shocked: it was the first time that a name had been put to our boating skills, and although Colin can laugh at his own shortcomings, naming the boat Mr Bean seemed a step too far. It took some time to persuade him that the new name was a good idea – although when we came to travel in France the name attracted so much attention he was glad I had insisted.

The previous owners, Margaret and Ron, had found it hard to agree on whether they wanted a plastic cruiser or a narrow boat built. The result of their differing ideas was a hybrid, and the boat they eventually took delivery of had a seagoing cruiser-style back with a long passenger seat across the stern and a steering wheel. The whole of the back area was covered in wet weather by what I described as a pram hood. The rest was a normal narrow boat.

As I've said, Colin and I were both sad to part with Humph but we had acquired a taste for boating and wanted to have the room to share the joys with the family. Hence, we agreed to invest in a bigger boat. But getting a bigger boat was about *all* we agreed on. I had been unable to get the hang of the steering on Humph:

with a tiller, if you want to go right you steer left, and I have always had difficulty telling left from right, so when I tried to steer we ended up zig-zagging from side to side of the canal. At 45 ft Mr Bean was the right length for easy handling but I was not happy with the inside layout: it was a shock having to use a porta potti. (Toilets loom large in my story, as you will see, and as time has gone on I have had to get used to even more primitive arrangements than a porta potti.) Colin liked the swim of the boat, it was well built, and a big plus for me was that it had a steering wheel. We bought Mr Bean as a compromise; and as with all compromises, neither of us were satisfied. I particularly did not like the tunnel layout with the walk way down the middle from front to back but in the interest of getting an agreement put my doubts to one side

Our first cruise was on the Chesterfield Canal as part of a convoy of Strawberry Island Club boaters. Peter was Commodore for this traditional Easter cruise; he and his wife Carol led the cruise every year. Carol is the guardian of the traditions of the cruise: she has Easter chicks, made by her daughter who is now a mother herself, flying up the wall inside their boat. Carol always makes a traditional Simnel Cake and a very tasty but lethal sloe gin. The cruise can hardly be described as healthy but is very enjoyable, and now that we're in 'foreign parts' it is something we miss enormously.

The route to the Chesterfield Canal is along 'home waters': the South Yorkshire Navigation and the Trent River. The building of the Chesterfield Canal was begun in 1771; the canal is entered by a lock off the river at West Stockwith, and the route from West Stockwith to Chesterfield was completed in 1777. Coal was the principal cargo, followed by stone, corn, lime, lead, timber and iron. The canal was at its busiest in 1848 when over 200,000 tons of cargo was transported in individual loads of 22 tons, all of it pulled by horses. From 1840, approximately 250,000 tons of stone from Anston was shipped along the canal to build the new Houses of Parliament. By 1904, the Norwood Tunnel only had headroom of 4 foot 10 inches owing to subsidence; by 1907, the tunnel finally closed the canal as a working environment began to decline and revert back to nature.

Today, it is hard to believe how busy the canal once was, now that it is given over to leisure boating. At the time we cruised on it in Mr Bean it was being restored from Worksop towards the Norwood Tunnel.

To the uninitiated, the countryside along the South Yorkshire Navigation from Stainforth (the nearest point on the canal to our home) to Keadby looks flat and uninteresting; much of the area was once bog and scrub, although at the time of the Norman Conquest the area was known as a fine hunting area. Beyond Thorne the area is still very rural; much of the area was drained by the Dutch in the seventeenth century, resulting in fine arable land. It is a country of big skies and little hamlets.

Our convoy arrived at Keadby at about 8 p.m. and we all had traditional fish and chips before settling down for an early night. We had an early start in the morning to catch the tide that would carry us up the Trent to Stockwith Lock and the Chesterfield Canal. The Captain and I went to sleep, confident in the strength of Mr Bean and comforted by the butterflies in our tummies.

In the morning we were up at 6 a.m. checking the engine, anchor, anchor lines, and of course Bob the dog, smart in her new harness in case her suicidal tendencies resurfaced. Bob had taken to Mr Bean: she had picked her spot, lying on the engine cover, an ideal place for a nervous dog. Bob would appear to be sound asleep in her spot but immediately the sound of the engine changed she would sit up and gibber.

The Trent is always talked of in tones of awe in the boat club. Conversations containing sentences like, "There I was, 'punching' the tide, when a huge wave came over the bow and we were swamped," were often heard. The received wisdom was that you had to get to your destination before the tide turned, or you were done for. At six-thirty we were all shuffling about in the large lock wearing the latest design in lifejackets, boat engines running. It was a tense time but I was unperturbed; I had seen the Trent from the motorway: it looked wide and peaceful – what was all the fuss about? At just past seven, the water in the lock drained out and the gates opened. I could see this sheet of silver water galloping past. 'God! That must be going at a hundred miles an hour', I thought. The Captain looked pale and resolute, his Denis Healey eyebrows standing to attention. With a mighty roar of the engine we followed our leader, leaning at a dramatic angle as we turned right and upstream with the tide behind us. We heard on the radio the lock keeper announce our departure and expected time of arrival at Stockwith. The Trent is the only river on which I have been on where I have been comforted by the knowledge that if we sank, someone would miss us.

The trip was fantastic: I read the charts and kept in touch with our fellow boats via the VHF radio. The view from the part of the Trent we were on has hardly changed over the millennia (a motorway bridge and four power stations being the obvious additions). What we could see from the river were the churches of the hamlets strung along the bank. I felt strangely in touch with the Britain of the past, the Britain invaded by the Viking longboats. I was too interested in my surroundings to be frightened.

I was more curious than concerned when I caught sight of our Commodore seemingly dancing on the roof of his boat and waving a long pole in the manner of Magnus Pike.

"What's he doing?" I asked the Captain.

"I've no idea. I hope I don't have to rescue him. I don't think I can slow down."

It was then that we remembered the radio and I asked Carol what Peter was doing.

"Oh, he's rescuing a sheep," was the seemingly unconcerned reply.

We slowed down as much as we could and watched in admiration as the sheep was guided with the pole to the bank where it scrambled up and disappeared without a backward glance. Sheep have no gratitude: that could have been a full scale Peter rescue alert.

Colin had insisted on the pram hood being down despite the cold, and as the morning advanced I was glad to be able to see all around us as we tried naming familiar places from this different vantage point. Exactly on time we arrived at Stockwith. The Captain revved the engine and made for the entrance, no messing about, positioning the boat by turning it round to slow us down and then making for the slack water at the side of the lock before negotiating an entry using the conventional method. We went in at a speed dictated by the tide to join Carol and Peter in the lock, stopping our boat with a noisy full-engine reverse (there are no brakes on boats, as the Captain keeps reminding me). We learned later that the lock keeper had asked Peter who the fighter pilot was, and remarked that he was well named Mr Bean. The Captain, knowing only half the story, was very proud of the impression he had made.

We moored up in the basin along with a lot of plastic boats. With our friends Carol, Peter and Richard, we had a quiet evening drink in the Stockwith Boat Club bar.

Peter, the commodore of the cruise, is an electrical engineer and the vice-president of Strawberry Island Boat Club; he was one of the few members who had faith in the Captain's ability as an amateur marine engineer. The Captain in turn had a great deal of respect for Peter's knowledge, ability and most of all he the way he never forced his opinions on you. If you asked for advice his replies always respected your abilities.

Peter is a large man in terms of height (over six foot), character and humour, though not in girth; our friend's energy and enthusiasm sometimes outstrips his physical dexterity, and some of his accidents and near misses were hair-raising. I sometimes thought that the two captains were similar in character: they both appeared to believe they could fly. I have seen Peter, in snow, take a leap from one side of a lock to another, miss, and slide gracefully down a mossy wall into the icy waters.

Carol, Peter's wife, and I have a lot in common: we are both children-and-family centred. There are differences between us too, though: Carol is tall, very elegant and much more practical than me; she can upholster a chair, organise and cook a dinner for a hundred, and, more important, make a mean sloe gin. Both Peter and Carol are very gregarious and an evening with them is guaranteed to be enjoyable.

Accompanying Peter and Carol was Carol's mother, a very cheerful and mischievous elderly lady who constantly wound up the collie pup, Macey. Macey was everything Bob was not: energetic, fearless and slightly mad; she was a good pal for Bob.

Richard, the captain of the other boat in the convoy, was a bachelor who lived on his boat. The Captain described Richard as a "typical railway man".

"What's that?" I asked.

"Well, he likes stoking his fire and is not too tidy."

The Captain also envied Richard's boat. It was "a proper man's boat – no frillies."

After a restful night's sleep we were up early, although not as early as the restless Commodore. The weather was awful, with a howling wind and driving rain. Peter was already out of the canal basin and waiting for us along the bank. For us, getting out of the basin was a nightmare. Until that morning, we had hardly had to manoeuvre the boat. I did not realise until many years later that you may put a boat's engine in reverse but you cannot steer backwards. As soon as we cleared the pontoon the wind got hold of us and spun us round to opposite the exit. In an attempt to override the power of the wind, the Captain revved the engine. Backwards, forwards and around in a circle we whirled in a lonely battle, to the increasing consternation of Peter who was galloping up and down the bank apparently shouting instructions. The Captain, encased in the pram hood I had insisted on keeping up, couldn't hear a thing and could see only slightly more.

"Go to the front and tell me what he's saying," I was instructed.

As I edged along the gunwale to the front I could understand the reason for Peter's increasingly panic-stricken signals. "Tell him to slow the engine down and use the forward to steer slowly," he yelled.

I tried to pass the message on, adding my own. "Stop the bloody boat!" I mouthed to the deaf Captain, who was devoid of lip-reading skills.

We continued at speed across the basin, finally impaling the superstructure of our boat on two arms of the anchor of a plastic boat. A crunch as our bow hit the boat amidships, setting the plastic boat rolling violently. A head appeared from below and a small lithe man with a squeaky voice screamed in the direction of the pram hood, "I was having me breakfast, what the bloody hell are you playing at?" Bits of breakfast were spouting in all directions like bullets. The man we now know as David would probably have liked to aim real bullets at the hood.

Before the Captain had time to emerge, Peter leapt from the bank onto David's boat and then onto ours, having decided to rescue the situation. We were all members of the same boat club, and I think Peter thought it important that, as commodore, he maintain the reputation of the club in foreign waters. Fortunately, there was no permanent damage to David's boat and we had only sustained two holes in our superstructure. Danger over, we all had a good laugh, but the Captain realised that he had gone to the bottom of the class again; he would have to learn to handle a new boat with the same problems as Humph, but bigger.

Despite the cold weather, the trip was relaxing and enjoyable. Carol gradually initiated us into the traditions of the Easter Cruise: alcohol could not be consumed until the invisible sun was "over the yard-arm", and Simnel cake and sloe gin finished the day; there was a BBQ and a big bonfire, cosy meals in pubs, and a shopping trip in the seething metropolis of Retford.

Gossiping, Carol and Colin guided the boats through the locks side by side, and at one point mended a puncture on Peter's bike. Peter and I worked the locks, travelling between them on the bikes. After Clayworth, the locks narrow to 6ft 10in, a great temptation to Peter to take a short cut from one side to the other. Well, the inevitable happened: he missed and took an unexpected cold bath.

The area around Manton was known to be plagued by vandals and the secret was to get through early: vandals only operate after lunch. It was just before Shireoaks Marina that Peter came into his own. A narrow boat was stuck fast in a newly restored lock which had apparently been restored on the kind of ancient foundation whose width is not always accurate enough for the designs of modern boat builders. Several people were trying to pull the boat; then Peter had a different idea: we would open the lock paddles and "flush" the boat out.

After a big discussion between British Waterways and English Heritage, the lock walls were later shaved to avoid further problems.

On our first cruise Low Treble Locks were as far as a boat could go. As there was no place to turn the boat to return, the route to these locks was still not open for cruising. Peter had an idea: he lashed Mr Bean's bow to his boat's stern and the two craft went forwards and backwards respectively until we reached the final lock gates at Low Treble. People came out of the nearby houses to cheer: we were the first boats there since the tunnel had closed in 1907. What a magic moment! I felt like an archaeologist discovering evidence of some forgotten time. (Since that first cruise, the canal has been restored as far as the tunnel, and oh! despite my fear, how I would like to be the first boat into Chesterfield from the Trent.)

Later that year we set off on our first long cruise, meeting up with our friends George and June to cruise on the Welsh canals. Bob was beside herself with joy, and as soon as we met up she immediately moved to her special place in front of their fire.

George and June were impressed by how well their pupils had progressed: for example, we now knew to go through tunnels fast in order to keep straight. Although I was impressed by the construction of the Llangollen Canal, without the company of George and June it would have been a very lonely time.

We left them, and, as we had hoped, our son Andrew came out with his family to use the boat while we came home. Poor Andrew and company had a very wet time as they travelled down the Shropshire, finishing their holiday moored in the centre of Stratford. Andrew still feels deprived to this day.

We continued our journey, arriving in Kinver on the day of a village celebration. The event kicked off with a jumble sale run by the playgroup. In the afternoon there was a tea dance, with Henry at the piano. I have never been to a more lively party. We sat with Miriam and her friends. Miriam was weighed down with heavy jewellery including huge rings on fingers with long, red, claw-like nails; she wore all her wealth to prevent burglars getting hold of it. She must have been in her mid-eighties, and was, according to her friend, "Brahms and Liszt". Miriam's other three friends were of a similar age and equally high spirits. The tea consisted of chicken sandwiches, mouth-watering trifles and cakes. The Captain, ever the gourmet, offered to marry at least three ladies, proving the old adage that 'the way to a man's heart is through his stomach'. Bob was not allowed in, but sat outside with Norman, who fed her a chicken sandwich, followed by other small titbits I was not meant to see. The dancing was far more noisy and energetic than Top of the Pops – there was much more dance than tea. We ended the afternoon with a rousing rendition or two of "You'll Never Walk Alone", after which the Captain and I staggered back to the boat to sleep it all off. We were both drunk on the atmosphere and sherry trifle; if that's old age, bring it on! We were recovered enough to enjoy an Alan Ayckbourn play in the school that evening, a perfect end to an enjoyable day.

The following year, we cruised to Waltham Abbey to the IWA rally. This was a very different cruise for we now considered ourselves "experienced boaters". We had enrolled ourselves on the escorted cruise from St Catherine's Dock to Hampton Court, and were the last visitor boat of the convoy; behind us was the back boat of our escort group, the St Pancras Boating Club. Getting to our destination "before the tide turned" was of vital importance. Over the VHF, the boat behind instructed us to get a move on just as we were about to pass the Houses of Parliament where the whole convoy had slowed to take pictures. As I have said, there are no brakes on boats, so the result of us speeding up while the other boats slowed down was a melee of bumping and bashing midstream. Most of the captains were of retirement age, and the canal rage they exhibited had to be seen to be believed: paintwork and pictures were definitely more important than the possibility of being swept past the London Barrage. It was on the way home from this rally that we began to hear the first towpath rumours of a convoy of thirteen boats going to Waltham Abbey in the near future.

The pram hood had continued to be a nightmare, with clear visibility only possible when looking straight ahead. Through the plastic at the side it was almost impossible to see anything at all. But the hood problem was finally solved when, unbeknown to us, our son crashed the corner of the window screen into a bridge wall, smashing the glass. Andrew did not realise when he put new glass in that he should have used safety glass.

Persuading Colin to make what I considered necessary alterations inside the boat was difficult, but I got help from two unexpected sources. Travelling on the Rochdale Canal in 1999, we met up with a lovely Glaswegian couple with a lively son of about eight who loved to come on our boat because Colin let him steer. We were warned in the navigation book about the peculiar low roof, combined with a dog leg, in the tunnel, but Colin, who was driving, was fully occupied with making weird yodelling noises with the young lad when we hit the dog leg with a mighty crash. The Captain stood there, silent (for once) and shocked, covered in wood chippings and splintered glass from the wheelhouse windows. When we emerged and stopped, the young lad ran back to his parents shouting, "Dad, Dad, Mr Wright's crashed big style!"

Instead of repairing the pram hood we took the opportunity to redesign the whole back. The bus seats went to the skip and the resident handyman built a smart new wheelhouse with collapsible windows and canvas roof. Later we also replaced the bunk beds. I turned over one night and found myself flying through the air and landing on my knees at the side of a sleeping Colin. At nearly sixty, it was not an activity I intended to repeat.

I had not been hurt, but taking advantage of the success of the redesigned wheelhouse I said to the reluctant handyman, "You may believe you can fly but I'm not the right shape for it." Sometimes it's not what you say but how you say it that counts; the unspoken threat was that I might break a bone and then there would be no more boating.

To reinforce my request, I began to have more difficulty in getting up and down the ladder into bed. I am a hefty lady and the possibility of landing on the Captain's stump concentrated his mind wonderfully. Another big problem was that once Colin is in bed he is literally legless; it's me who has to get up and repel boarders in vandal-infested areas.

Alterations to the inside layout were begun, and only properly completed as we sold the boat. Once an owner alters one thing in a boat, everything else has to be redesigned, so eventually I got the boat to my liking: new kitchen, bathroom and a state-of-the-art porta potti.

We were now more experienced boaters, so we did not have the "adventures" on Mr Bean in England that we had had on Humph. But talking to a chap in a lock one day, I found out that a group of narrow boats were going the following year to France. It was pouring with rain at the time and I fancied a bit of sun and wine. Years earlier, we had cycled and camped all over Brittany and really enjoyed the experience, the locals being really taken with the image of "ze man with ze wooden leg" riding a bike; I felt that fate was pointing its finger in the direction of France, as that same year the way was suddenly clear for the introduction of the Pet Passport scheme.

Chapter 2

Preparations for France

"We're going to France next year, but not with the man we met," I told Colin. "Our Graham will do the transporting cheaper." My brother had by now forsaken a life on the water and was working for a shipping company, arranging transport for containers all over the world. I knew that if we got the trip cheaper than our informer, Colin would be up for the expedition. I contacted Graham, who told us to get more information, such as where could we put the boat in the water.

At the end of the season we went to reconnoitre northern France. Of course, on the trip we only saw what we wanted to see, big wide stretches of empty canal, often lined with trees. We asked passers-by for directions to moorings, and a combination of my poor schoolgirl French and the lack of mooring places led to some interesting situations. At Amiens a passer-by told us about the Hortillonages, which sounded an ideal place to drop the boat into the water.

We went to the tourist office. In my feeble French I explained that we wanted to launch our boat into the Hortillonages, and was met by a completely blank look. Irritated, I explained three more times using differing pronunciations of the same message to no avail.

"They're bloody thick," I said to Colin, "shouldn't be allowed to work in a tourist office. We will have to use the map."

Three hours later we found the Hortillonages. They were allotments, most of whose plots were surrounded by very small, three-foot wide irrigation canals . . . Colin's face was a picture, he was both impressed by the scale and design of the allotments and irritated by the time, effort and, more important, the petrol we had wasted.

Back at home we did some further investigations and found out that before we could go to France we would need to obtain a certificate to say we were competent boat handlers. We duly enrolled on Tam and Di Morrell's boat-handling course. The course lasted four days and was held on their boat, Friesland, based in Cambrai. There cannot be a better couple to teach elderly people new skills: Tam taught the driving and Di the rope skills, as well as cooking some excellent meals. We students were two couples, and the other pair tested Tam's diplomacy to the limit. The man was a large rumbustious consultant doctor who was constantly asserting he didn't need to be there as he had yachted all over the world and was a *more* than competent sailor. (In the event, though, I passed the test before him.) The woman was also a doctor. Although Petra (not her real name) was well into middle age she was sick with puppy love for Bob (not his real name) who, for the most part, was coldly indifferent to her attentions. I learned later Petra and Bob were not a couple. Petra told me she had come on the trip in the hope of altering the situation. The moment we met Petra asked me to swap rooms, as Colin and I had been allocated the cabin with the double bed. Affronted by the assumption that we had no need of a double bed, I coldly refused her request.

Tam, our instructor, with his long pony-tail, fisherman's smock and generally gentle demeanour, reminded me of a sixties flower child; but his patience was sorely tried by his pupils on this trip. One afternoon Petra constantly anticipated wrongly Tam's instructions. We banged from bank to bank in a large boat like a dodgem car then I heard Tam's very calm quiet voice say, "Petra, if you carry on ignoring what I say we are seriously going to have to renegotiate our position."

I was angry that these two people who, in my opinion, should know better were spoiling our time on the boat; and the more I thought about it, the angrier I became. When I am in that sort of mood, I tend to withdraw into myself. I became silent and inadvertently mysterious to Bob who began to follow me around the boat like a love sick puppy telling me what a brilliant doctor he was, all the while ignoring the equally puppyish overtures from Petra. I can still see Petra's agonised looks as she espied us sitting together outside the wheelhouse; if she had looked closer she would have seen the irritation registered on my face.

It became so bad that my inner rage threatened to break out and Di, probably fearing for her financial future, had to take me for a long walk as soon as we stopped boating that evening. Colin, oblivious to the swirling hormones, concentrated on learning how to handle the boat, and despite his lack of formal education, passed the course first and with flying colours. To my surprise, I also obtained my certificate, and was the first to do a figure of eight through the arches of the bridge, one in the eye, I thought, for our two pains in the neck.

At last we were ready for our great adventure on the canals of France.

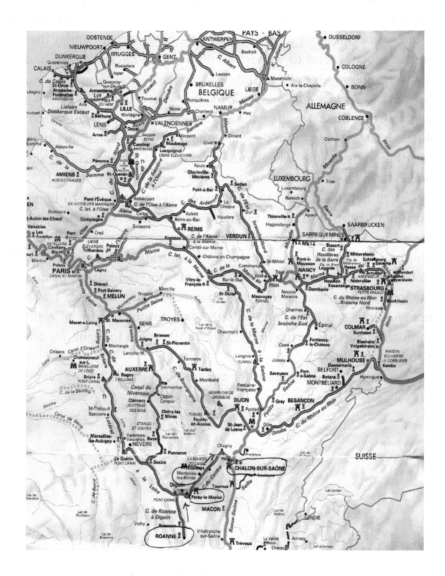

The canals of France and Belgium

Chapter 3

Vive Voies Navigables de France

I had been recommended a boatyard in Migennes that had a crane and was run by an Englishman. I was anxious to get to warmer climes quickly and I had also heard horrific stories of narrow boats travelling on the big highway of the Grand Gabarit. We decided to pay for the extra mileage and take Mr Bean to the boatyard by road. Chantier Fluvial de Migennes is on the River Yonne; about a mile downstream towards Paris there is a turn to the right followed by a lock which is the entrance to the Canal de Bourgogne. Turn left from the yard upstream, and it is a day's boating to Auxerre and thence to the prettiest canal in France, the Nivernais. Paris is about a week's boating north and downstream from the yard.

Our move to France in the year 2000 coincided with the foot and mouth epidemic in Britain. For weeks we were marooned at Thorne, away from our home mooring, finishing the alterations. Eventually the boat was lifted out onto oil drums and then Mr Bean's bottom was sterilised with a high-speed pressure washer. With all the certificates we could think of to confirm we were sanitised, the boat was ready to be craned onto the lorry for France.

A small crowd of family and friends gathered for the lift and departure. Almost as soon as the lift began, Colin had doubts about the competence of the crane driver, as he was busy chatting away to me and not watching where he was putting the slings. The slings fixed, the operator got in his cab, started the engine and the boat began to rise. The front rose out of the water but the stern did not follow until ten seconds later.

A look of horror and then rage showed on the Captain's face. He shouted to the crane operator, "Put the bloody thing down, the slings are in the wrong place."

It took several attempts for Colin, increasingly frightened and red in the face, to alert the operator, by which time the rocking boat looked as though it was about to take a nose dive to the floor. Eventually, the operator heard our shouts and the crane lowered the boat towards the ground.

"Come on, Andrew, we'll have sort it, he's no idea about bloody balance," Colin shouted at his son.

I was mortally embarrassed by the behaviour of the Captain, and as the crane operator came and stood by me redundant I tried desperately to distract him from the vibes that were coming through the Captain's back. It was during this rethink that the crane driver told me he had appeared on You've Been Framed, dropping a boat from a great height.

It was with some relief, therefore, that we eventually saw Mr Bean onto the lorry. The Captain was so relieved to see the back of that "daft bugger" that he broke open his wallet and gave Sally

£30 and told her to go and get everyone bacon butties in a nearby café. Colin to be spending any money unprompted is truly amazing, so much so that his gift was greeted by all the kids with stunned silence instead of thanks.

Later, we followed the boat on its journey to Migennes, David, our middle son, taking us and the dog as far as Calais in his car. We journeyed on to Migennes by train. Amazingly, considering all the hype in the papers about the French not wanting to buy our "contaminated" meat and sterilising the lorries, we were informed later by Jo the *patron* of the yard that the driver of our lorry had told him no one had ever asked to check the boat's papers.

We arrived at the boatyard in Migennes to find Mr Bean already in the water. The River Yonne had been in flood, but by the time the boat was launched the water had retreated to just below the bank. There he was, Mr Bean, riding high in the sun, waiting for the start of our big adventure; and by the time we left the yard four days later, the river had already fallen so much that the boat's roof was level with the bank – the first intimation that things were much bigger and quicker on the continent.

On the appointed day, Jo let the lock keeper know we were setting off at *neuf heures*. Our first introduction to French locks was a frightening experience. At six metres, the lock was deeper than anything we had experienced in England and we were not alone in there. We were at the front, with plastic boats of assorted sizes milling around us. For ages it seemed there was no one there, and we could see nothing above but the lock walls and a patch of very blue sky. We both felt very nervous bobbing around trying to avoid the other boats, some of which also had very inexperienced captains' mates who were intent on warding us off with the points of boat hooks. No one seemed to speak English, or even French.

Eventually, a three-pronged hook was lowered on the end of a rope by a very surly sallow looking man who, we presumed, was the lock keeper. The rope and prongs were shaken about until we got the message to hang our rope on the prongs. The lock keeper had bottle-bottom glasses, with a yellowish tinge, worn very close to his eyes, very black straight teeth, and a soggy roll-up hanging from his lip; it seemed to us that, for him, work was an interruption to his life and that he no intention of helping inexperienced, frightened boaters. The hook with the rope hanging from it disappeared from sight, and we were left with only just enough rope, Colin having to hang onto the stern rope with his hands above his head.

Finally, after much shouting and poking, we were all tied up. But waiting in the "black hole", we had no intimation of the drama to come. The water came in with such force from under the boat that we could barely hang onto the ropes; first Mr Bean attempted to attack the boat next door, and then the boat behind. The noise was horrendous and I was terrified; no one else seemed to be aware of the dire danger I felt we were in. In the lock, the wider plastic boats were easier to manage and now that they were anchored to the bollards, and their crews were chatting to each other unconcernedly as the boats rose rapidly in the lock. It wasn't long before we could see the port of Migennes above the locks walls, and it became apparent what our difficulty was: our boat was the wrong length for the bollards. The distance the rope had to travel back to the boat was too far to secure the rope to two bollards, which meant that, as the water came up, the rope slackened − not enough to manually tighten but enough for the water pressure to swing the boat across the lock, thus tightening the rope so much that I had no chance of pulling the boat alongside the walls. Keeping the boat safely straight along the lock walls was a difficulty that was to dog us throughout our voyages in France.

The scene that greeted us at the top of the lock was what we had seen in the brochures, a huge, sparkling expanse of water with a hire-boat station at one end, a café behind it and railway lines on the other side. A few other boats were moored at the quay; but we were excited and anxious to be on our way, and so, without stopping to chat, we were out through the broad canal at the end of the port. The canal was lined with pollarded trees, bright with new green leaf. It was leading us, we believed, towards new and exciting adventurers.

Our cruise plan was to travel south along the Canal de Bourgogne to Saint Jean-de-Losne. Turn west and upstream on the River Saône, continuing west along the Canal de Centre, and then North along the Nivernais Canal, which ends at Auxerre, then onto Yonne, and finally back to Jo's yard for the winter. We were to cruise in a great circle covering the oldest canals in France.

To us at the time, these canals were huge; to the French they were out of date and very rarely used for commercial traffic, although on our first trip there was a lively hotel cruise boat trade. I was amazed to learn that the cost of a cruise was £2,500 a week per person.

Despite being in commercial decline, the locks were operated as though commercial boats were still going through in numbers. On the Bourgogne, all the locks were operated by the lock keeper or *éclusier*. Crews were not allowed to operate the locks; all we were allowed to do was open and close gates under instruction. On the Canal du Centre, the locks were automatic, operated by aiming a zapper at a fixed point – a fantastic idea as long as certain rules were adhered to, such as sticking to agreed boating times, and if in a convoy, staying with the convoy. Failure to do either of these things resulted in a long wait while the *éclusier*, in a distant control room, got round to answering your call for assistance. In England we had been used to pleasing ourselves when we travelled; now we had to book an *éclusier* before we could start our journey. The lock keepers always asked us for instructions on start and finish times, and then announced what time we would start and finish. The midday lunch break was sacrosanct; if the lock doors were open when you went in and the lock cycle could not be completed before noon, that's where you stayed, in the bottom of the lock with the pounding of the water from the open paddles in your ears (they did this to move the water lower down the canal). We soon learned that despite what we had requested, all stops were pre-planned by the *éclusiers*. During the summer, many of them were students, and levels of competence varied widely, and many hair-raising events were caused by the student *éclusiers'* inexperience.

The Bourgogne canal is 375km long, with 192 locks. At the northern/upstream end is the port of Migennes, which still has commercial traffic. Boats use the port to load up, mostly with grain, and then usually sail downstream on the Yonne and Seine to the northern canals and ports. At the southern/downstream end of the canal is the large leisure and commercial port of St Jean de Losne. From there, boats can go south along the Rhône to the Mediterranean or along the Rhône au Rhine Canal to the Rhine and eastern Europe. The canal travels through rich productive farmland, forests, and eventually vineyards. There are no big towns until Dijon, the ancient capital of the Dukes of Burgundy. The northern end has views of Châteaux and abbeys; the area both sides of the summit, Pouilly-en-Auxois, is remote, and we spent a lot evenings watching the deer graze. At the summit is a 3.3km tunnel, which, unusually for France, has no lights.

Our first mooring was at a small town, Brienon, where we were amazed to find free toilets, showers and electricity. Everything about the mooring was immaculate. Colin had become obsessed by the mosquitoes, so we set off to the shops to buy ourselves a net. The main street was long and unattractive; the French in rural areas, I learned later, spend money not on their houses but on living and flowers, and there were many houses in Brienon that, to English eyes, needed some TLC.

There was only one shop that looked likely to sell mosquito nets, so in we went. The *patron* turned his shop upside down in an effort to find what we wanted, and eventually, in a dusty box, he found it.

"Voilà," he proclaimed.

We all cheered and I asked, "Quelle prix?"

"Gratis," was the shopkeeper's reply.

We were very touched, and with many "Merci beaucoups" we returned to the mooring for tea. We spent the evening watching the locals playing *boules*, followed by wine with a group of very jolly Germans. Despite my threats, Colin did, of course, *mention the war*. But the Germans were not offended, and we had a very interesting discussion: all of us had been born just before or during the war, and we exchanged information as to how we had all been affected. After a good few years of living in France, I now feel there will be no repeats of the mistakes of the last hundred years.

The next day we said goodbye to our new German friends and cruised to Saint-Florentin; here we decided to get the bikes out and visit the abbey at Pontigny. At 10km it was just within our range, and we were well rewarded for our efforts. Here is an extract from a letter I wrote to a friend about what I saw there that day:

We went on the bikes to Pontigny Abbey, it was 10kms on an N road which was enough distance but worth the effort. The Abbey is Benedictine; they believed in austerity, poverty and simplicity. The abbey reflects those beliefs. The soaring white gothic arches are made of rubble covered in plaster, a fantastic piece of engineering. The windows let in natural light; there is no ornamentation or furniture, just a bank of candles on a stand in front of the Lady Chapel. The church is dedicated to the protective saint of England, St Edmund, who is buried there ... how come we have ended up with St George as our patron saint? It seems the reason was that St George was more warlike. I was so overcome with the beauty of the place I lit a candle for my family, a big departure for a non-conformist. Fortunately, I reverted to type as we cycled home through gently rolling country alongside fields of green corn and occasionally through avenues of trees bright in their spring green. If there is a god, I thought, he is a tree, not a building, however beautiful.

I had first begun writing to friends to pass on my excitement about what we were experiencing; later, it would be to assuage the feelings of homesickness and fear I often felt.

My friends were amused by our adventures and passed the letters round. It was not long before there was not enough time to write to all the people who requested letters, so I bought a word processor at a car boot sale and the group letter was born. Time and memory alters one's perception of events, and as I want to convey how we thought at the time I will reprint quite a few of the letters in this chapter. Here is an edited version of the first letter I wrote in our first week on the Bourgogne:

Ancy-le-Franc
25th May
A misty morning in Château country, France.

I can see the sun behind the mist and make out the outline of the cruise boats moored in the small port. On the canal side is a three-storey house with gardens; you would know you were in France just by looking at the house. The Captain manoeuvred the boat under the back of a flower-decked large cruise boat and the front of a similar one. The passengers, mainly Americans, watched from the rails, wine glasses in hand, as we squeezed between the boats last night. Later we entertained a stream of visitors all fascinated by the smallness of our boat; the Americans are very friendly but so nosey; they want to look everywhere and question you intensely until they know your whole life history. In return they tell you all about themselves and how the next stop on their tour is the UK to search for their roots in ten days. Apparently we are "cute" and what we are doing is "wondeeerful". I couldn't help liking them. I got the impression, particularly among the men, that they were bored silly. After they had all gone back to their boats for dinner we had a brief respite and then we entertained, counselled and laughed hilariously with the crew as they drank all our cheap plonk. The crew are mainly young, carefree and English, the American customers elderly, enthusiastic and, as they have paid £2,500 for their trip, demanding. Bob was a surprise beneficiary of a kindness: one of the crew approached early this morning with a parcel of best steak left over from the meal last night. Colin and I had a marital when he laid claim to poor old Bob's steak. I won though, and Bob had most of the steak.

The second part of this first letter was written the day after:

We decided to stay another day, as travelling behind the cruise boats is so slow and Colin wanted to do 'man' things and I wanted to get a wine refill. Colin took the bike with an oil drum on the carrier at the back to fetch diesel. When he came back he was white and shaking. "What a bloody scare I've had. I got the diesel from the garage at the top of the hill, fixed the diesel drum on the back carrier, and set off. Coming down the hill, the weight of the drum pushed the bike faster and faster. Me load was too heavy for the brakes to work. The pedals were going so fast I had to take me feet off and hold me legs out – that cooled me parts, I can tell you. I could see a gaggle of old ladies up ahead, crossing the road to the Château. I shouted all kinds of things in French but they took no notice."

"What were you shouting?"

"Does it bloody matter?"

"Course it does, that's probably why they took no notice."

"Oh! I shouted, 'Assistez vous' and 'Yo Ho'."

assistez vous !!!!!

"Well no wonder: 'Assistez vous' means 'Help you'," I replied, annoyed that he could be so daft. "Did you hit anybody?"

"No, just missed: there was a gap in the middle of 'em and I shot through. Bloody stupid old people!" (He always says stupid like Captain Mainwaring).

"I'm going to have to build a trolley, can't do that again, I might damage me false leg, then we'll be stuffed." He sighed with exasperation.

Colin embarked on the new project, building what the French called a "chariot". It was amazing how in no time at all complete strangers in passing boats were asking how the chariot was progressing. Colin enlisted the help of shopkeepers and engineers along the canal side to assist in buying and manufacturing parts. The French were really interested and generous; much of the metal work was done gratis, Colin explaining what he wanted by waving his arms talking slowly in a 2 year olds' French, assisted by drawings on pieces of card made from cut up Cornflakes packets.

The boats and people using the canal were a veritable united nations, the only country not represented appearing to be the French. When I read our log for the eventful two days at Ancy-le-Franc, all Colin had written was that he had watched a duck lay an egg, which he was about to have for his tea.

Despite all the company we had on the canals, the villages and small towns en route often seemed very quiet. Although the shops were open, there seemed to be no one about. This was a big surprise after the bustle of the UK – and it was about to get even quieter.

At Montbard we moored up with some very exuberant Australians who were about to hire a minibus to visit the abbey at Fontenay. They asked if we would like to join them. We had a very enjoyable trip, and on our return Bob spent the evening on their boat. The port of Montbard was the furthest the cruise and most of the hire boats went.

From this point we prepared to go over the summit through over thirty closely positioned locks and finally a long tunnel. Because the canal is very short of water, the lock keepers like to fill the lock with as many boats as they can, and they do this by making boats in front wait for boats behind to catch up and then moving them all on together. It was in this manner that we caught up with a hire boat containing four Swiss-Italians, and a very small solar-powered boat. For us to be together made sense: the hire boat was short and fat, we were longer and thinner, and the solar-powered boat could fit alongside us and behind the Italians with room to spare.

The solar-powered boat was manned by three very old men and a younger, middle-aged man. Two of the men were identical twins, thin and well over six foot, both dressed in above the ankle blue bib and braces, with long flowing white beards and equally long smooth shiny white hair. Only one of the men, I learned later, spoke English, and he flapped and shouted in a flat cap and long shorts, seeming to be trying to be in charge. The other old man was very smart, with a trilby-style hat. He drove the boat, the twins worked the locks, and flat cap tried to keep up with them while they seemed to ignore his presence totally.

The two boats were waiting as we entered the lock, manoeuvring carefully. Colin positioned our boat alongside the solar boat. A waiting Italian put our rope on the middle bollard. As he walked to anchor the back rope, a streak of blue with a while tail spinning leapt over the front lock gates, and as our back rope went on, the front rope came off and was chucked down on top of our boat. Not a word was spoken as the Italian, having missed what had happened, went to close the back gate. The other twin started shouting and waving at him not to shut the gate; I was also shouting, as our front was now drifting into the solar boat, which I was trying to fend off with the boat hook.

I couldn't understand what anyone was saying, except the Captain, who was yelling, "Get him to tie us up. What's he bloody playing at?"

All I could see most of the time was legs. The Italian's head appeared over the lock and I passed him the front rope. Almost immediately, the back roped clanged onto the boat.

By now the lady on the Italian boat had climbed on their roof and up onto the lock. I could tell both twins were on the same side of the lock, but, with the front fastened, our back was now swinging out. The face of the driver of the solar boat was rigid with concentration; he hadn't time to shout, his boat was slow to respond, and he must have been terrified of being crushed.

Solar driver just managed to move to the front-side of our boat before our back end hit the wall. Poor old Bob was shaking all over and trying to be invisible as the Captain revved the engine in a vain attempt to straighten up the boat. Colin and I had no idea what was going off; all we could hear was shouting, engine noise and the pounding of water over the front lock gates. Eventually, though, we were fastened by the Italians at both ends and the lock began to work. As we rose in the lock, we could see an Italian man on guard at each of the bollards to prevent further assaults by the twins on our ropes. The Italian lady approached, and told me the situation was "complicate": apparently, the twins had decided that they didn't want our boat in the lock with them, and by taking our ropes off they were indicating to us to get out. The lock keepers were not going to interfere: as far as they were concerned it was all of us in the lock or none at all, and they expected the boaters to sort things out while they had a fag.

We were to travel with these two boats until we were the other side of the summit. We became friends with all but the twins, who remained distant and largely a law unto themselves. We learned that the elderly German driver had bought the boat on the spur of the moment at the Paris Boat Show; flat-cap man was assisting the driver to take the boat part way to Saint-Jean-de - Losne where the German had a mooring. The twins, who were in their mid-eighties, were French and were friends of the German; they didn't understand German or English. The seller of the boat had found the twins to be a nightmare, refusing to take instructions and so obsessed with safety that they were a danger – to wit the kerfuffle in the locks.

We reached the summit, and after a more than thorough inspection of our safety equipment by the *éclusier*-in-chief, including the bucket and paddle, we entered the tunnel. We were the lead boat and were in the dark for forty-five minutes before emerging into bright sunlight followed by the Italians. We waited and waited for the solar boat. Half an hour later, the little boat emerged, the twins paddling in unison. No one had thought about the lack of sun in a tunnel, and their batteries had gone flat. The flat-cap man had decided to walk over the summit and meet the boat as it came out; I suppose this confirmed to the twins the belief held by many Frenchmen, that when the going gets tough the *rosbifs* clear off.

We were now coming down in the locks. At the first, the twins hung onto the front and back ropes for dear life. The water fell; the boat stayed where it was. Legs akimbo and stringy arms straining, they stood their ground, ignoring our shouts. Eventually, the driver realised that he should not be looking into the Captain's eyes, and shouted at the twins to let go – which, contrary as ever, they did at once. The boat landed with a splash, and shortly afterwards flat-cap man was seen to depart in his car.

let it down slowly
you daft buggers

We parted with our Italian friends at Vandenesse-en-Auxois. As we came through the lock we saw tables and chairs and a sign saying "épicerie". As soon as we had moored up I went to have a look at what goodies I could buy. Behind the lock there was a barn, and at the side there was a large tent with tables and chairs. I went into the shop, the bell clanged, and a moment or two later a young lady with a small child came in. The place had all sorts of goodies for sale: paté, bottled fruit, wine, honey, cheeses – you name it. I didn't know where to start.

Through halting conversation I learned that this was a new venture and that the shopkeeper was a chef – and yes, I could book for a meal (there was only one dish, rabbit) tonight. I booked, and excitedly returned to the boat.

"We're going in that tent for a meal tonight, so you can get cleaned up I'm putting a frock on. We're having rabbit."

For once, Colin didn't grumble.

We arrived on time for the meal, and were the only customers in the tent. After a starter of paté and salad, the main course arrived: a huge pot of rabbit stew. A few minutes later, a black, long-handled pan was put on the table, half full of green beans. There was a huge basket of crusty bread and a large carafe of *vin ordinaire*. The sweet was a homemade apple tart.

What the meal lacked in style and ambience was more than made up for by the simple, well-cooked food; the meat in the rabbit stew was melting off the bones, and the wine was the best I had tasted in a long while. Despite being the only customers, we enjoyed ourselves and I left hoping that the young lady would be able to make a living from her new enterprise.

A few days later, at Pont d'Ouche, we picked up our children Sally and David, Sally's daughter Jenny and Dan, David's son. Despite a dramatic change in the weather – low cloud and rain – we were all excited to meet up. We celebrated by going out for a meal in a restaurant, and for once David was able to eat everything on the menu.

We arrived in Dijon a week or so later in pouring rain and mist, but nothing could dampen our spirits. We opened a bottle of wine or two and ended up dancing in the fog and dark on the pontoons. Dan started practising his German with some of our neighbours, who had come to see what the racket was about; they were on their way into the city for a meal and Dan decided to join them.

We had been in bed a while when there was an almighty bang, clatter and swearing. The boat rocked as someone moved from the wheelhouse to the front at speed.

"Don't you dare be sick Dan or I'll kill you."

"God, he's only had a bit too much Sal, calm down," I heard David say to his sister.

"It's that bloody net thing: I got wrapped up in it and fell over," Dan slurred.

"You bloody fell on me, frightened me to death," laughed David.

Sally was not laughing. "Where's the bucket? If he's sick, me mam will go mad."

That's a bit rich, I thought: here I am, so calm that I am pretending to be asleep.

"Bloody hell, Aunty Sal, get a life."

"Go back to bed. I'll see to him," said David, well aware that Sally and Danny are petrol and a match.

The boat rocked again, and I could hear the sounds of Dan, complete with mosquito net, being put into his sleeping bag. As he was already asleep, there was quite a bit of thumping about.

Both the sixteen-year-olds spent the next day in bed. David cleaned the boat while Sally, the Captain and I drove to the beautiful old wine capital of Beaune. As nurses, we were both very impressed by the thirteenth-century hospice.

We were very sad when the family finally left us and decided to have a bus trip into the centre of Dijon a couple of kilometres away. Bob the dog, Colin and I boarded the bus bound for the city centre. Fifteen minutes later, we were sure we were heading in the wrong direction. After a heated debate we decided to stay on until the terminus and then head back.

We must have travelled ten kilometres before we reached the terminus. The driver insisted we get off the bus and go to the other side of the road. The bus pulled up and I prepared, with Bob on the lead, to board.

"Chiens interdit," the driver said.

"Pardon?"

"Chiens interdit."

I could not believe it. "But we came on your bus," I said in English.

"Chiens interdit," the driver said again, his gestures indicating that Bob should be muzzled.

We had no alternative but to get off. We were in the middle of a high-rise estate, no people, no shops, no phone, and my French was not up to getting us out of the mess we had got ourselves into. Colin could not walk far; I would have to walk back in the heat with the reluctant dog and then come back in a taxi.

My mind was blank with panic as we sat on a wall and watched the bus disappear. When it had gone we walked for a bit, looking for inspiration, but still no one about. Eventually, we saw a bus coming up the hill the way we had come. The French buses have separate entrance and exit doors, and I said to Colin, "You hide behind this tree and I'll get on the bus and distract the driver while you sneak on at the back with the dog."

I got on, and pretended not to understand any French or the composition of the euro. I made the whole interaction last five minutes, and was relieved when I turned round to see Colin sitting innocently at the back.

"Where's the dog?"

Colin indicated under the seat: for once Bob had not made a fuss. The ploy had worked.

The journey home was tense. We feared exposure at every bus stop, and every kilometre was a relief. Finally we were back at the port.

"Bugger the town centre, I'm going back to the boat for something to eat," said a relieved Colin as he got off the bus.

It was a year later before we made a more thorough exploration of the lovely city of Dijon.

By the time we got back to the boat, we had been joined by another narrow boat, Albert, and met a couple with whom we were to become firm friends. John, the captain, was an enthusiastic, rangy chap, one of the few men I've met who look at ease in shorts and a floppy hat. He spoke in a very posh accent, but as the tone of his voice was friendly and humorous I did not hold that against him. John and his wife, Sue, had met in Kenya, where Sue had been working as a nurse and he as a tea planter. They had left Kenya in the sixties, and after a rocky start on the job market (there is not much call for tea planters in the UK, although he told me he had tried at the job centre) they ended up owning and running a post office and then retiring to a flat on the Isle of Wight and life on Albert in the summer. John loved gadgets, bargains and very cheap wine. Sue complemented John perfectly, a calm, interesting family woman, and I was devastated when she died in 2005; we used to text each other whenever we felt lonely, and she always managed to cheer me up.

We decided that day in Dijon to travel to Saint-Jean-de-Losne together, starting at nine o'clock the next morning. That day was very hot, even at nine o'clock, and the canal was flat and uninteresting with very little shade. At noon Albert pulled up at the only tree for miles so we could have lunch, and we stayed there all afternoon. Sue and I followed the shade round the tree, talking for

England. Colin and John viewed each other's inventions and generally did man things. After tea, John and I drank the one euro a litre wine and Colin and Sue drank tea. Later, Colin had to assist me to bed.

We arrived in St Jean and moored under the trees and whenever we emerged from our haven the heat hit us like a furnace. The town of St Jean sits in a valley and surrounds a large port basin that opens onto the river Saô ne. It is known for having a micro climate being colder in winter and hotter in summer than other parts of the area. There are hundreds of boats of all kinds there, moored in several leisure and commercial marinas. I could not believe my eyes: during the first two weeks on the Bourgogne we had seen very few boats on the canal compared to the UK. John, a real David Livingstone character, doesn't like staying anywhere long, so he is keen to get on with the next adventure. We had only one more day together before we said a sad farewell. We turned right and headed upstream on the broad River Saône.

Our first stop was Verdun-sur-le-Doubs and I quote an extract from my letter home:

This village is how you imagine a French village to be, we got here by going behind an island in the river, passing old houses clinging to a cliff. The moorings are pontoons at the bottom of a 15-metre wall. On top of the wall is a line of pollarded trees which border a square. We awoke this morning to the sounds of a market being set up, so we grabbed our bags and money and climbed the ramp to see what was going off. As we got to the top we could see a huge spread of summer flowers in baskets and pots, all for sale. The perfume of the flowers mixed with the strong smell of sweaty socks from the cheese stall. There was a stall selling music tapes and discs and playing French accordion dance music, and along the top of the walls were stalls selling pantalons and all-over aprons as well as the usual tee shirts and shorts. After we had bought supplies we had a very black coffee and a croissant at a table outside a cafe while Bob played to the audience. Colin had stuck an apple label on Bob's forehead, which attracted the attention she loved: all approaches were graciously received with a paw-shake. By one o'clock the market had gone and everywhere was empty and quiet. We decided to continue on our journey. Big mistake! By six o'clock we were tired and grumpy and could find nowhere to moor, and eventually the Captain decided to ram the point into the bank of a midstream island and tie up to a very weedy looking tree. He kept saying, "We must be on our way at 5 a.m. or a big boat will pass us and the wash will ground us and probably hole the boat." The captain ostentatiously set the alarm, but I refused to bite. I am an adult: if I have to get up I will. The Captain needn't have worried: we were attacked by thousands of mosquitoes that night. Colin fought back with the tea towel, and we then had a marital as the tea towel was covered in mosquito blood. Apparently I am "too hygienic". As Colin was hot and sweaty he was wildly attractive and the mosquitoes enthusiastically bit him. I tried to stay cool but was only slightly less bitten. We had only a couple of hours' sleep but were under way at 5 a.m. without the need for the alarm.

The locks on the Saône are very big and are operated by unseen people in observation towers. If you're lucky, they don't contact you; a sequence of lights tells you when things are going to happen. If the *éclusiers* contact you it's a nightmare: I have never been any good at deciphering 'tannoy speech', and when the words are in gabbled French it's ten times worse. Usually asking for clarification via the VHF only increases our confusion.

At the first lock after Verdun, ten minutes were spent wondering what the instructions meant, until finally a small figure came down the steps of the watchtower and sped towards us. From the way the chap walked you could tell he was annoyed.

He stopped above me and made seat belt signs.

"Ah! He wants us to put lifejackets on," I shouted to the Captain.

Clearly irritated, the *éclusier* stormed off.

this feels like a coffin

The big river locks were so much easier than the canal locks. The water came up slowly from the below the boat and we rose gently, unlike the horrendous gushing speed of the canal locks. Also, we were able to secure ourselves so much more safely, often to floating bollards fixed in the lock walls which rose or sank level with the boat. The locks on the Bourgogne were not only fast-filling but the bollards were positioned for much bigger boats than us; it was always a nerve-racking experience getting ourselves safely tied up, never helped by the Captain's continual stream of "helpful" commands.

We did not know it, but getting through the locks was about to get worse: we were coming into 'tele command' country; but more of that later.

As we approached the next lock, the doors slowly closed. "Oh bugger! It must be dinner time," Colin exclaimed, "Now, make sure you lasso that stanchion first time, it's a bloody disaster if you miss it."

At the time, I really believed that we would be swept away and sink if I missed the stanchion, and probably Colin did too. Now, though, having missed a few, I realise that it caused the inconvenience of having to turn round in water with a current in order to try again, but it is hardly a disaster. Luckily, this time I managed to get the rope on the hook and we tied up to have our lunch too.

We were on to the sweet course when we saw a small boat circling, and I must admit it did look scary for them. We signalled to the boat to "breast up" with us, and went back to our meal. Suddenly, Bob was on the back deck, barking like mad; we went out to have a look to find Bob backing up, tail going mad, and a man in a Viking helmet, with a plastic penis on his nose and carrying an axe, boarding our boat.

"Good afternoon, I am a '*wiking*' and I have come to pillage your wine."

We willingly let him and his 'wiking' partner pillage our wine for half an hour; then, in merry mood, we allowed him to lead us into the big lock, not forgetting the lifejackets. As we came out of the lock, the 'wiking' swiftly disappeared and we were on our own again.

The Canal du Centre is the canal that links the Rhône and the Mediterranean with the western canal routes to the north, and the lock that forms the entrance to this canal is enormous. Its guillotine doors slowly descended, and as we moored to the floating bollards, the stone walls rose over thirty feet, covered in dripping green slime. We were the only boat in a lock that appeared to be about a hundred feet long. Although the lights had changed from red to green at our approach, no one had acknowledged our radio message verbally. Was it coincidence that the lights had changed? I wondered. Did anyone know we were buried alive in this big wet slimy hole?

After a few minutes, my query was answered as we rose slowly. It was so quiet compared to our other lock experiences that it seemed a miracle. I could not take my eyes off the bollard; I think it worked on water pressure – but what if something leaked? Somehow I felt that if I kept watching I would avert disaster.

We came to the top and Bob leapt off for a sniff, a pee and a paw-shake with the lady with the clipboard who was waiting for us. The lock lady welcomed us with a cheerful, "Bonjour," took our details, and gave us an information leaflet about the canal and the zapper with which we were to operate the locks.

It was three days since we had spoken our own language, and the difference between the comfort of the crowded waterways of England and the emptiness of the French canals was beginning to get to us. Loneliness is not the big problem now that it was then in 2002, as there are more English speakers on the canals and our French has improved. The housing boom in the United Kingdom has meant that more boaters of a certain age are "opting out" and recreating the irresponsibility of the youth they wished they had had. After the passage of seven years, I find it difficult to believe my thoughts and feelings on this first cruise, as expressed in a letter home:

The Canal du Centre is "désolé". I like that word in French, it means "sorry", and what a sorry state this canal is in. The locks have been electrified, and seem lethal. We have a zapper to work the lock, which we have to point at a detector. If we are lucky a light comes on at the front of the lock to say the signal has been received. Sometimes there is no light and a huge marital results as we have to turn around on the canal to try again. At times the lock refuses to work and we have to manoeuvre so I can jump off and speak in appalling French to a disembodied hole situated in a hut wall. A torrent of words comes back at me and I have to hope I have been understood. Colin, ever a Job's 'comforter', constantly says, "They don't know we are here," and nags me to go through the procedure again. We are in a constant state of anxiety about whether the lock will work. The French mobile éclusiers usually do respond, arriving on either little mopeds or small white VNF vans. Compared to the leisure-orientated English canals, this canal seems deserted and neglected. There are no waterside cafés or pubs. Many of the lock houses have just been abandoned, although at certain houses someone has planted flowers, we too feel abandoned, especially when we finally get into the lock. We are going up the canal so before anything can happen we have to find the 'tirez'. A 'tirez' consists of two metal bars, one red and one blue, which are fixed to the lock wall; the blue starts the lock and the red is the emergency stop. To activate the lock the slimy bars have to be pushed upward to make a connection. For some reason, the side on which the tirez is situated can change – another source of disagreements if I don't anticipate the correct side. Manoeuvring the boat in the lock is difficult with the flow of water over the front doors pushing us all over the place amidst the roar of the water.

In very deep locks there are bollards set into the wall of the lock and I have to move the rope up from one green slimy bollard to another while the lock continues to fill and the boat is swinging about. If the lock is not too deep I have to put the loop of the rope on my pole and fish about for an unseen bollard on the top and then drop the loop over the bollard without the rope dropping off the pole too soon. There are usually wear-marks on the lock kerb to indicate the general area of the bollard but it is still a hit and miss procedure. Once secure at the front, the idea is that the Captain uses the engine to push against the rope and so keep us to the side. Because the length of our boat is smaller than that of French péniches, for whom the lock was built, if the boat is secured to the front bollard we cannot reach the tirez to start the lock working. We have tried all sorts of solutions, all involving much shouting and panic; finally we decided to tie up loosely at the front, move back, push the tirez up and then frantically pull the ropes tight under the front bollard before we are overwhelmed by the force of the inrushing water and are unable to stop the lock filling. Sometimes after I have pushed the tirez up and Colin has moved the boat forward we find that I have not pushed hard enough. Usually this is because of my difficulty in getting enough of a grip on the weed covered slimy bar to get enough upward momentum. When I make a successful connection a loud bell rings but there are times when I do not notice that the bell has not rung and we have to start again. Moving a boat backwards is a nightmare as boats have no steering in reverse. Even when we start the lock, before we are sorted the water starts pouring in, the boat leaps about the lock, the Captain bawls and shouts, the dog, lying on the Captain's left foot, trembles thus preventing the Captain from jumping up and down in frustration at my perceived slowness as I try to pull 12 tons of boat into the side of the lock against the flow of the water. The noise is horrendous, and all in all I get very frightened and don't need know-it-all Colin telling me what I should have done. The worst thing is, once the lock has started we are too far away from the tirez to stop the bloody thing. These locks are all geared for commercial traffic, not dinky narrow boats.

We have gone for several days not seeing one boat; then one day I was making a drink and I heard Colin yelling, "Bloody hell, what's he want now?"

I dashed up the steps. "What?"

"Look. Look, a boat!" he yelled, setting off a tremble in the dog. A small boat approached and gave us a wave as he passed.

"There is life out here somewhere then," I remarked sarcastically as I returned to making the tea.

Colin and I need people to dilute our relationship, neither of us are really interested in scenery (after all, as the Captain often says, a tree is a tree) or ancient buildings. Very often, as you will have noticed, we can remember who we have met in a day but not where we have been.

It was after we had parted from the Americans for the first time that Colin admitted he felt as lonely as me and suggested that maybe we should go home for next year. Then we came into Dijon and saw a hundred moored boats. Where had they all come from? We met a lady walking her dog, who turned out to be from Brighouse. Norman and Audrey chatted to us and we told them how depressed we felt. The following day, a Sunday, Norman came over to invite us for lunch; we stayed until the early evening, sat on the top of their large modern Dutch cruiser in the sun and wind. Next day they called to see us again and we entertained them for a couple of hours. Audrey sympathised with my feelings of loneliness and said she and Norman, who, like Colin, did not suffer from homesickness, had agreed that she should go home for holidays frequently. Norman also said he thought the French canals were not really suitable for narrow boats and small people. They also gave us a few how-to-manage tips. Apparently, if a narrow boat comes out of a lock too fast the sensor doesn't register that you have left the lock, so the next lock does not work. The solution is to go back, bend over the bank and wave your shoe in front of the sensor. Apparently the English have particular problems with speeding out of locks.

After Norman and Audrey had gone we felt restored and full of energy we cleaned and touched up the paint on the boat. This morning we have set off and are heading in a slightly different direction, so the sun is not directly in our faces. We have crossed the valley of the Loire via an aqueduct, and all in all things are improving. It depends how things go from now on, whether we stay another year. Nice as it is today, we have still only seen six boats in over a week. Audrey told us that all the English speakers get to know one another and keep meeting up around France. It conjured up a picture of all the "oldies" who missed the swinging sixties trying to recapture those times in the land of cheap booze (a substitute for pot?) by having boozy 'do's' whenever they meet up, the rest of their time being spent looking forward to the next 'do'. As France is a very big country, I would think boozy 'do's' are few and far between unless moored up at known gathering places, and then what's the point of having a boat? For us it seems a depressing way to exist. These people cruising the canals must seem like aliens to the French; at least the immigrant North Africans speak the language and work. For Colin, the boating adventure is all about keeping the boat going mechanically in "foreign parts", and for me it used to be about all the exercise I got from working the locks in

Britain. In France exercise is now "interdit": we are allowed to open and close a gate if the lock is a manual one, but here all the exercise I get is from rowing with the Captain. But, for now, we are travelling cheerfully, revitalised after having company.

Our mood continued to improve as the Americans, in the big old Dutch barge, caught up with us. We had met Charlotte and Harold briefly when we moored in Paray-le-Monial and we had sat on the bank, with Bob, watching them do jobs around the boat. Charlotte was very dark, small and slim; she wore shorts that revealed a pair of very fit-looking brown legs, despite her being in her late seventies she acted as though in her fifties. It was obvious to us, even before we knew officially, that Charlotte did all the driving; she was the "captain" both of the boat and her partner. In that capacity, she spent a lot of time shouting, "Harold!" although her shouts were mostly ignored. Colin and I both were reminded of Steptoe and Son. Charlotte's Harold was also small, but very stocky and blond.

We just had to get talking to this interesting-looking couple, and, under the pretence of examining the old boat, we struck up a conversation. We learned that they were from Boston and had spent seventeen summers in Europe on the old boat. Harold was quite deaf as a result of working on the deck of an aircraft carrier during the war; later, though, we learned that some of his deafness was selective . . . Harold was of Polish extraction; his wife (his third, he told me) had Russian ancestry. As a couple they were content with their own company, but circumstances fortunately meant that we would travel together for over a week, and a lovely friendship developed. Here is an extract from a letter about our journey together:

It's now Wednesday and we keep parting and meeting up with the Americans as their boat is faster than ours. Charlotte drives; she is so small that only the top of her head can be seen through the wheelhouse window. Harold stands at the front and guides her steering, using a whistle. Harold drives Charlotte to distraction; he stands on the prow, whistle at the ready as bridges approach. From where Charlotte is steering, the bridge appears nearer than it is. Anticipating his immediate decapitation, Charlotte abandons the wheel, pokes her head around the wheelhouse door, and screams several times, "Harold!" He ignores her cries but at the last minute he ducks. I am sure he does it on purpose. The shouts of "Harold" echoing along the canal amuse me and Colin; it seems Charlotte falls for it every time. On a wet, cold afternoon we followed them into a lock and noticed a photographer on the bank; it looked like he was from a magazine as he was accompanied by a girl with a notebook. What a performance! Harold stood on the prow, whistle to his lips, while Charlotte posed, leaning on the wheelhouse door, best leg towards the camera. Colin demanded his bowler hat. Bob refused to pose and stayed inside near the biscuit barrel: she is the star or nothing. Eventually the reluctant dog came with me to the pointy bit and gradually we rose in the lock under the eye of the lens. Strange: neither Bob nor I felt the usual fear as the lock filled; obviously vanity overcomes fear.

As we journeyed along I learned more about our friends. Harold was a Harvard professor, something to do with medical machinery; he invented the first blood infusion pump and made a fortune from the invention of a humane killer, a guillotine, for laboratory rats. Charlotte had done lots of philanthropic things and with her first husband had been part of the social scene in Boston. I did not realise until I cooked them a meal with pork and mustard sauce made with sour cream that they were Jewish ... They ate the *meal enthusiastically all the same. Harold in particular enjoyed it, whispering to me that "Charlotte's a terrible cook"!*

Further along this canal, things began to get very surreal. We spotted another narrow boat and decided to moor up for the night to investigate while our friends decided to continue. The owners of the narrow boat were Christian evangelists who ran a book-swap. On the French canals, being able to swap books is a life-saver. When we came to France I had not realised the importance of having a book to read en route and had set out on our journey with no books at all. A very kind gentleman had given me two, which, after I had read them, I swapped for three, and gradually built up a collection. In Saint-Jean-de-Losne a very stern Scots lady, who managed the bookshop in the tourist office, measured your books: you could only take away three inches if that is all you brought in. Anyway, in true Christian spirit I was allowed to take as many books as I needed from Roy's library. The couple were pleased to see us and showed us around their converted wine store; everything was recycled, I never realised there were so many uses for wine crates.

Roy and Audrey had very little money and tried to live by bartering (they called it "donating"). I invited the couple for tea and scones on our boat, and was rewarded by a bunch of daisies from Roy and a tin of Heinz beans from Audrey. The following day, Roy visited and said they were going for their monthly shop in Moulins and would we like to go for a ride with them. We put some petrol in the car for them and off we went. On the journey, Roy gave me the realities of boating in France. France is a big country, the largest in Europe, with nearly the same population as the UK, and most French live in the towns and cities; on the canal, where we were, the best time for company was May and June when everyone heads for the Mediterranean, and September-October, when people are coming back from their summer holidays and it is wine-festival time.

Moulins is the regional capital, and there we were taken by Roy and Audrey to the café which they said was the model for the Moulin Rouge in Paris. Apart from Colin being totally embarrassed in an ironmonger's shop by a lady with what goggle eyed Roy called "une grande balconée", I remember little else of our visit to the city: I was too busy catching up on talk time.

We had enjoyed Roy and Audrey's company, but decided to move on to try and catch up with the Americans. After leaving the Lighthouse, we caught up with Harold and Charlotte at Gannay where we were to spend Bastille Day, along with an unusual number of mainly French boats. At the moorings, as well as the usual services there was a parked caravan with a corrugated Perspex-covered, wood-framed structure attached to the side: this was the port restaurant. The weather had been awful for the past two days and the ground was very soggy even inside the structure; nevertheless Charlotte and I decided to lift our wet mood by getting dressed for dinner. Charlotte's dressing for dinner consisted of a long frock and loads of bling; Colin put his bow tie on and I put on a flowing, summer frock. Charlotte took centre stage among the tables, avoiding the puddles, and from this vantage point she put on a star performance, chatting to everyone in superb French, her flirtatious manner belying her seventy-odd years. The taste of a very basic *coq au vin* followed by yoghurt was improved by the vast quantity of wine we consumed. Charlotte proclaimed the *coq au vin* superb and looked to Harold for confirmation; but he had long ago switched his hearing aid off.

The meal over, the tables were stacked and the dancing began. The hem of Charlottes dress became caked with mud as the dance-floor became a quagmire. Harold managed to sleep through all the noise, only waking to escort an exhausted Charlotte back to their boat about midnight.

The next morning, Harold was up bright and early, dressing his boat and finishing off with the huge Stars and Stripes that had covered his brother's coffin. His *pièce de résistance* was a massive horn that used compressed air, which he intended to blow. Colin also had a horn that worked by his own lung-power, and they agreed to blow simultaneously. Unfortunately, at the appointed time Colin's lungs worked and the compressed air machine blew up with a loud bang. Here is an excerpt from a letter describing what happened on the day:

The Irishman in a £400,000 boat (he's a house-builder on the Isle of Wight) started drinking at 9 a.m., took a dinner-break at midday until 1 p.m., and continued until nearly midnight, when he decided the holiday was over. He gathered various crew-members and set off at speed into the night. Unfortunately he had forgotten to disconnect the electricity, and the resultant break in the wire caused all the lights to fuse and the port to plunge into darkness just as we heard a loud splash. The body overboard meant much shouting and swearing as rescue was attempted in the dark.

The Frenchman had started drinking even earlier, and, contrary to French custom, had not even managed "mange"-break. He and his wife were already pirouetting very prettily in the middle of the canal when the Irishman set off. I think the man-overboard incident was caused by the big boat's crew trying frantically to prevent the French boat from mounting them, using poles.

By this time I had had enough: as is their wont, both drunks had repeated themselves all day; the Irishman insisted on believing we were heroes, having crossed the channel in "that little boat"; he kept repeating, "I tell you, I went to Barcelona and I was terrible scared what with the mistral an' all – you are so brave." The Frenchman, meanwhile, was fascinated that his wife and I shared the same Christian name. "She Yvonne. You Yvonne. Bonne!" After the hundredth repeat I was losing the will to live. Colin escaped to the village on his bike, to return with the news that all life was in the port. That news was the last straw: I went to bed, and the carousing went on until the early hours. Next morning everyone was up early and we and the Americans shared the lock at 7.30 a.m. The Irishman had already departed the other way at 7 a.m.

The rain, which had been intermittent on Bastille Day, poured down now, soaking through my wet-weather protection; it wasn't until we approached Decize that the sky began to clear. The sun came out, and Charlotte invited us for a barbeque on their boat later on that evening. We had known the Americans long enough to have begun teasing one another, and Charlotte told Colin that the *piece de resistance* that evening was to be frogs' legs. The Captain did not believe her.

Here is an extract from a letter I sent home describing the feast:

Yesterday we were invited to a barbeque on the American couple's antique Dutch Barge. We sat on the worryingly spongy deck above the saloon with Harold whilst Charlotte prepared the meal. Every now and then there came one of her shouts — "Haro-o-old!" — so reminiscent of Steptoe and Son. Colin and I had difficulty keeping straight faces. Eventually all the items were on the table and with a flourish Charlotte removed the lid of the tureen. The dish was full of frogs, their legs chopped off at the creatures' waists. The legs were swimming in butter and there was a very strong smell of garlic.

The Captain's jaw dropped and he exclaimed, tactfully, "I can't eat them, they look bloody awful."

Oh God, he's gone too far, I thought. "Don't be such a stick in the mud and try something new," I growled, reaching for a pair of legs myself.

The taste was absolutely appalling, so bad in fact that my stomach revolted; meanwhile, Charlotte and Harold were enthusiastically tucking in.

"There's no taste in them," declared the hostess to the host, "and I put 13 cloves of fresh garlic in, and some dried garlic. I should have put some more in."

As for me, I just couldn't manage more than one leg. The

Captain, though, after my rebuke, ate five pairs and then came across a solitary limb. "I can't go on, Charlotte, a one-legged frog is too close to home," he declared.

We put the tureen under the table and hit the wine. Later, when we helped clear up, we found frogs' legs all over the place. Bob, who will eat anything from horse-muck to tissues, had tried to steal the starter and had been defeated by the garlic, thus chucking legs all over the place in an attempt to find an edible pair.

Harold moved to the bow to barbeque while we sipped the wine, soon the boat was covered in clouds of smoke, so much so that I was worried we might have a visit from the pompiers.

The next course was to be barbequed chicken, bread, couscous with mint, lettuce and tomatoes and a dressing that included mud (unintentionally, I think). There were potatoes as well, but Charlotte had forgotten to cook them. Harold declared the chicken done and another leg plopped onto Colin's plate, this time very black and crispy. Colin took up his knife and fought his way into the thigh. "It's raw," he said.

"For God's sake shut up moaning and eat it," I muttered out of the corner of my mouth. But it was too late: Charlotte had heard.

"Haro-o-old," she yelled, "how often do I have to tell you it's dangerous not to cook chicken properly? Give it back to him," she ordered a shamefaced Colin, who was well and truly caught between two bossy women.

Harold returned the mangled chicken leg to the barbeque to continue its cremation; the leg that was returned to Colin's plate was black and crispy inside and out. Both of us were stricken with a fit of the giggles, and to cover his embarrassment Colin rolled out one his stories from childhood. Apparently, a game he had played now and then was to catch a frog, stick a straw up its bum, and blow. When the straw is removed and the air comes out, the frog *makes a farting noise as it leaps away. I made disapproving tut-tutting noises while the Americans laughed disbelievingly, and so the evening ended on a happy note. Our friends agreed to try and follow us as we were to turn north on the home stretch to Migennes.*

The Canal du Nivernais links the Loire basin with the Seine basin and roughly follows the course of the River Yonne. The Nivernais finishes close to the city of Auxerre, where it joins the Yonne and eventually the Seine. The canal is 174kms long and has 112 locks. It is fed at the summit, Port Brule, by a feeder canal from the beautiful Panneciere Reservoir, although the summit is generally considered to be Baye. Construction of the canal began in 1784 and the canal was completed in 1841. But it was never a commercial success. It was built to aid the *flottage* of timber from the forests of the Morvan to Paris via Clamecy. Huge rafts of logs were floated down on the canal and river, guided by men known as *flotteurs*. The importance of the canal faded with the arrival of railway in the nineteenth century, and it is now given over exclusively to the leisure industry after narrowly escaping closure. It is regarded as one of the loveliest canals in France. On our trip Harold was worried that the bridges might be too low for the wheelhouse of his boat, but our enthusiasm – plus a consultation with a navigation expert from the VNF – convinced Harold that all would be well, just!

On the morning of our planned departure Charlotte decided to have her hair cut in the town, so we set off from Decize, in the pouring rain, without them. We agreed we would meet up for the evening at Cercy-la-Tour. We arrived at Cercy at around four o'clock, expecting the Americans to be not far behind, as they usually made much faster progress than we did. We waited and waited and began to get quite worried: a high wind had got up, it was now a quarter to seven and the locks closed at seven.

At nearly seven we saw a shape through the almost impenetrable rain. What was it? There seemed to be huge flapping covers blowing out from the sides of what we could now make out was the American's boat. As they approached the moorings we could see that in place of the wheelhouse there was what can only be described as a metal-framed tabernacle, covered in loosely-attached blue plastic sheeting.

"Oh! What a time of it we've had," Harold told Colin ruefully. "The first bridge we went under took the wheelhouse off. It was a good job Charlotte's small or it would have decapitated her as well. As it was, she was covered in broken wood and glass."

We were horrified. "Is Charlotte alright?" we both asked together.

"Oh yes," Harold responded. "But somehow I've got to secure this sheeting or we'll be flying."

He was right: the wind was so strong that the sheeting was acting as a sail and making it almost impossible to secure the boat. Colin and Harold spent the next couple of hours in the wind and rain, tying everything down – a monumental feat considering Colin has one leg and only full manoeuvrability in one arm, while Harold was in his mid-eighties, with a huge scar from major heart surgery as well as being an insulin-dependent diabetic.

I felt that the men and Charlotte, who seemed unfazed by the near miss, needed a reward, so I cycled up to the very posh restaurant in the town and booked us a late meal; it was to be my treat. We spent a very convivial evening together, but it seemed a long way back to the boat, even though it was all downhill. Charlotte and Harold had got to the restaurant on their little motorbike, with its US postal service box on the back for the shopping. Harold was an early and enthusiastic recycler: the metal poles of the temporary wheelhouse, for example, had found their way into a skip from some refurbished hospital.

Sadly, the couple's troubles were not over. Mooring up the following night, Charlotte hit a concealed rock and bent the rudder; there was no chance of us doing anything to help, and I was amazed when Harold got into his trunks and went underwater for a look. Poor Harold! He was desperate to do something practical, and, unable to mend the rudder, he started removing the old windows.

"I can't stand it," the Captain said to me, "he's no idea about joinery. I'm going to help him."

Later, Harold said to me, "I think it's truly wonderful how Colin treats me as his son." Very tactful.

Harold and Charlotte were an amazing couple and in just a few days we had become very fond of them.

After a couple of days in Châtillon-en-Bazois, a truly idyllic mooring at the foot of the Château, we decided to continue on alone, as Sally and Peter were coming to cruise with us from Clamecy. We were to continue our friendship with the Americans for a few years until Harold no longer replied to my e-mails; they had to give up the boat in 2005 after Charlotte began to have memory problems and Harold was not physically fit enough to maintain the boat. But all that was a long way off.

Chapter 4

Vive La France

The first day after we had left our friends seemed very strange. "It's like we keep having bereavements," Colin remarked to me, and I agreed. Our saviour and lifeline was the mobile phone. I was an avid texter, and it was only years later I learned that the family failed to grasp the meaning of my cryptic messages most of the time.

The weather had picked up and we were travelling in scorching sunshine. We moored up for the evening, along with several other boats, at the side of the canal, as there seemed to be no people about. I decided to have a communications session, texting various members of the family. But as I jumped off the boat I dropped the phone.

Plop. The phone disappeared from sight.

I screamed at Colin, "Get the sea magnet, I've dropped the bloody phone!"

I dared not take my eyes off where the phone had entered the water. Colin turned up with the magnet, but various attempts proved fruitless. Raising my head, I saw a phone box on the bridge fifty yards away. "I'm going to phone our Sally and get her to ring me and then we will know where it is," I said.

I shot off to the phone box with my phone card. It was our granddaughter Jenny who answered.

"Ring my mobile now!"

"Why?"

"Cos I've dropped it in the canal, and when it rings Grandad will know where it is."

Jenny replied in a tone that all youngsters use when talking to old people who they think have lost their marbles. "Grandma, the phone won't work under water."

"Why not? Watches do."

"Well, phones don't. You've lost it, that's it, you will have to buy another one."

"Oh ! I don't think I can get one in France. Never mind, give my love to your mam."

As I returned disconsolately to the boat I was unaware until much later that Jenny had phoned her mother at work and soon the whole hospital would be aware that this mad old lady thought mobile phones worked underwater. But the last laugh was on me: just as I got back to the boat, Colin "caught" the phone with the magnet.

With my scream of delight, about eight men of different nationalities appeared from nowhere, and all of them had different ideas about what to do next. The Italian, who had brought a huge fishing net to catch the phone, insisted on grabbing the phone rushing to his boat and attempting to dry it with a hairdryer. He seemed totally unaware the atmosphere at 70 degrees was almost as hot as the air from the dryer. As the phone screen looked like a small aquarium, I could see drying out was going to be a long job. All the men except the Captain continued to hold forth as to what could be done and after about half an hour they all decided the phone was beyond rescue. I just wanted everyone to go away and let me wallow in my grief at the phone's demise.

Part of the Captain's character is his dogged determination to try and make the impossible happen, especially when it will make me very happy. This is not an altruistic trait, more self-preservation: he reasons that if I am happy then he will be allowed to be happy. Carefully, he drilled a hole in the phone's screen and the water poured out; then he put it on the scorching hot roof of the boat to dry out.

After two days of "cooking" we decided to try and use the phone. It didn't work.

"I bet the battery needs charging," I guessed.

A few hours later, the battery charged, I phoned my daughter who was at work.

"Oh," she said, "have you managed to buy a phone then?"

Did I catch a hint of sarcasm?

"No, it's the old one."

"How's that?"

"Well, somebody phoned me and I found it," I lied.

"I don't believe you," Sally replied.

I was so proud of the rescue that I couldn't continue with the lie, so I told her what really happened and she told me that the whole of the hospital knew about her dotty mother.

It was to be three years before we replaced that old phone, and then for purely cosmetic reasons.

The weather continued to be hot, and the cruise to Clamecy was uneventful and restful. Clamecy was all you'd imagine of a small French town: old stone houses, cafés, alleyways – even the new buildings in the centre managed to be in keeping, with a fountain spurting from the path. It was at Clamecy, in times past, that logs were made into rafts to be floated down to Paris, and every year there is a raft race on the river to commemorate the event. In honour of that past a favourite sweet is ile flottante, a light meringue floating in a caramel sauce – very light and tasty, and deadly for your figure.

The port on the canal was full, so we moored further back, alongside the bank, a good spot for us, as Bob could have a wee on the grass. We were still charged for mooring, but the *Capitainerie* was a young Canadian who had married a French woman. He told us about a *son et lumière* at a Château called Saint-Fargeau; the event took place every two years and many local people took part. I thought that if we got the chance we should go to it.

After two days Sally and Peter arrived, bringing with them Colin's new car. Peter had very soon explored as much as he could and was anxious to be off on our cruise. I was worried that Peter would not enjoy himself, but I needn't have been: after the first day of gadding about sightseeing, calm descended and he began to really appreciate the slower, warmer pace of life. By now the flowers on the locks were in full bloom, the sun shone, and the very expensive wine and eggs we bought from the lock keepers tasted delicious.

We came through the last lock of the canal and onto the River Yonne, and shortly after that we sailed into the city of Auxerre. We were all overwhelmed by the prospect before us as we came under that main road-bridge. On the right were boats of all shapes and sizes, moored as many as three abreast. To the left, high on a hill, was a huge Notre Dame-type cathedral, and to its left, also on hills, two smaller churches. Along the riverbank there were pollarded trees, and behind them a broad stretch of land with cars parked on it; then a road, and then cafés and restaurants with tables and umbrellas outside. Along this bank were the moorings for passing boats.

Peter and Sally could hardly wait for us to tie up before they were off to discover the city. Auxerre, a lovely city without too many tourists, usually attracts people who are travelling at speed to the south of France (and missing all the great things in between). The only negative – and this applies less now than it did – is the "land mines", or piles of dog poo. I could not believe that French dog owners would stand directly in front of our boat and let their dog do its daily business. The authorities had coped with the problem by using a machine with an attachment similar to a vacuum cleaner extension, which they went round with sucking up the piles of poo.

Since that first visit of ours many ports have put up posts and boxes containing biodegradable poo bags; on that trip, though, Sally and I had a heated exchange with a French woman, me waving a shovel at her, and her claiming, "Vous aggressive!"

Sally and I went back to Clamecy by train for the car, my first ride in the new machine. On the way back I decided to book tickets for the Saint-Fargeau *son et lumière*. I was not very popular: the others thought the trip an unnecessary expense. But oh, how wrong the rest of them were. What an experience! Peter still talks about it to this day. Below is an extract from the letter I sent home:

It seemed a long way to the Château at Saint-Fargeau. I would have enjoyed the ride into the hinterland of the canal if I had not been so worried as to whether I had made the right decision or not. Peter and Sally had already done o lot of driving, and Colin is never very keen on exploring the countryside by car at the best of times. We arrived about 9 p.m. but the show did not start until after 10. The car park was a good way from the Château and in a rough-cut grass field: not a good start. We walked up to the small village along the only street, and a fantastic scene greeted us. The courtyard was full of life, light, and noise. There were stalls selling all sorts of things from crêpes to souvenirs. There were at least two competing musicians, one with a barrel organ, and several restaurants with outside seating, the whole surrounded by the high stone walls of the Château. Peter was (as we say in Yorkshire) gobsmacked. I was relieved that things were looking up. Perhaps a word here about Peter: he, like my dad, thinks he is very laid back about holidays –

being off work is sufficient, he says. But the vibes I pick up from him are the exact opposite: I think he has high expectations, and when he comes to visit us I do my very best to meet them. He had to be persuaded to come on the trip, so my worries about whether he would enjoy himself were very great.

After we had eaten some sausages with thin frites washed down with some vin ordinaire, we noticed people seemed to be on the move. We followed the crowds to a big amphitheatre; the seating was illuminated and there seemed to be no stage. After a few minutes the lights went down and the show began. After a moment of complete darkness, a purple spotlight picked up a small, Merlin-type figure beyond a grass arena on the far side: a wide expanse of reflective dark water. Behind the Merlin figure were trees silhouetted against the lighter sky. Merlin waved his arms as a deep ghostly voice intoned from the loudspeakers. The commentary was in French, so I did not understand the meaning of most of it, but the spectacle was very atmospheric. After a long speech from Merlin, the light broadened; men on foot and riders were seen approaching from even further away to the right. Some of the horsemen carried fluttering pennants and were in medieval armour; the others running alongside the horses were obviously unarmed. Merlin disappeared from view into the darkness from whence he had appeared. The spotlight was now following the knights and company. The horses plunged into the water and the foot-soldiers embarked in small medieval-looking boats. Slowly, to sombre music, the horses crossed the lake, the effect of the spotlights giving the illusion that the horses were actually crossing on the surface of the water. Boats were rowed towards the grass arena where eventually the group disembarked. The spotlight turned mauve and the huge battlemented Château was illuminated. The knights and company raced to the walls and began climbing ropes to rescue the damsels that had appeared in the high windows miming distress. The area covered by the spectacle was huge; as well as using the Château as a backdrop, there was the lake, with a forest behind in the distance. Facing the seated audience was a huge grassy arena with exits left and right.

Darkness returned as all the lights went out, and there was an expectant silence. When the lights went up again the scene before us was a medieval joust. Watching the joust was a stand of ladies who graciously bestowed their favours upon the participating knights. Music played throughout the tableau, medieval in style, including the famous "Greensleeves". The knights were obviously acted by local people; they were enthusiastic and daring, if not very competent, riders. More than one fell off his horse before he could be knocked off. Finally, the joust over, the winners were cheered and all the horsemen chased off towards the Château accompanied by the ladies in decorated carts.

For the next tableau (a bit I did understand), the arena was fully lit up and a peaceful village scene appeared. There were farmers ploughing, shepherds herding sheep, cows being milked by milkmaids, pigs driven along by peasants, babies fed by mothers, youngsters playing games of jumping and skipping, and couples falling in love; there was water drawn from wells and food in the process of cooking on real fires. To accompany all this activity, "Greensleeves" was again played softly on the speakers. (Odd! I thought: our King Henry VIII composed the tune.)

Suddenly, the music became warlike and threatening, and from the side a whole host of horsemen appeared. The pennant fluttering from the front rider's hand was the Dragon of St George. The English! It was absolute mayhem for the next half hour. Health and safety issues were completely disregarded as cooking pots were overturned, peasants were set on fire and animals ran completely amok. I am not sure all of the action was acting. The final glorious moment was Joan of Arc being burnt at the stake, a very realistic re-enactment with a real stake and fire burning Joan.

The scene over, it was the interval, a time to stretch our legs and rest our bottoms. The wicked English had certainly taken up more than their fair share of time if the show was to move on to modern times. I wondered, in this day of European Union, how the organisers were going to tackle three wars against the Germans in the last hundred years.

The second half began with two more long pieces, one on the French Revolution, where the guillotining of aristocrats was played down, and the other being a demonstration of the Belle Epoque: finely dressed people paraded around as though on the Champs-élysées, and men demonstrated French inventions and achievements. Now, I thought, how are they going to stage the First World War in time? The music played a soft sad song of loss from the period as the lights rose to half-light. The mist was back, now representing the fog of war as five men in First World War uniform wandered through it in front of the crowd, reading letters to loved ones at home. Annette and Yvette were among the girls left behind. In a flash the soldiers disappeared and we were had the full cast before us for the Roaring Twenties and the Charleston. The dance faded into sombre music and then came an enactment of an episode from the time of the Resistance. I noticed that all the "enemy" men were small and stupid – obviously boys. The Resistance men were tall, handsome and moustachioed. I wonder if the older generation, with their memories, delegated the young actors to be the enemy.

The lights went out, and from the loudspeakers, at full volume, came the beat of "Yankee Doodle Dandy". The lights went up to the roar of engines as several tanks and jeeps entered the arena. The music changed to the American National Anthem, followed by, as the music faded, a sonorous voice speaking over the public address system. I did not understand all the words but I did understand the last sentence: "There will be no more war ("la guerre" heavily emphasised), for we are all children of Charlemagne". As these words ended, there came the sounds of the European anthem "Ode to Joy", followed by "Land of Hope Glory". Through the tears streaming down my face, I gave Peter my translation, assisted by my German neighbour. It was only later that I wondered to myself how the French version of history came to be so different from the English. The time spent in the show on raping and pillaging by the English was disproportionate to the time spent on two world wars – plus I always regarded "Land of Hope and Glory" as the real national anthem of the English, and here it was ending a very French saga. Also, the British contribution to the war effort was totally disregarded. But more puzzling than anything was my reaction to the spectacle: I was crying and shouting "Vive la France!"

All our multinational neighbours agreed that it had been a fantastic experience.

We had a day to recover, and then it was time for Sally and Peter to return home and for us to continue our journey back to the boatyard at Migennes. Quietly, and unbeknown to our conscious minds, the decision had been taken. Mr Bean was staying in France, and we were coming back for more adventures on her canals next year.

We were lifted out of the water by Jo and his crane, and parked on oil drums at the back of his sheds where we had had our first experience of life in the boatyard in Migennes. The next two weeks were spent painting and winterising the boat. In breaks from our tasks we watched an elderly French couple work on their boat, the sleek yacht cleaned and painted to a high gloss. We were very impressed, and said so to Jo, who grumpily remarked the boat was "a heap of shit". At that time Jo was not particularly friendly towards Charlie because Jo had put a basket down by the dustbin, lost it, and then spied it, full of plums, on Charlie's table. But even I could see that Charlie was a bit of a 'womble', and the boatyard was full of things crying out for recycling.

Charlie was small and wiry; he worked "French hours" on his boat, and we learnt that before his retirement he had been a bargee and now renovated old boats bought cheaply at auction. Charlie always wore a flat cap; his wife, who worked as hard as him, spent most of her time working on the boat. Both of them would get absolutely filthy as they hammered and cleaned off the rust from inside the boat. At six o'clock at night, Madame Charlie would go for her shower; on her return she would put up the umbrella, set the table and disappear into their small caravan to cook the evening meal while Charlie completed his ablutions. We were invited to join them to drink Chablis and feast on their newly picked plums nestling in Jo's basket.

The couple's routine went on for a couple of days, and then came the dreadful moment when Charlie hammered a hole right through the side of the boat. He was devastated, and very dramatic in his grief; with his head held in his hands he begged Jo for a solution. Jo was very busy, but despite his earlier bad feelings he set about the highly skilled job of welding a patch onto the paper-thin side of the boat.

It was the first time I heard Jo's definition of an optimist: a person "not in full possession of the facts". Charlie, according to Jo, was an optimist as anyone but Charlie could see that the boat had gone past its sell by date.

Despite his harsh words, I saw a soft side to the *patron*.

A big friend of Charlie and champion Chablis drinker was Daniele, a retired joiner; he lived with two big dogs in a decrepit white Transit type van. Daniele was "helping Jo out", and like his friend he spoke virtually no English. It was in the yard that Colin and I learnt the power of drawing and mime, and thus we had an enjoyable relationship with Charlie, Madame Charlie and Daniele.

One evening, Daniele had a visitor, a buxom blonde. There was only one shower in the yard, housed in a primitive building along with a disgusting Turkish toilet that I tried not to use. The evening of Daniele's friend's visit, I went to have my shower as usual. As I approached the building I could hear shrieks of laughter, along with sounds of slapping. What a place to have a bit of slap and tickle, I thought, as I turned back to wait in the boat until they had finished.

Half an hour later, after I had seen the blonde lady talking to Charlie, I decided to try again. As I walked to shower around the other side of the building, a figure approached wearing flip-flops and carrying a rolled up towel, but wearing no clothes. It was Daniele.

I looked him straight in the eye as he spoke. "Bonsoir, Madame." And there was not a trace of embarrassment.

"Bonsoir, Monsieur," I replied as we passed each other. Gosh, I thought, as I rushed my shower in order to text home with a bit of spiced up gossip. We Anglo-Saxons get so hung up about naked bodies and I knew which friends would tut tut.

Thereafter, Daniele was known by Colin as "Dangler Dan", mischievously he would raise his glass to "Dangler Dan" who had no idea what he was drinking to.

It was in high spirits that we headed home, already planning next year's cruise route.

BOOK THREE – FRANCE AGAIN

Chapter 1

Voies Navigables de France

The telling and retelling of our story had increased our enthusiasm for our return, the start of which was not auspicious. We had not yet learned to listen to the weather forecast and the shipping news on the radio; if we had we would never have set off. From Leicester, our journey to Dover was horrendous: the rain lashed down and the wind howled; the traffic crawled along. Even though we had allowed plenty of time, it became clear that we were going to miss our sailing, so it was with some relief that I learned that all sailings had been abandoned for the day. We were near Ashford when we began to look for somewhere to stay for the night. Everywhere we tried in the darkness and pouring rain refused to admit Bob, and we were getting increasingly desperate, particularly Colin.

"It looks like Bob will have to sleep in the car," he said, with no sympathy for the dog in his voice.

"I tell you what, if they won't have Bob we will *all* spend the night in the car," I snapped back. I always feel with Colin that his comfort has to come first.

Eventually we found a Formula-type hotel. I booked a room, insisting on the ground floor: I had a cunning plan. I went to look at the room and expressed my approval, locked the door, went to the window, and beckoned Colin waiting with the dog. The rain was still lashing down and the wind blowing a gale as Colin tried to lift the sodden dog high enough to make it through the top window-vent. For Colin the task was difficult, as his right arm is fixed at a right angle and the dog was in a lumpen, panic-stricken state, her brain completely defunct.

Colin managed to get Bob's head through the window, but that was all. We had a rethink and tried bottom-first; the tail went through but that was all: despite much coaxing from me and many "Bloody stupid dogs" from Colin, nothing was going to work. Now we were faced with the prospect of sleeping in the car when we had paid for a room, but at least we could use the toilet.

As I walked past the reception desk on my way back to the car, the bored young man looked up. On the spur of the moment, I said, "If I told you my husband is diabetic (prophetic words, I'm afraid), has one leg and is nearly blind but refuses to leave his dog outside in this weather, what would you say?"

"I would say I'm just going for my tea break. I'll be about ten minutes," the bored young man muttered, not looking at me.

I shot outside, grabbed the dog and the bags, and made with great speed back to the room before Colin had time to gasp in amazement.

Two minutes after my arrival there was a knock on the door. "What the hell's going off?" said a wet and short-tempered Colin.

"Shush, the young man's gone for a tea break and there's still life in the old girl yet," I triumphantly replied.

Sometimes Bob did use her brain: there was not a squeak out of her all night.

The next morning we needed a strategy, as the shift change had meant that a young lady was now in charge of the reception desk. Colin went on ahead; he is very adept at looking lost and vague. Eventually there was a knock on the door. Bob and I made a beeline for the exit and made it back to the car without being noticed. We took Bob for a walk in Dover and managed to get on the Hoverspeed for the short sea crossing to France and the start of another boating year which we hoped would be full of adventures.

The weather was not much different when we got to the boatyard in Migennes. The boatyard seemed to be the same, and yet it was different: Charlie and his wife had gone, as had Dangler Dan. Jo was the same, wary and yet friendly, up to his neck in work and trying to manage on his own. I didn't know it at the time but I was about to start a training course in patience: just because we had arrived did not mean we were to be put in the water straightaway.

Having the car made a difference, and luckily we had discovered French car boot sales, or *vide greniers*, which means literally "clear out your barns". The French boot sale is very different to the English version; in France the *vide grenier* is part of the village fête, with the village closed to road traffic. Most of the stalls belong to villagers, and it is difficult to describe some of the junk that is deemed saleable: galvanized buckets with holes in them, chicken feeders and pre-war gardening implements, along with more familiar fare such as children's toys, clothes and antique computers. There is often a stall selling CDs, and the sound of the demonstration recordings of accordion dance music fills the air. Near the centre of the village usually there is a stall offering glasses of the local wine for sale; next to it will be a marquee where local volunteers labour over barbeques on which locally-made sausages sizzle. One memorable *vide grenier* had men making the Boudin sausages in full view of passers-by. I was nearly sick. The small, galvanized baths seemed to be filled entirely with blood; the men wearing aprons, bent over, up to their elbows in the blood, stirring the mess by hand. We sat next to some locals eating the deep red sausages with very thin *frites*. Colin, using mime and additional words from me, teased our neighbours about their "black pudding". Eventually, in desperation to prove the deliciousness of their sausage, the French ladies gave to the ignorant Englishman one from their plate. I could not believe that Colin would actually eat the thing, but he did, pulling a face as he chewed. Our jolly neighbours laughed: I think they thought we were wimps.

Colin was quite happy to be in the yard, though; there was always something to see and do – from small beginnings do love affairs begin.

Eventually the day came when we set off, heading south again; but instead of turning west at the end of the Bourgogne we planned to turn east before heading north. We had really no idea where we would end up, we were just glad we were finally going.

The cruise started off very differently from the previous year. This year we had some sense of what we were doing; but we were puzzled by the lack of other boats. There were no tourist boats or cruisers and we seemed to be on our own for most of the time. The weather was cold and rainy; occasionally we saw a boat going the other way but apart from the *éclusiers* we saw no one.

Our spirits sank; what we wouldn't have given to be on the dear old Leeds and Liverpool looking forward to an evening of jazz in the pub at Rodley. As it was, the towns were as deserted as the pubs.

We approached the mooring in Montbard with the icy cold wind blowing the water into small waves. I knew that from Montbard you could catch a fast TGV and be in Paris in an hour and a half; from there, six hours tops, I could be in my own village having a meat pie in the Bay Horse with people I knew. We were all miserable; even Bob was reluctant to take her evening walk, which she usually considered the most important act of the day. The Captain announced that there were breakers on his coffee.

The next day we were accompanied by a lady *éclusier* and it wasn't until we were mooring up for the night at Veneray that I realized we had acquired a companion, a small plastic boat. It took a lot of effort for us to moor, as the wind kept blowing the boat away from the side —and as usual in these circumstances the Captain takes charge.

He Who Must Be Obeyed from his steering position cannot see the front, he has no idea what I am doing with the ropes, but still this doesn't prevent him from telling me what I should be doing.

"Throw the rope! Jump!" he commands.

"Bugger off!" I yell back.

He can't see that we're six feet away from the side and moving ever outwards.

"Bloody hell! Yvonne, jump or we will drift off," comes back the desperate voice.

"But where will we drift off to"? I think to myself, "the other side." "Wow big deal"! When I do not feel it's an emergency I can slow-time 'Him Who Must Be Obeyed'; It helps that the Captain is slightly deaf (although he always denies it) and with the noise of the engine, while I can hear him he can't hear me.

Eventually we come close enough for the lady *éclusier* to catch my rope and I jump off to tie the boat at the front, leaving the irate Captain to his fate.

"Neuf heures demain," I say, the first French boating phrase I ever learned.

"Le canal est fermé," the éclusier replies

"Pourquoi?"

The *éclusier*'s face was full of concentration as she struggled to tell me why the canal was closed. She eventually said, "Pluie," making rain signs with her fingers.

I thought I must have heard wrong so I asked "Pluie"?

"Oui, pluie." More rains signs.

My question "Quel jour canal ouvert?" was met with a Gallic shrug.

By now the Captain had managed to stop the boat drifting and had brought it straight alongside the quay.

"Before you start you can shut up, we have a bigger problem," I said. Something in my face must have warned Colin to keep his opinions on my rope-handling skills to himself.

One of the biggest problems facing canal travellers is how to manage the arrival and departure of visitors. While canal maps do show railway lines, they don't always show stations, and without contact numbers and language skills it's impossible for us to find out what buses are running and when. If our visitors are arriving by train, we have to be there or have some way of instructing them how to get to us. We also have to ensure that the cruise we take them on ends at an appropriate place to catch a train home. And if our visitors come by car, the end of the cruise has to be somewhere where a bus or train can take them back to their car. An additional problem for me is that I like to show our visitors the best of our life on the canal, so the cruise has to have a lot of locks for sunshine and exercise, and beautiful cities or towns for social and cultural interest. As in Britain, there are few rural trains here, and most lines run north to south.

Well, I had arranged to meet Peter and Sally in Dijon in three weeks; plenty of time under normal circumstances. In a completely over-the-top hand-waving panic, I said to the *éclusier*, "Mon Dieu, mes enfants sont à Dijon!"

Looking very unhappy, the *éclusier* uttered a phrase I was hearing for the first time, one I often use as a mistranslation because I like the sound of it: "Je suis désolée." The word in French is an apology

What a word *désolé* is, so much better than the "desolate". We have made it our own and use it to describe complete and utter misery.

We spent the night poring over maps, reaching the conclusion that there was no way we could meet the kids in Dijon: we would have to turn back, which Colin really hates doing, and perhaps take the kids for a cruise along the River Yonne.

Next morning, the weather had not improved as Colin started the engine at 9am. The little boat that had moored with us was already underway, heading over the choppy waters of the port. As I was about to cast off, the *éclusier* lady approached. "Le canal est fermé. Pour vous le canal est ouverte temporaire," she said.

I thought I had misheard. "Pardon?"

"Le canal est fermé. Pour vous le canal est ouvert droit de l'écluse."

I had no idea what was happening, but had the feeling our luck was in. By now we had cast off and Colin was aiming to catch up with the plastic boat, which was turning left onto the canal.

"Go right," I yelled as I sped back signalling to the wheelhouse, the Captain looked gormless. "Go right."

"Right? Why?" Colin repeated

"They have opened the canal for us."

"Why?"

"I don't know."

"Are you sure?"

"No . . . just go right." I was beginning to get irritated by his slow response

We shot into a deep lock. Nothing!

"Now look what you have done, we'll never get out

backwards," Colin grumbled in an I-must-be-tolerant-of-the-less-able tone.

"But they said they were opening the canal for us."

"You must have got it wrong."

"We had better shout and see if anyone is there."

We shouted, but our voices seemed to get lost in the sound of the water pouring over the lock doors, when suddenly a head appeared over the wall. The head appeared to have no neck; the complexion was sallow, the eyes framed in horrendous glasses with black frames and lenses that enlarged the eyes out of all proportion to the size of the face. The whole head was topped by lank greasy hair. We had seen that head before.

With a soggy cigarette hanging from its mouth, the head spoke. "You speak English?"

"Yes, Yes," said the two supplicants in unison.

"The canal is closed but for you we will open it temporaire."

"Oh, thank you." We grovelled in worship to the head.

By now Bob had stopped trembling and was sitting posing at my side, looking straight at the head. It went on shouting above the noise: "You will do as I tell you OK? You understand you will do as you are told by me?" As the mouth moved, black teeth were revealed. For once, him for whom rules are made especially for him to disobey pledged his troth to complete obedience; it was not a problem for me: I would do anything to meet the kids "à Dijon".

We nodded and spoke in complete agreement (for once). The head disappeared and then its body appeared with a lady on top of the lock. They were talking to each other and taking no notice of what was happening to the boat in the lock as they quickly wound the paddles up. It was a good job we were now more experienced boaters: as Mr Bean rocked we were too busy saving our lives to worry about what was happening on top of the lock.

As we emerged into daylight we realized there was another man waiting for us. By his demeanour and appearance he seemed to be the boss. As we reached the surface there was a conference during which we were again asked to repeat our promise after being informed of the terms of the agreement. "You will do 18 locks today, 19 tomorrow and 18 the day after. There will be no stopping unless we tell you. Do you understand?"

The message was translated for us by the "head", with the boss nodding his approval. We looked serious and piously agreed to the terms. The boss got into his van and we started the journey to the summit of the Bourgogne.

For two days the rain poured down but as we travelled we could see there was hardly any water in the canal; only a narrow boat could travel in such shallow water; there had to be a big leak somewhere. Our two *éclusiers* continued to ignore us; they were obviously attracted to each other, and as they chatted away, waiting for the locks to fill, they consumed vast amounts of cigarettes. The *éclusiers* vanished at noon and reappeared half an hour later, otherwise we travelled non-stop until they decided sometime around six p.m. to depart with a brief "au revoir." By then we were absolutely shattered and Bob was going stir crazy. Without negotiation, each night I took Bob for a walk while Colin performed his "boaty" tasks. I then prepared a meal, Colin washed up and took Bob for the evening wee, and we were in bed before nine. To think that most of our family and friends were envious of our "wonderful" life.

Late on the third day we arrived at Pont Royal to be informed that we were to have a change of *éclusier*. In Pont Royal there was a restaurant, closed, a boulangerie, closed, and no other great signs of life; but we thought it did have possibilities and the rain had stopped.

"I don't care what they bloody say, I have had enough, we are stopping," announced the Captain, reverting to form.

"I think we should let the *éclusier* know," I replied.

"Oh, they'll not be bothered."

"Well, I think they will. Get the bike off."

A grumpy Colin got the bike off Mr Bean, and much against his better judgement I cycled to tell the new *éclusier* that we were leaving at nine in the morning. I could not believe it: the new *éclusier* was at least six foot tall as thin as a pole, he was wearing green overalls with a thick leather belt cutting his body in half. What was astonishing was the man's glasses: I was looking up into yellow lenses in huge black frames yet again. Were we in a land of aliens or had the local optician obtained a job lot of "Starship" glasses?

"Nous restez at Pont Royal partir neuf heures demain," I said to the *éclusier*.

"Non. Non. Vous continuez." The glasses bent over towards me threateningly.

I backed off. "Okay, okay, we continue. Pardon. Pardon."

I turned and sped back to the boat to find that Colin had already got the chairs out and was dreamily sat stroking Bob.

"You can forget that, we have got to continue. Go! Vite, vite!"

"What! Why?"

"Don't argue, just do it."

"Bloody French, what would they do if we just refused?"

"We wouldn't see the kids, that's what."

Feeling like naughty children we finally reached the summit and the tunnel. This time we passed over the summit through the tunnel with no problems and began the descent towards Dijon. We again stopped at Vandenesse-en-Auxois to see if the lady with the *épicerie* in a barn and restaurant in a tent was still in business – which she was. As we were coming in to moor, I saw someone walking away from the premises with a fantastic looking quiche on a big plate. Ah! I thought, I bet the lady is doing takeaways. I dashed over with my mouth watering. And yes, if I provided the plate, she would bake me a quiche. I thought it would be a nice surprise for the Captain.

The quiche was exquisite, if a little expensive. I worried about the lady: if the other side of the canal stayed closed for any length of time, how was she going to make a living? She had made so much effort. The barn was full of wonderful specialities of the region, and it was a temptation to spend more than we could afford. She really was, if not a chef, then a very good cook.

The weather improved and we spent a happy few days cruising into Dijon. On the way we heard from the kids: the date and time of the proposed visit had been changed, we were glad as we were able to slow down and enjoy the journey. After leaving Saint-Jean-de-Losne we turned east onto the River Saône. We saw hardly anyone before we entered the Rhône au Rhin Canal at Saint - Symphorien. We moored up at the boatyard there and the owner, an Englishman, made us very welcome, but the yard was home to very big boats and we were moored well away from the quay and felt very much the poor relations among the long-term and mainly American residents. We decided to move on as, at that moment, we were not particularly keen on Americans.

It was about midday, and we were just passing through Dole when Colin caught sight of a familiar motorbike with a United States postbox on the back. "Look! It's Harold."

Frantic waving had no effect, but soon, under a tunnel of trees, we saw "Skutsje". I couldn't wait for Colin to faff about getting his boat equidistant from the mooring pins; I was off shouting, "Charlotte, Charlotte."

As Charlotte emerged, Harold sped up on his bike and helped Colin to tie up. Harold and Charlotte had decided to spend the summer under the trees not far from their winter mooring at St Symphorien; I think the wheelhouse decapitation and the rudder bending had made them decide to take it easy from now on. Harold had got the situation well organised: the lock keeper had agreed to provide the boat with fresh water and electric, there was a café in the park nearby for dinners, and he had plenty of jobs to do.

We gossiped the afternoon away and they agreed with me that some Americans abroad are absolute pains; they had used their boat as a floating B&B in the past until one group of New Yorkers had driven them to distraction and they had abandoned the project. The final crunch had come when there had been complaints over the bottled water: numerous varieties were tried but none were approved until finally Harold filled bottles from the lock-side tap, to universal satisfaction. We also discussed the American health system. As a war veteran, Harold got the best of treatment, and we were surprised to learn that in America the idea is to visit the doctor before you are ill, since by doing so your insurance remains valid.

It was then Colin told Harold about always being thirsty, and Harold took the Captain's glucose levels with his machine. Shock horror! The reading was over nineteen. I could not believe I had been so blind.

From then on I tried to keep him on a diet. Dieting means keeping to rules and as I have said before rule-keeping is not Colin's strong point. French cooking in the country is not a problem for the dieter: we reckon there are only six puddings: *ile flottant*, a meringue floating in crème anglaise; *tarte*, or as one waitress said to us, "pee of the day"; *mousse chocolat*; *crème brulée*; and then *glace* or *yaourt*.

After a while puddings are just a memory of something you have in England, but the cakes you can buy in the *boulangeries* are another thing. They have to be seen to be believed – but of course they are full of colour, artistry, sugar and fat.

Colin did not have an auspicious start to his diet, as Harold and Charlotte said they would take us out for tomorrow's midday meal at 'Jeanine's'. We took Bob for a walk later that evening to the park where 'Jeanine's' was situated. It was a wooden hut – what sort of meal would we get from this place? Charlotte and I decided not to get dressed up for the occasion; we were too busy gossiping, and Harold and Colin were messing around with Harold's gadgets, which seemed to have multiplied alarmingly. When we arrived in the park the following lunch time, the hut had undergone a transformation: now there was a bright awning over a serving hatch, and numerous tables were spread over the grass, at most of the tables sat men in overalls. Sitting on each cloth covered table were carafes of wine and water, and a little vase with a single flower. The sun was shining, the grass and trees were green and the temperature perfect, an auspicious start to the meal.

We were shown to the end of a table where there were already six French men seated. Charlotte and Bob responded to the workmen's interest and started playing to the crowd: Charlotte fluttered her eyes and swapped jokes with the workmen. Bob made a circuit of the tables offering everyone a paw. The first course came out, a huge platter of fresh salad with every ingredient known to man and a delicious dressing, accompanied by baskets of fresh crispy bread. It was absolutely fantastic, and I ate fast, as the English do; the French on the other hand savoured their food interspersed with sips of wine and loads of chatter.

Half an hour later came the second course. I could not

believe it: the large roasting pan contained a huge amount of black lentils, and sitting atop the lentils were whole hocks complete with skin and a thick wodge of fat. Haricot beans accompanied the meat course. I was appalled: there was no way I could fight my way through the skin and fat to find the lean meat. But Colin was ecstatic. "God! We used to have this as kids, I never thought I would eat such food again, it's fantastic." (He had not been impressed with the salad.) In no time at all the new dieter had polished off his hock and lentils and was starting on mine.

Finally there was pudding, no surprise there: it was one of the six, yoghurt. A small espresso followed. As we finished coffee, the workman stood up as one and all went to a row of bay trees, stood in a line with their backs to us, and peed. Then, with shouts of farewell, they left, and the four of us were alone.

For a moment Colin and I were speechless, after a minute we burst out laughing. "Don't even think about it," I said seeing envy on Colin's face.

Although we were sad to leave Harold and Charlotte we felt so much happier for having chanced upon them, and were looking forward to meeting the kids at Besançon. From Dole the canal becomes a canalised river, the Doubs. We had joined the canal from the Saône/Rhône link at Saint Symphorien. There were 73 locks to reach the summit of the Rhône au Rhin, and 39 locks before we would drop down to the Rhine at Niffer. The canal is 238 kilometres in length and travels through beautiful and varied countryside. We started on the artificial canal across the plain of the Saône; then we would follow the contours of the rugged tree-covered hills of the Jura. We would be sailing on the Doubs river interspersed by the canal and locks as we wound our way between steep cliffs. At Voujeaucourt the canal leaves the Doubs valley to join the Allaine valley, followed by the Bourbeuse, and finally the Ill. By now the canal is high up over the fields and unprotected by trees, and offers wide views of the surrounding farms and fields. The lock at Saint Symphorien is a modest 38 metres, whereas the lock at Niffer at the entrance to the Rhine is capable of accommodating several boats of 2,000 tons.

I was so excited about Sally, Peter and granddaughter Laura's visit that I hardly remember the journey until we emerged from the Tarragnoz lock just before Bescancon. We decided not to go through the tunnel that cut off the loop of the river that encircled the citadel and centre of Besançon, but to follow the river. And oh, what a circuit! To our right there were huge Gothic buildings fronted by beautiful greensward. In front of one building a bride and groom were having their photos taken surrounded by their guests. The ladies' pretty summer frocks were blowing in the wind.

For this year's cruise, Colin had made a sun canopy to put over the wheelhouse; he called it the "surrey with the fringe on top". The canopy was made of a bright blue silky parachute-type material with a white fringe. It altered the light, so we looked out on the scene in front of us, a bright sunshiny vista through a delicate blue haze. All Colin could say as he stood in his "Eric Morecambe's" on his milk crate (his feet did not reach the floor if he sat down to drive) was "Bloody hell, Yvonne! Can you believe it? It's so beautiful. What a place!" I agreed, enviously looking onto the scene just as the bride sat down, her dress settling in a diaphanous circle around her. The groom was bending over, holding her hand and looking into her eyes. It was a fairy-tale picture and I hoped for this unknown pair the fairy tale would continue from the sunshine of today to the twilight of old age.

Two thirds of the way around the circle we came to some

pontoons under the canal-side trees. "Oh, let's moor here," we both said. We did not know at the time that the mooring was reserved for small boats and the Tourist Trip Boat. The trip boat captain was very helpful, and with a bit of shuffling about we were finally settled. We soon had the chairs and table off Mr Bean, setting them up under the tree on the bank above the boat. Bob, always glad to get off and meet people, settled herself under the table and then had a surprise visitor, her "doppelgänger", no less. At first we thought the new dog was Bob, and it turned out that the two dogs not only looked alike but had similar characters too. In no time at all we were sharing dog tasks with the trip boat captain. Walks, for Bob, were so much more interesting when you had a companion. We were in an ideal spot: from the mooring pontoon, a steep slope flattened out under a group of trees before resuming its climb about ten feet to the top of the bank. At the top, turning right, the road led to the lock keeper's house, and to the left a park and over the bridge to the city. On the other side of the road was a wide expanse of the shallow Doubs, where there were often children cooling off in the water.

After the first mad enthusiasm of exploring the city on our bikes, we sat in the shade awaiting the arrival of our visitors. The trip boat captain showed us a new use for wine corks: soak them in white spirit and hey, presto, you have a sure start for your barbeque.

Nothing is ever straightforward with our children. We had a phone call to say they were on the train and very near Besançon, so we had a final mad spurt of preparations and then heard nothing for a couple of hours. When the phone did ring it was to tell us they had passed the stop and were in Montbéliard, miles away. When they finally arrived, Laura was in a teenage sulk because, in the darkness of a tunnel, Peter had "attacked" her and mussed up her carefully arranged hair. It took Laura quite a while to work out who the culprit was, when she did she was determined to make him (and us) suffer by being monosyllabic and moody.

Over a meal, we decided that we would take the kids for a cruise on the Doubs Canal to Baume-les-Dames and then return to Besançon in time for them to visit the city. We set off the next morning, for most of the time cruising through the wide, shallow, rocky water of the Doubs. Every now and then we would be back on the canal, passing through locks. The lock keepers had put a great deal of effort into making the approaches to the locks beautiful, with pots, troughs and hanging baskets bright with summer flowers. Sally and Peter, like sunflowers, turned their faces to the sun and basked in the beauty of their surroundings; even Laura began to relax and enjoy herself. We were all enchanted to hear the clunk of cowbells as we sailed along: the Swiss border was not far away.

A memorable event on our journey concerned nine (yes, nine) Germans. As we set off, we noticed a hire boat being loaded up via the bank of the canal from a small car. The loading seemed to consist mainly of crates of beer. Two of the Germans stayed by the car as the others set off in front of us. Like many hire-boaters, the passengers found it difficult to appreciate the difference between driving a car and a boat, so speed was of the essence.

The Germans soon left us far behind. We arrived at a point on the river that was particularly wide, curved and shallow, and were surprised to find the Germans stationary. As we approached, they seemed to be looking pleadingly at us: they appeared to have grounded. Colin rang his big red fire engine bell, fastened to the roof of Mr Bean, to alert them to the fact that rescue was at hand.

"Ooh! I just love the idea of rescuing the bloody Germans,"

he said gloatingly. "You go to the front and yell them to throw their rope."

As an obedient wife I went to the front, and, using hand signals I indicated to them to throw the rope. I fastened it to Mr Bean's front cleat and Colin gave the engine some throttle, clanging his bell at the same time. Clouds of smoke and noise, the rope tightened, and . . . nothing happened. Mr Bean was leaning over with the strain.

"Let the rope go," Colin shouted at me. "Get the back one."

By now Colin was in full "Mein Führer" mode, no please or thank you passing his lips and for the moment I was doing as instructed without protest. The rope was tied at the back, Mr Bean took the strain, and again nothing happened, while the boat leaned over alarmingly. The kids stood by and watched in amazement as their normally stroppy mother obeyed the captain robotically.

"Right, we have to do something different; you tell 'em." The Colin instructed me.

"No. You tell them, you are the one who speaks German," I said sharply, coming to my senses. The Captain's German had been learned 40 years previously as a tank driver stationed in Dortmund. He started shouting in "pidgin" German, waving his hands about in illustration, telling the Germans to line up on the far side.

"When I shout 'Hup', you all jump up together, Verstehen?"

"Ya, we understand," came back the shout of reply.

The Germans lined up on the far side of their boat. Mr Bean's engine roared, smoke poured out of the back, but despite all the engine's effort the boat still leaned towards the Germans.

"Hup!" yelled Colin.

I could see the German figures bend their knees in preparation to jump, and as they did they saw the name of our boat. "Mr Bean! Mr Bean! Das Boot Mr Bean!"

The German's jump was aborted as they all fell about, sounds of raucous laughter could be heard across the water (Mr Bean is extremely popular on the Continent). Colin's pride was wounded and he retaliated with angry words and actions. "Stuff the lot of you. You'll need me before I need you. Cast the rope off, Yvonne" he shouted.

The rope was cast off and we sped away at Mr Bean's maximum 8 kmh. As I looked back, the Germans were still laughing, they had beer cans in their hands, which they raised in victory at our retreat. It was the next day before they passed us again, waving a cheery, "hello." We stuck our noses in the air and ignored them.

Telling our tale some time later, we realised that the Germans could have walked to the bank if they had wanted to, the water was so shallow; an even more radical solution would have been for them to dump some of their beer supplies. As it was they must have had to wait quite a long time for the hirer to rescue them.

Peter, who is habitually stressed, gradually relaxed. He was content to sit at the front of the boat with his arm around Bob, watching the beautiful scenery drift by. For Sally it was harder, as she felt for Laura, who had come on the cruise with preconceived ideas of loads of shops, other teenage company and of moving by boat from one metropolis to another. All Sally could do was try her best to keep her entertained.

After four days cruising up and down the river and canal we returned to Besançon for sightseeing, shopping, haircuts, and sitting under the tree. Beautiful as Besançon is, it's the challenge game of *boules* we had with the lock keeper on our last night together that Peter remembers best. The lock keeper and his friends were surprised when Peter, after watching their game for a while, went up to them with five euros in his hand and challenged them. Peter plays any sport that involves a ball, although his favourite is cricket: he is an indifferent batsman but a notorious medium-pace bowler. In our local team Peter likes to be known as 'the Difference' because his bowling has in the past changed a losing game into a winner. 'The Difference' psyched up his team and they went into our game with the French with all the confidence of Henry V at Agincourt. Unlike King Henry's, though, Peter's army let him down badly and they lost spectacularly; Peter was convinced he had been led into a trap by the dastardly French and offered double or nothing. For a while the French team politely demurred from playing another game and taking easy money off the English; but at last they were persuaded, and wiped the floor with Peter and his team amid much shouting, laughter and wine.

When the family leaves I am always grief-stricken I have never got used to an empty nest, and for a while I am not good company. Also, the events that overwhelmed us when we eventually sailed on the Rhine tended to obliterate memories of the cruise to the Rhine after Besançon. I quote from a letter sent from Boofzheim, the first port on the second part of the Rhône au Rhin canal:

Dear All,

I think I have gone mad! We were sat in this port recovering from a near-death experience when all these men dressed in dark clothes, very shiny brass helmets with brass neck protectors and masks poured out of fire tenders carrying hoses, and rushed towards the canal. Some of the men fell on one knee and others supported the hose as a stream of high-pressure water was directed into the centre of the canal. There was a lot of shouting, engine noise, and running about. There we were, sitting under a plum tree, savouring the fact that we are still alive and suddenly all hell breaks lose. The only object in this port is us and we are certainly not on fire; Mr Bean might be slowly sinking but he is too exhausted to even think about a fire.

I feel so traumatized by the whole experience of being on the Rhine that I can hardly remember the journey to the lock at Niffer. I first saw a big boat at Mulhouse, the Pandora, moored near the Port de Plaisance. I was shocked at the size of it and a little bit scared, although the captain did give me a cheery wave. Next morning we set off, and after the enclosed environment of the Port in Mulhouse it was pleasant and interesting to journey along the new, dead straight 13km canal to the lock and the entrance to the Rhine at Niffer. There were lots of young people rollerblading or cycling along a new concrete towpath; the whole area adjacent to the canal had been beautifully landscaped and was verdant with new young trees and grass. We arrived at Niffer and moored for the night. If we had been a boat over 15m we would not have been allowed on the Rhine without a special licence but under that size we were considered a plaisancer or sport boat. To the right, upstream of Niffer, 19km and one lock away, is the Swiss city of Basel; to the left and downstream, where we were heading, is 75kms and 5 locks before we re-enter the Canal Rhône au Rhine (branche Nord). That evening we walked to look out on a river as calm as a millpond, and despite our sudden fear when we saw the big boat in Mulhouse we were quietly confident: after all, we were experts at travelling on the Trent.

The next morning, lifejackets on and anchor ready for emergencies out on the bow, we were the only boat in a lock as big as two football fields. We attached the securing ropes to the "floating bollards"; we had been told by "experts" that the bollards would float down with us. I did not trust these new contraptions:

what happened if they sank? I was on full alert watching for such a possibility, though with no idea what to do if it happened.

The gates closed and we began to slowly sink. Everything was calm and quiet; there seemed to be a long delay before finally the floating bollard began to sink with us. I have no idea how the bollards work but I assume it has something to do with water pressure. Down we went, and as we sank the silence was disturbed by a choir of eerie wailing noises at different pitches. The noise of the choir was coming from the floating bollards. Gradually the sky became a small patch above us as we dropped, Colin estimated, 25 metres. It felt as though we were entombed with ghosts. Eventually we reached the bottom and the gates opened, and we sallied forth towards the mouth of the canal. As we reached the junction, a "block of flats" passed in front of us – a ship with containers piled three high on the deck. I was too amazed to be frightened, and grabbed the camera. It took three pictures to get the whole of the ship in.

It was a clear, sunny day, and after the "block of flats" we did not see another boat as we approached the first lock. I called the lock keeper on the VHF and in my best French I requested passage through. There was no reply, and we had a heated discussion as to what we should do before, miracle of miracles, the lock light turned to green. Once again we were the only boat in the lock, and the let-down was slow and calm as before. But that was the end of our luck. At the third lock, there was again no reply to our VHF request to enter, so we hung about in the middle of the river. "Hanging about" is difficult in a boat, especially when there is a current. A boat cannot be steered in reverse, so in order not to drift into the side we have to steer while going forward, but to avoid hitting the lock gates we have to reverse. I call this manoeuvre "dancing about", and sitting at the front I have always found it extremely stressful. Bob, sensing my stress, follows suit, gibbering and shaking and trying to sit on Colin's foot, much to the Captain's annoyance. We were "dancing about" and arguing, the Captain insisting I call the lock again. I was reluctant to nag the lock keepers, though, and feel that Colin is often too impatient; but I did as I was told, very badly. "Monsieur éclusier, permission to enter the écluse? Merci." Silence, and then doors began to open and the light changed to green. "Hurrah!" shouted Colin, and we headed for the opening as fast as we could.

We had just got past the open doors when I looked behind me. My heart sank and my legs went to jelly. "Oh my god, look at that big bugger."

I had read somewhere that big-boat captains cannot see immediately in front of their boats, and I really believed that this boat would not know we were there and would crush us. I signalled Colin to look behind; his face was white as he turned back.

"Hurry up. If we are not to get crushed, let's get in the lock first, then he's bound to see us."

We tied up at the front floating bollard, and incredibly slowly the "big bugger" followed and stopped behind us. A small man built like a tank looped the big boat's front rope over a bollard; he had a piece of paper in his hand and started walking towards me. I was convinced I had done something wrong so my legs, already jelly, went to water.

"Bonjour, Madame."

"Bonjour."

"Do you speak English?"

"I am English." My voice was shaking as I replied: I was definitely going to be told off for something.

"I have noticed that you speak to the lock keepers in

French," the man said in a soft voice, using surprisingly good English. "Going upstream on the river you must use German. I have written out what you must say on this card to help you."

"Oh! You are so kind!" I was so amazed that I burst into sobs which seemed to come from the bottom of my stomach.

"Why are you crying?"

"I was so frightened. I thought I had done something wrong," I gasped between sobs.

"Oh, you are doing fine; there is no need to get upset."

By this time, Colin, seeing me crying, had come to investigate. Finding out that all was well, he asked the péniche captain where we could stop for the night.

"Go through the next lock and two kilometres further there is a mooring place just off the river," he told us.

With many thanks we all got back on out boats and went down in the lock. It was only when the big boat had passed us after we emerged that we realised it was the same boat we had seen in Mulhouse, The Pandora. There is something about Colin when he is anxious and travelling on a straight road or river: he has to turn a corner. Despite my protestations, he could not wait for two kilometres to turn into the mooring that the péniche captain had told us about; he saw a sign for a port and before I could speak he had turned and refused to turn back. We were off the river for the day. We had a huge marital but he was determined this was where he was going to stay the night. The port was obviously going to be expensive: it was full of huge modern boats and the charge turned out to be 25 euros a night. Well, I was determined they weren't going to get any more money out of us, and I was also determined, despite the searing heat, that we were going over the bridge and into Germany.

Halfway into my "stand" I felt horrible: it was obvious that the heat was affecting Colin's stump and walking was difficult for him; but I also think he was milking it.

The town was uninteresting, but that was maybe due to the mood we were in. On the way back we sat at a table in front of the campsite café. We were joined by an elderly English lady who, we learned later, was in her eighties. We were amazed to find out that the lady was on her way, in a 12ft boat, to the Danube. Yes, she was cruising on the Rhine in training for travelling on the Danube.

"Don't your family worry about you?" we asked.

"Oh, I ring them every Sunday to let them know I am alright. Mind you, I had a scare the other day: I ran out of petrol at the bottom of the lock at Niffer."

I looked at the old lady in horror, but she was laughing and at the same time eating her sausage and chips with relish.

"What happened?"

"Oh, the lock man had to get his little boat out and come in and rescue me," she replied in a tone of unconcern. "Have a chip, I can't eat all these."

Colin, never missing an opportunity, moved in and finished the feast.

"Did the lock man tell you off?" I asked.

"Oh no – but I don't think he was very pleased," she replied.

"Weren't you worried?"

"No, not really."

That's my problem, I thought: I am always trying to be the "good girl". I felt a complete wimp and decided I must get a grip. We had as much right to be on that bloody river as the big boats, I tried to convince myself.

Next morning we set off, part of a little flotilla of "sportboats"; there were no big boats to be seen. Numbers four and five locks were enjoyable because of all the other small boats. I felt we had a right to be there; in fact, just before the doors opened on number five I was happy. There were no more locks on the Rhine for us: as soon as we were out of the lock we would cross the river and into the second half of the Rhône au Rhin canal, and thence onto Strasbourg. We were the front boat as the doors opened, with five smaller boats behind us; and there behind the opening doors was a monster of a boat, his bow very high, waiting to come into the lock. Suddenly, as we came out, all the little boats passed us at speed and, turning behind the monster, began to cross the Rhine, heading for the entrance to the canal. We followed them into a maelstrom of crisscross bow waves. Mr Bean seemed to alternately growl and scream as we pitched alarmingly up and down.

"God, what's that noise?" I asked, while a stern white-faced captain wrestled with the wheel, paralyzed with fear. Even Bob had forgotten to whimper and shake. At the same time I looked at the little boats in front of us and felt sorry for them as they were thrown up, down and sideways by the wash. The first boat had missed the opening to the canal and was desperately trying to turn round and come back against the current.

He's had it, I thought abstractly. "What's that screaming noise?" I asked again.

"It's the propeller coming out of the water. I think we have lost the anchor rope; go to the front and drag it in, we are done for if it gets round the propeller: it'll stop us dead."

I fought my way down the boat to the front. One moment I was walking uphill, the next I was slithering down. I opened the door at an uphill moment and dragged on the anchor rope. Fortunately it was still on board, although it was clearly on the move. I pulled the rope onto the floor of the boat well, wondering if I should leave the doors open – it would stop us rocking. I decided against the idea and closed the doors just as we were going into the deep, and water pounded over the front. I pushed with all my might against the doors, deciding to bolt them; the idea of being in an air bubble had come into my mind. As I turned and headed back, a figure hurtled past the door and crashed into the side of the wheelhouse. The captain had been thrown off his milk crate by the force of the water on the steering wheel. He lay stunned, his back against the wall of the wheelhouse, with his wooden leg at a funny angle. I helped him get back on the crate, and as he got up I looked over the side and saw two big boats heading at speed, seemingly for us. We were in the middle of the river; if we weren't sunk by the water, we were going to be crushed by the boats.

"Turn back! Turn back!" I screamed.

"We can't turn back, we have to go on."

Well that's it, I thought, we are done for; and for a minute all was calm as I imagined our memorial service, given that our bodies would never have been found. I thought of a certain conventional and opinionated acquaintance telling the vicar, "I told them they should have had a caravan at Bridlington."

My reverie was broken by the Captain shouting, "Lasso that bollard and DON'T miss."

I didn't miss: I caught the bollard and whipped the rope round the cleat – and stopped us dead. Once again the Captain took to flying, but this time he got up in euphoric mood, shouting to all the other captains, "That was a brown underpants job!"

It was amazing, all the other captains, of several different nationalities, seemed to be yelling the same thing, as well as jumping up and down in triumph.

We were at the entrance to the canal but still on the river; the next task was to get through the lock. I couldn't believe it, the French were on their lunch and we had to wait half an hour. Typical: there we were facing death and the French were calmly having their *lunch – revenge for Dunkirk I suppose.*

Next big stop is Strasbourg where I have booked us into the Motor Boat Club at Bassin de l'Hopital. Our friends Helen and George are planning to join us. For now we are just glad we are alive.

Our arrival in Strasbourg was a strange coincidence: I am one of those people who struggles with left and right and I had given our contact – a person who it seems also struggles with left and right – totally the wrong information as to where on the canal circle that runs around Strasbourg we would be arriving. So it was lucky indeed that, as we approached Strasbourg, we saw this figure waving at us. Another huge marital had been diverted and soon we were happily moored up amid a very friendly and welcoming group of people.

Our tea planter friend, John, had told us that one of his favourite activities while he was moored at the boat club was to sit at the front of his boat and look over the canal in order to watch "the ladies of the night" working along the road in front of the hospital. And John was right: watching the activity across the road was indeed fascinating; cars would often do several circuits, stopping to talk to possible partners; the cars would then speed off without picking up the lady of the night, only to return later. We presumed the car drivers were negotiating prices and terms. We observed a very long negotiation which involved a man on a bicycle. After three circuits he was not seen again; was he successful, and if so what happened to the bike?

Halfway between Paris and Prague, Strasbourg is known as the "crossroads of Europe". I was not impressed by the futuristic European Parliament building just off the historic centre; I was even less impressed when I learned that parliament members divide their time between Brussels and Strasbourg and vanloads of paper "stuff" are transported between the two.

Soon we were joined by Helen and George – and what a performance from Bob as she told Helen a long story about her adventures in France, involving much whining and paw-shaking. Bob regarded Helen definitely as her soul mate.

After doing the usual touristy things exploring the many canals of Strasbourg, we were ready to set off on our travels again. I remember very few of the day to day highlights of our cruise, as I was too busy enjoying the rest from being Number One. I spent the days gossiping and cooking with Helen while George took my usual role as general boat dogsbody; the odd moments I do remember were when I heard Colin shouting instructions to George, and George, not the shrinking violet I am, answering him back: "Make your mind up!" Oh, sometimes revenge is definitely sweet.

At night Helen and George journeyed back to their hotel in Strasbourg until we reached Saverne when, after a visit to the tourist office, Helen and I decided to book for the *son et lumière* at Haut Barr. Helen booked an overnight stay at Saverne and we parted company to "dress" for the occasion which in Helen's case meant a cool, elegant long skirt and blouse. Château Haut Barr, known as "The Eye of Alsace", lies to the west of the city and commands the vital pass of Col de Saverne. The chapel of the Château is situated at the top of a huge rocky spur. The tourist office had laid on a bus, as the event started at 10pm and was aimed at the car-less boaters visiting the city.

We picked up the bus outside the tourist office; the journey to the top of the rock was hair-raising; from the bus windows I looked down on a vertical drop. After buying our tickets we went through a door to the sound of Elvis Presley; so far I was not impressed. The idea was that from the top of the rock to the bottom was Mankind's journey through time, right back to the discovery of fire. We had gadgets on our head that provided a commentary in English, but they were more of a nuisance than a help, so in the end all of us took them off and guessed what was happening.

It was very dark as we journeyed down a narrow path; at times we were scared out of our wits as the skeletons of dead plague victims launched themselves out of coffins and made a grab for our pens, glasses, bags, etc. Helen, whose job entails elements of Health and Safety, was not impressed as the edge of her long skirt brushed a Neanderthal fire, I found her disapproval really amusing, and her muttered comment, "wouldn't be allowed in England."

We really enjoyed the night, although I think the Saint-Fargeau *son et lumière* was better, as I felt more involved. And the Sputnik helmets were a real nuisance.

After our trip to Haut Barr it was time to move on to our next port of call, Lutzelbourg. For the trip, Helen and George stayed on the boat, the first non-family to do so, and it worked very well. Lutzelbourg is one of the most beautiful villages in France, and geared to the boating fraternity, with a long quay offering all the facilities. The weather was glorious; I thought Helen and George were reluctant to leave us, and my intuition proved to be right, as a month later much to our delight they came to visit us again – although by the time of that visit everything had changed; but more of that later.

The station at Lutzelbourg is small, and we were impressed when the station master greeted us in full uniform. After our visitors' departure we felt flat, but fell into conversation with a German who offered to let us have a map of the German waterways: "Come for a drink on my boat and I will give you the map."

Without a second thought we followed him, thinking Bob was following us. Two hours and a good deal of wine and schnapps later we staggered home.

"Best take Bob for a wee," one of us said.

And then: "Where *is* Bob?"

We were in a panic; we had never given Bob a thought, and guilt overwhelmed us. Colin got the bike and went one way and I went the other, and soon many boaters were looking for "Bob the dog".

As I got near the railway station I saw Bob sat patiently waiting at the bus stop where we had stopped while Helen and George crossed the track to catch the train.

"Oh Bob. You poor thing, you really are missing Helen, aren't you?"

Whines in response from Bob; and when I got back to the boat I said to Colin, "That poor dog, what a life she is having at the moment, frightened to death on the Rhine, scared witless by the French thunderstorms when you won't let her in bed with us for comfort – no wonder she wants to go home with Helen."

"That bloody dog's frightened of a paper bag. But I agree, we should have been more careful tonight, I never checked she wasn't behind us."

The Captain and I agreed that to make up we would do what we did when the kids were little and we felt we had been bad parents. We would have an "I love Bob" week. As a result, it was with a happy dog that we moved onto our next experience. The boat was sealed into a lock on the inclined plain at St Louis and then was lifted 45 metres to the canal higher up. For the first time we had to show our papers and all the fuss added to the episode. We were no sooner out of the lock than we were plunged into a 2,306-metre tunnel, followed by a 475-metre tunnel, both of them much higher and wider than the "rabbit holes" that had frightened us so much in England, not to mention lit with electric light.

A few days later we came into the Port de Plaisance of the city of Nancy. We moored in a free mooring that appeared to be at the end of the High Street, and quickly became an item on the tourist itinerary. In French, the narrow boat is known as a *cigar*, and initially most of our tourists were under the impression that we had crossed the channel in our *cigar*.

Being a tourist attraction is a mixed blessing, especially when you have broken your false teeth and do not want to open your mouth to anyone. The night before we arrived in Nancy I had attempted to eat the toughest steak I have ever bought in France; a resounding crack echoed in my ear, and my mouth suddenly seemed full of dislocated bone fragments. In the shower I attempted to put my face back together with Blu-Tack – and the repair worked, as long as I did not move a muscle.

A lovely young lady called Alice came to my rescue. Alice had black hair and blue eyes; she was Welsh and worked as a singer with Nancy Opera. She lived permanently on a boat moored in the harbour with her husband. Alice took me under her wing, but even with all her powers of persuasion it was three days before my teeth would be repaired. Oh, what a peculiar time: Alice showed me all over what is a truly beautiful city, even introducing me to the market coffee specialist, who gave me a thimble-sized sample of his wares and nearly blew my head off. I would then return to a boat full of mainly French tourists, all intrigued with the *cigar* that had been on the Rhine. Colin, who by this time was fluent in mime, was thoroughly enjoying himself – and of course had to mime for the benefit of everyone but me that my teeth had fallen out.

and Mrs Bean will be starting the guided tour in 5 minutes   only $20

A highlight I vividly remember was a visit late at night to the vast Stanislas Square. There are four entries to the square, all of which are guarded by enormous gold-painted wrought iron gates. The square itself is surrounded by Georgian buildings with decorated balconies. It was a Saturday and the cafés around the edge of the square had spread their tables into the usually empty space to accommodate extra diners. We could hear all around us the sound of hundreds of muted conversations, not a fight or a drunk in sight – a truly amazing sight, coming as we do from South Yorkshire, where a booze-up and a fight are prerequisites of a good Saturday night out.

In conversation with Alice I learned that for their holiday she and her husband were delivering a large boat to Namur in Belgium. Alice told me what a lovely route it was down the Meuse, which, she assured me, was not a bit like the Rhine in terms of big-boat traffic.

The part of the Meuse we were considering travelling on was through the French battlefield of Verdun. David, his son and another grandson were to be our next visitors, and we thought it would be an interesting cruise for them. We picked our new visitors up at Commercy and the cruise turned out to be very rural, with few activities for a fourteen-year-old boy away from his parents for the first time and with a pocket full of money.

As we approached Verdun Jo said to Danny, "I hope there's somewhere to spend my money here." There were no slot machines, so in desperation he bought a fishing rod. I attached a magnet to the fishing line and encouraged him to go fishing in the port for First World War shells.

All went well until the line got caught on an object in the middle of the port and Colin insisted it was a torpedo. Despite the assistance of a boater on the other side, the line had to be cut and the "torpedo" was lost. Then Colin and Jo had to enlist the help of a small boat to recover the remains of the line.

It was while David was with us that Mr Bean's engine first began to give us trouble; all of a sudden it just cut out. Colin diagnosed "muck in the system", and in a short while he and David had got us going again.

David and the boys left us at Stenay and Helen and George rejoined us. Stenay was the German headquarters during the First World War and it was good to have with us friends who could appreciate the significance of the area. We had a fantastic tour of the castle in a major thunderstorm, very atmospheric. The scenery on our cruise down the Meuse was really spectacular as we headed for Charleville-Mézières, a city with one of the finest squares in Europe. By now Colin was increasingly having to sort out "muck in the engine", so after Charleville we headed back to Pont-à-Bar where we left Bob with his favourite person while we went back to fetch the car. The weather was lovely but very autumnal. Unusually for France at Pont-à-Bar there was a boatyard with a crane. Moored along the canal was a chap with a small sailing boat covered with a tarpaulin; I cannot remember the name of the chap but he had a dog that made friends with Bob and consequently he with us. One of this chap's constant refrains was, "I am a loner, I am." Nevertheless, he took several walks a day to chat to us, interrupting valuable Helen-gossiping time. In order to escape, Helen walked along the towpath gathering Mirabelle plums, with which we made a fantastic crumble. The chap's future plans involved sailing to Sens to work as a welder for Simon, the boatyard owner there, but it was clear the man's health was dodgy and he feared he wouldn't make the trip.

We took Helen and George to the railway station to go home. Once we got back, Colin set about repairing Mr Bean's heart properly. Mr Maubacq was having none of it: cutting a hole in the fuel tank to enable Colin to clean it out was "Not possible. Dangereuse". Colin's inability to repair Mr Bean, along with the autumnal weather, got to the Captain, while the autumnal weather, homesickness, and the "I don't need anybody" chap got to me.

"I wish we could go home," I said to Colin.

"I do too" he replied.

"I know, let's ask our Graham if he can arrange it," I said.

"I had better check with Monsieur Maubacq first," replied Colin.

Yes, Monsieur Maubacq could lift the boat with his crane, and yes, Graham could arrange transport.

The day we decided to go home was Sunday; by Tuesday, less than a week since Helen and George had left us, the transport arrived to take Mr Bean back to England. I did not intend to come back: my love affair with the French canals was over.

Mr "I don't need anybody" asked if I had any maps; I had, and I sold him the lot for 25 euros, something I was to regret later on. A year later I told Jo the story, and he told me what he had heard had happened to the "I want to be alone" man. Apparently, as planned, he and his dog had turned up at Simon's boatyard with the idea of working the winter. "There's something wrong with my dog and I am too frightened to take him to the vet," he said. It appears Simon offered to accompany the chap to take his dog to the vet. "I cannot face it, if the vet wants to put him down will you take him while I wait in the car?" the chap said to Simon. Simon agreed. The vet could find nothing wrong with the dog. On his return to the car with the good news, Simon found the chap dead.

On hearing the story, the first thing Colin asked Jo was, "Have they sold his boat?" Jo did not know, and asked if Colin was interested in buying it. "Oh, no. It's just that if the boat is not sold and we know where it is we might be able to break in and get my maps back."

I was mortified but not surprised: Colin is ever the pragmatist.

Before the lorry came, we went into Charleville and bought a load of wine, stacking it in boxes in the salon. We were comforted when the lorry arrived to find it was from Howden, twenty miles from where we live. It was new, and the pride and joy of the young man who owned it; he had brought his father along for the ride. As it was only 8am and the lift was not due to start until the legendary *neuf heures*, we all had coffee and croissants and the young man indulged in a bit of polishing. Promptly at nine o'clock, Monsieur Maubacq started his crane and Colin sailed Mr Bean into the slings that were to lift him on to the lorry. Smoke puthered and the crane engine roared, and the crane track treads began to lift off the ground. I think M Maubacq swore as he immediately stopped everything. We were not sure of the weight of Mr Bean, but if we were correct his weight was very nearly the crane's limit.

"I bet all that wine has tipped us over the top," I said. "I'll have a word with M Maubacq and offer to lighten the boat."

But M Maubacq was having none of it. With arms gesticulating and a flurry of invective in French, he stormed off. "Merde" and "Dangereuse" were the only words I could catch.

Later, when he had calmed down, the boatyard patron said he would send for a mobile crane. An hour and a half later, an Osama Bin Laden lookalike turned up, complete with laptop computer. Osama's French was terrible; I could not understand a word. But by this time a group of Germans had become involved. The man could understand Osama but could not speak English, so he told his daughter what Osama was saying and she translated into English. I can understand a lot more French if it is spoken slowly, even Algerian French, so it wasn't until I got into bed that night that I realised that as a result of all the translations we had bargained up the price with Osama. What had started out as six hundred euros and a nine o'clock start had turned into nine hundred euros at eight o'clock.

The two lorry drivers were mesmerized and not a little relieved when I told them the fault was ours and we would of course expect to pay for their wait. The lorry drivers' only worry was, how were they going to get a shower? Throwing all caution to the winds, I said, "We will take you into the campsite in Charleville for a shower and then out for supper." I refused to think about the fact that the wine in the boat was rapidly becoming the most expensive wine in history.

We had a wonderful night out, the lorry drivers saying that they were envious of our boating life. Huh!

The next morning the mobile crane arrived promptly at the usual French start time. M Maubacq was nowhere to be seen; he had washed his hands of the stupid English. The lift began again, and this time the tracks began to sink.

"I don't bloody believe it!" exclaimed Colin.

I began to believe that bankruptcy might be a possibility.

Osama had an idea, and for once it did not involve spending more money. After a lot of arm-waving we finally got the message: sail the boat down to the nearest road bridge and the crane would lift us from the bridge on to the lorry behind the crane.

It was with relief that we saw the rest of the operation go smoothly. The lorry shot off to catch the evening sailing, leaving us to follow in the car.

By the time we got to England, Mr Bean was safely ensconced on trestles in the boatyard in Thorne. We learned later that even in transit Mr Bean had continued his adventures. After checking in at customs in Calais, the young lorry driver had told his dad he was going aloft to check that the ropes on the wheelhouse were tight; to his surprise, as he moved the tarpaulin covering the well of the bow, he sensed movement. Curious, the driver looked under the tarpaulin – straight into three pairs of dark eyes. At some point in the short journey from customs to the lorry pound, three refugees had managed to climb up the lorry and into the well. The driver was relieved to find them: if Customs had found them at Dover he would have been fined; but the event has had a lasting effect on me; I felt somehow personally involved with those unknown people fleeing who knows what to a country that, despite all our grumbles, allows us to do just that, and on a full stomach most of the time.

It took Colin two weeks to eradicate the "muck in the system". We had joined Thorne Cruising Club and Mr Bean was given what I considered the best mooring in the club. There he was in the bright autumn sunshine, lying along the canal bank opposite a jolly pub, and, more importantly, three miles from home. For Mr

Bean, a new life had begun; and although it was not to be with us, and it involved a name change, the boat will always be Mr Bean to me: another boat with a stout and courageous heart.

BOOK FOUR – KOOPMAN WELVAREN V

Chapter 1

Colin Has another dream

I thought our foreign adventures were over until I overheard the Captain telling a friend of ours that he thought he had unfinished business in France. We began to look on the internet, and as usual could not agree on what to buy. I wanted a boat with a flushing toilet, bathroom, and shower, preferably square in shape and big enough to fill the lock. I took it for granted that any boat would have a kitchen. Colin had fallen for an ex-police launch with fantastic speed, headroom for a midget, and no facilities. Eventually we saw a boat for sale in the boatyard at Migennes. The Captain remembered the boat, moored on the bank, being repaired; he had liked the look of it, so we decided to view.

It was the middle of January 2003 when we returned by train to the boatyard at Migennes. As we walked from the station we could see the familiar shape of the crane above the roofs of the boatyard sheds. We walked across the yard and round the corner of the shed, and there was the boat, just as Colin remembered, sitting on trestles on the bank between the workshop and the river. Oh! it was so pretty: blue and white, with a lovely Dutch barge slipper-back. What's more, to me it seemed big and well capable of sailing the larger canals of France safely.

Jo came down the yard to meet us; everything about him and the yard seemed homely and familiar. By this time we had got to know Jo enough to trust him. Despite his surname, Jo Parfitt is English; he left the UK over twenty years ago to work repairing holiday hire boats; later he bought a disused railway yard at the side of the river Yonne to open a *chantier fluvial*. Jo is six foot tall, dark haired, usually has a beard, wears glasses, and walks with a slight limp, the result of a motorbike accident in his youth. I always think of him as foreign-looking. At the time we met him, he was in his early fifties, and in character very mercurial. As a psychiatric nurse, I have been trained to anticipate unexpected changes in behaviour, and Colin can usually get alongside everyone he meets. With Jo, we really enjoy his company and appreciate his kindness, generosity, tact, and sense of humour; and he has undoubted skill and an encyclopaedic knowledge of all things mechanical and "boaty". At other times we have raged at his dismissiveness, opportune "forgetfulness", tactlessness and general bolshiness. He is known all over the canals in France, both for the quality of his work and his character; to mention to a stranger that you know Jo is a sure-fire way of making a friend, drinking wine and generally having a very convivial time. I think at some time most of the boats and boaters on the canals of France have been guests of Jo and his yard – and usually for longer than they anticipated.

After the usual French-style greetings, Jo gave us the key and left us to look at the boat. As I expected, Colin was impressed, and to my relief all thoughts of the police boat disappeared. Despite much more room, however, the living conditions were primitive: two gas rings, a sink, and a horrible sea-toilet compartment. On the back bulkhead behind the sink there were some fantastic antique Dutch tiles showing children playing games; the tiles, plus the beautiful round wood edgings, persuaded me that a bargain could be struck.

I said to the handyman, "I need a kitchen with room for a washer."

Colin looked shocked but by now he was imagining sailing the boat down the canal, so a new kitchen was agreed. Strangely, neither of us thought it necessary to discuss what would become essential alterations: the installation of a shower and beds that allowed you to sleep in something other than the foetal position. I think I was too taken with the shape of the wooden edging and the old Dutch tiles, and Colin was enamoured of the boat's sexy shape.

We told Jo we had decided to buy, subject to "sea trials", and to seal the deal he took us to the café in the port for midday lunch and wine. We drank a toast, and both of us looked forward to rescuing Koopman Welvaren V. We were so excited we totally ignored Jo's repeated comment that the boat was a "summer boat". Even if we had taken notice we had no idea what "summer boat" meant.

By the following year we had found out the hard way.

Koopman Welvaren V was built in 1905 and is in traditional Dutch Beurtschip style with the lovely half-moon slipper-back which Colin believed would give the boat a good swim. A Beurtschip is a work boat. We later found out that Koopman had been built to carry calves, milk and cheese from the farms along the narrow Dutch canals to the market at Amsterdam and was part of a fleet of sixteen such boats (we have only ever seen one other). The boat was 14.88m long and 2.8m wide, about half as wide again as a narrow boat. To us at that time it seemed huge.

Koopman had been converted from a working boat into a leisure boat in the 1960s at a boatyard in Sneek in Holland. It had a small bedroom with two four-foot-ten-inch bunks, a roomy saloon and a very high wheelhouse with a sundeck behind. When we finally sailed, Colin could hardly see over the wheel; even the milk crate did not provide enough lift. We have never been able to work out the thinking that lay behind a design that required a six-foot-ten man to drive the boat and a four-foot-ten man to sleep in it. The toilet compartment had a sea-toilet, a huge hand-basin and a cupboard in historic bottle-green Formica – but no shower. Despite its lack of modern facilities, though, the workmanship of the conversion was of a high standard, something that Colin would do his best to live up to.

By the spring of 2003 we were all set to buy Koopman. Our friends Helen and George had bought Mr Bean and we had sold a small field at the side of the canal at Barnby Dun to fund the purchase of Koopman. Because of my limited French we decided to buy most of the things we wanted to install in England. We went on a spending spree, buying kitchen equipment, hot water systems, a washing machine and an inverter. We also intended to take the boatman's stove out of the kitchen at home.

Two of our sons said they would help Colin transport the stuff and three grandchildren went for the ride. Iain packed his white Transit full of the goodies. When Andrew suggested they take sleeping bags, I said it wasn't necessary: "They have bedding in France," I told him sniffily, assuming he was intending to use a sleeping bag in a Formula Hotel.

When they returned from the trip I was attacked from all sides and Andrew was the loudest: "You said we didn't need sleeping bags, we were bloody freezing, we thought we were going to die."

"Which hotel did you stay in?" I asked in surprise.

"Oh, we stayed on the boat," he replied.

"But it's March. Whose idea was it to stay on the boat?" I replied, incredulous.

The answer was a cacophony of grumbles along the lines of, it's a long night when there is no pub to go to, no light, no TV and worst of all no heating.

I knew who was responsible but I had a premonition of who would be blamed. To the leader of the expedition it was logical to spend thousands of euros on an old boat and save on a warm bed and shower for the night – although he did at least treat everyone to a meal in Auxerre. The prospect of suffering for a cause brings out the worst in Colin, and he is still very much the patriarch, so the stroppy six-foot two-legged forty-year-old sons and bolshie adolescent grandchildren went along with the ideas of an elderly one-legged man. In addition, the boat was not even ours. I am sure Jo, safe in his snug bungalow, had no idea of what was happening in his yard. Colin, as the senior of the party and smallest adult, had been given the four-foot-ten bed in the prow.

"All I had was the towel to cover me. I never even took my clothes or my leg off," Colin moaned pathetically.

I could not believe they thought it was my fault. Andrew chipped in, answering his dad but wagging his finger at me. "You were lucky: we had nothing at all to cover us and playing 'I spy' for six hours in the bloody dark on a Friday night is the pits. It was too cold to shiver and have a fag. Don't deny it, it was you, Mam, who said don't take sleeping bags," he ranted as only he can.

There was worse to come. Laura, our fashion-conscious thirteen-year-old granddaughter, who, we all knew, associated France with bikinis, had filled her suitcase with "appropriate" clothes. In the land of Haute Cuisine, Laura had absolutely refused to eat anything other than a McDonald's. Iain and Andrew had wasted time in a useless effort to find a pub – although Iain did find a bookie's. But then he does have a nose for those places. Not one of the kids had thought to overrule their dad and organise a comfortable bed for the night. I had no sympathy with any of them.

For my part, I was appalled and disappointed. I had anticipated that the family would enjoy a taste of the France I love; instead, they had taken South Yorkshire to a country that regards itself as the epitome of culture. I am pleased to say their education began there and has progressed well. We later found out that "summer boat" meant that there was no insulation throughout the boat. On the night of the sleep-in, there had been a hard frost. Despite the stiff limbs and lack of proper liquid sustenance, the men had managed to unload all the stuff from the van into one of Jo's sheds.

A month later I emailed Jo with Colin, Bob's and my estimated time of arrival at the boatyard. Jo did not reply; but that was usual for Jo.

The first thing Jo said when we arrived was, "Didn't you get my email?"

"No – why?"

"The crane's broken and I have no idea when it will be mended. I have sent to Hong Kong for spare parts."

All I could think of initially was that we couldn't put Bob the dog through that journey again so soon. I was also totally unaware of boat-buying procedures in France; when we had bought Mr Bean we had given the owner a cheque and sailed away. I had given Jo the money, so why couldn't we live on the boat until the crane was repaired? I truly thought we would do a few bits and bobs to the boat, put the kitchen equipment in, and sail away. Jo was sure the boat would do well on its sea trials. Oh how wrong we all were!

We told Jo our plan, and he said he would ask the owner if we could stay on the boat until the crane was repaired. He came back to say it was OK. Somehow, despite the lack of sea trials, we felt that we were already the owners. None of us anticipated how long it would take for those sea trials to take place.

So that Bob could get into the boat, which was on trestles and at least six foot in the air, we built scaffolding with poles, ladders, planks and bits of carpet. It took two hours of coaxing to get Bob up the tower; for once, a trail of food had no effect, and in the end she was dragged up the ramp by her collar. Then we settled in, had a meal, and surveyed our new project. Full of plans, and having forgotten what we had bought, we went to survey our future home, which was stored in Jo's shed. Colin is incapable of doing nothing, so in no time at all he had the sliding doors off the wheelhouse and began restoring them, laying them on trestles on the ground.

A week later I was hanging washing on the boat rails when I noticed a man watching us. I climbed down, went up to him and asked him if I could help. I knew enough French to understand that he was the *patron* of the boat, and he was mystified as to what these people were doing on and to Koopman.

It never gets easier for poor old Bob the dog

I was mortified, but Colin, as usual, saw the funny side, and began laughing. A swift kick on the shin shut him up. By this time Jo had arrived from the workshop, muttering that he had "forgotten" to tell the *patron* that we were living on his boat. But Jo must have convinced the owner we were trustworthy, because soon we were chatting away to him in pidgin French. He told us he had bought the boat on the spur of moment because he thought it so pretty. "A real boat," he said. His wife, who was chronically ill, had not been impressed and had insisted that he sell.

Apparently Koopman Welvaren V was at Jo's because it needed repairs to the rudder, among other things. But even the news that the boat needed essential repairs did not put Colin off; it seemed that come hell or high water he was going to give new life to the elegant old boat.

We did not, however, realise what breathing new life into the old boat was going to cost in terms of blood, sweat and tears, and the next four months were an emotional roller coaster. As with Mr Bean, we found that one small change had a knock-on effect, making other, more difficult, time-consuming and expensive changes necessary.

Chapter 2

A boatyard Odyssey

The boatyard known as Chantier Fluvial de Migennes is a rough square of about five hectares. It is entered by car from the road from Migennes. On the left side of road lies a field and then the abattoir. Behind the field, facing the boatyard, are the campsite and sports fields. The road continues to the right, bridging the river Yonne. From the gate on the right near the start of the rise to the bridge, there is a wide rough track leading forward. Boats are stored either side of the road. After about 150 metres, the track in the yard diverges to the left and right to sweep round the back of various buildings that run parallel to the road and river. The track comes to the front of the property between Jo's bungalow on one side and the mobile paint shed. The track runs in front of the buildings, with the River Yonne on the other side marking the front boundary.

The space in front of the buildings is the main working area, and the crane is usually somewhere along this frontage. Various boats are usually sitting there awaiting repairs. About twenty metres to the side of the bungalow more boats are stored. There is a gate in the fence and a path under the road bridge to the recreation field, and a kilometre further, a plantation of trees – a wonderful shady walk for me and Bob in the heat of summer.

Behind the paint shed is a fence, also with a gate. Through this gate is a shortcut to the port of Migennes. The path runs past the sewage works and under the railway bridge. The whole track system is similar in pattern to a flattened lasso. The land once belonged to the railway, and there are buried heaps of tar that melt in the summer, as well as stacks of cut-up rails. The buildings are a mishmash of brick, concrete and corrugated sheeting – but they are not in as bad a state of repair as you would expect from the look of them. The area is prone to flooding, so no new buildings are allowed by the local authority. One disgruntled customer of Jo's told me that he did not intend to spend the summer living near a railway sandwiched between an abattoir and a sewage works. I was surprised at his attitude: I saw the beauty of the walk through the trees and heard the nightingales singing all night in the wood the other side of the river.

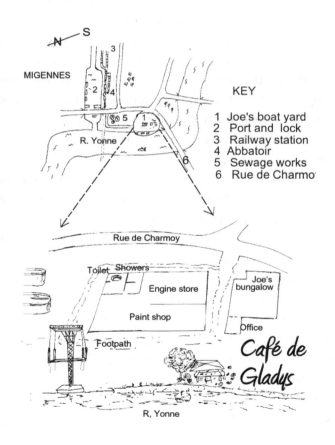

KEY

1 Joe's boat yard
2 Port and lock
3 Railway station
4 Abbatoir
5 Sewage works
6 Rue de Charmo

Admittedly, the yard is a dustbowl in summer and a quagmire in winter. Jo needs a clear view for craning boats in and out, so the only trees in the yard are in front of the bungalow on the riverbank, apart from a small fecund cherry tree. The major drawback to life in the yard is the sanitary arrangements: the shower and toilet are in a small cubicle at the side of and halfway down the main workshop. There is a very efficient hot water boiler and sink in the entrance, and then two cubicles, one housing a shower and the other a square porcelain base with a hole at the back and a flushing system above. A so-called Turkish toilet, and an absolute nightmare for women, as it necessitates getting completely undressed. Colin reckons it is easier for men, owing to their "angle of dangle". Usually the floor of the place was filthy with mud from the yard, although I have to say that the porcelain base was very often clean. I got to absolutely dread using it though, preferring to bucket and chuck it with a receptacle bought for the purpose. There was one unexpected pleasure to living in the yard: I am an avid fan of soaps, and the yard was like living in the best soap ever.   That year, the year we bought Koopman, turned out to be the hottest for many years. I quote below an extract from a letter I sent on August 12th:

The hot weather continues day after day with temperatures in the high 30s and low 40s Celsius. We are officially in drought. In Paris cars are restricted to 30kms per hour because of the poor air quality. The wheat harvest has been in a long time but the Indian corn does not look like being worth harvesting. Since we came in May, it has rained only one day and a few times during the night. Bob is thin and a filthy grey colour; we spray her with cool water several times a day – she refuses absolutely to go in the river. After we have sprayed her with cool water, her routine is to go and roll in the dust.

The French see the British as abandoning France as they head home in droves for their woollies and fleecy slippers. The Americans are not even bothering to come; many of the cruise ships are laid up, as are many of the small hire boats. The hotel in Paris that accommodates the Americans prior to their cruise is eighty per cent empty. Mind you, the falling dollar might also be exacerbating the situation. Worst of all, the leaves are falling from the few trees around the perimeter of the yard. The dog pants all the time, plodding around the yard with Jo's very old thin dog that is too tired to even stop to poo. Only Colin remains defiant, in true Dunkirk spirit: every morning as the enemy (the sun) appears over Jo's shed, he puts on his red sweatband, Eric Morecambe shorts, gentleman's short sleeved shirt and odd socks to wave his insulation board and, in the manner of Ian Paisley, cry, "No suurendurr!"

go back yer bugger ...come back in a month

Tar is seeping up through the dust and the boatman's stove we brought from England has stuck to the floor of the shed. Colin tried to move the stove today and got tar all over his wooden leg. He used white spirit to get the tar off – but the leg melted, so once again it's a big Elastoplast on the hole and we are back to Colin sounding like an Espresso machine when he walks.

Unlike the canals in England, there are very few marinas and boatyards in France, and consequently there are always too many customers. During the summer of 2003, the boatyard in Migennes was packed with boats not being repaired or launched until the crane was mended, and everyone pestered Jo for news.

The story of the crane parts was, for many of the more cynical of Jo's customers, difficult to believe. The main part seemed to have become involved in a multinational swap. A more important customer than Jo had laid claim to the original part, offering a removed preventative maintenance part in exchange. All these exchanges took time, and in the yard tempers rose along with the heat. Valuable boating time was being lost; more important to Jo was the amount of money he was losing.

When the spare parts for the crane finally arrived, Jo and his son worked long hours into the night to make the repairs, and eventually the "praying mantis", as Colin called the crane, lifted us into the water and our sea trials were underway.

Perhaps, if the trials had happened when we first arrived in the yard, we might not have bought the boat. But by the time he was in the water we had lived on him for weeks and were emotionally committed. There were two main problems for Colin: he needed a couple of milk crates in order to see where he was going, and the old steering system, involving chains, wires and pulleys, needed a pilot as strong as Atlas, and not a man with restricted movement in one arm.

We decided to ask Jo if he would install a hydraulic system as well as do some other "simple" modifications. Jo was already up to his neck in work that he had planned to do months ago, and while he agreed to do the work he did not say *when*.

During the next few months, despite the dirt, dust and heat, we had some good times in the yard. Jo was very generous with Colin; he allowed him to use one of his sheds as a workshop and lent him tools; the only stipulation was that Colin ask him first. He also encouraged Colin to do many repairs for himself under his guidance. For me it was more difficult: for years I had worked in a mainly female, structured environment where I was in charge of my own agenda, and at times life in the yard drove me mad, especially when Colin abandoned what he was doing in order to join all the able-bodied men in hanging onto a rope as Jo lifted this or that boat in or out of the water. Here is an extract from another letter home:

As soon as Colin heard the engine of the praying mantis start up, he was out of the boat in a flash with his red bandana on his head, and spent the next hour being shouted at. In a temper, I once called the yard "Tonka Land": suddenly I have been reduced to acting as gofer, tea maker, cleaner and general assistant, and as someone who has always been in charge of her own work programme I find the situation particularly frustrating. We have decided to move the sink in the boat, but as we started to take off the beautiful old Dutch tiles at the back of the old sink we realised that the boat was not insulated. The glue had bonded the tiles and steel together so hard that we only managed to salvage a few. The lovely old wood needed to come off in order to install the insulation. We also realised that the only windows in the boat that opened were a few portholes and a Velux, which could only be opened if the mast was raised. The boat became a furnace inside, and poor Colin is so hot and dirty fitting the insulation and trying to make the new wood in the boat look like the old we had removed. At one point we had twice as many left-hand curves as we did right.

Revolution is definitely in the air: a roly-poly Dutchman and his wife have just arrived and gone straight to the top of the list; not only is the small hole in his boat being repaired almost immediately because Queen Philomena once stepped on his boat, but Jo has made a metal crown and is welding that over the hole. The rest of the boaters on the list are furious with Jo and feel guilty about Rene, who is a jolly kind man but the butt of our anger because, through no fault of his own, he is getting his work done while we have all waited so long. For Jo and his son Herbie, the working day is long because of the amount of work there is to do. For the customers, the working day is long and for the most part boring; there is a general belief that if the customer cannot be seen by Jo he will be forgotten and then he will slip down the list. In one respect Colin and I are lucky: there is so much we can do ourselves and lessen the stress of waiting. Everything Colin wants to do, the first question I ask is, "Does it involve Jo?" and if it does, the second question is "Can we manage without doing the work?" The heat is unbelievable and the air is cooler in the evening, so that is when most work gets done. I have invested in a very large red umbrella and have a table and chairs set up in front of a very small cherry tree. To the side are some large rocks which I use to store "stuff". Other boaters stop to chat and have become a substitute family; we exchange gossip, usually about positions on the list and strategies for gaining Jo's attention. Jo has given us nicknames: Colin is Arkwright; mine, as you may have guessed, is Gladys (I think the nicknames are a reflection of our broad South Yorkshire accents).

The idea of the café started by accident. By the time we were finally in the water after the sea trials, when we discovered the boat was almost impossible to steer, I was so happy I believed I would never have to use the hole-in-the-floor toilet again. I was the happiest I had been for weeks until I tried to use the toilet and found the flush pump was broken. Colin could not mend it as he had no spare parts; Jo said he had some, cheering me up for a moment, and then "forgot" to give them to Colin. The "forgetting" seemed to go on for a long time. In the end, overwrought, hot and dirty, I accosted Jo en route to an "important" job. Out of my mouth came a torrent of self-pity regarding women's attire not being best arranged to use holes in the floor for bodily functions. In the end I was so sorry for myself and angry at Jo's thoughtlessness I could not speak for crying. Jo seemed to be amazed by my carry-on and offered to help Colin repair the toilet pump. At last we had a working toilet made out of bits from three toilets, all tested in a bucket of water. That afternoon Jo appeared with a pretty box tied up with ribbon for me. When I opened the box it contained beautiful cakes, and accepting the peace offering I made some English tea.

The Café de Gladys was born. Most of the time I accept my role; at others I really get fed up at things not moving as fast as I think they should. I have become a people watcher and the yard is very fertile ground for that occupation. I realise there are two main types of boater, those who want to travel, stop, sit on the back deck drink wine and socialise (generally they have the money to pay so they do not get dirty maintaining their boats); the other type are those who love working on boats. There two types in this category: the "big hammer boys" and the perfectionists. Colin would like to be a perfectionist but I am a "big hammer woman", and in the heat there are many disagreements between us over what standard the work is to be done to. Jo does not help in these disagreements *because he has high standards: he is not slow or diplomatic in telling Colin when he thinks he can do better.*

At times I began to think the boat would never be finished. Another characteristic of Jo's is his acute observation of human behaviour. He has several sayings which I find amusing: "An optimist is a person who is not in full possession of the facts" – very relevant for newcomers to the yard who have not encountered the vagaries of the "list" before; "Some people are 'Cling-ons'" – a very brief description of how many English behave: they come to France because it is full of mysterious and attractive French people and then huddle in English enclaves eating the food they have brought out from the UK. Then there's "No cash, no splash" – this quote has never been said to us but is something Jo uses for big expensive boats with miserly owners. Jo also has very apt names for people; Colin really is an Arkwright – I leave others to judge whether I am a Gladys.

Meanwhile I entertain myself watching the behaviour of the other residents of the yard. In my next letter I will tell you about some of the residents of the boatyard at Migennes.

As high summer progressed to late summer, the weather became ever hotter and even the shade offered by the Café de Gladys was not enough. I took to sitting in the three-foot shade offered by Jo's shed while I listened to and worried about "bandana man" banging away in the furnace that was the boat.

At this time, because of the teapot, I had become a counsellor for many of the inhabitants of the yard; I think this was because Jo "took tea" at the café and it was thought that I had his ear. Oh how wrong they were! Jo, I have found, is consistent: in one thing at least he works to his own list of "priorities", a process I have never been able to fathom. From my chair I had observed that many of the boaters would promenade around the sheds in the hope of bumping into him "on the off chance" to enquire as to their progress up the list.

I was busy observing the scene when Paul strolled up; he had had an unsuccessful promenade and was in the slough of despond. Paul told me he had "sat on the toilet in the boat this morning strained away and the bloody thing fell to bits."

"What do you mean?" I said.

"There I was sat on the floor, bits of toilet around me."

"God, was there any in your bum?"

"Lucky for me, no, but I've got visitors from America next week. Jo's got to see to it. It's his fault, he hasn't winterised the boat properly, I know that because there's bird shit in the boat as well."

This information was too much and I fell about laughing. Paul was a handsome, sophisticated, interesting man who wrote travel books, and here we were discussing bird shit in a hot dusty boatyard.

"What's my chances of getting hold of the King and getting a toilet?"

"None, it's lunch time!" I exclaimed.

Paul and I had taken to calling Jo "the King" to reflect our feeling that he had almost feudal power over our lives. When eventually Jo appeared, heated words were exchanged over my head, Jo insisting that the toilet's disintegration was due to old age, and Paul insisting it was the work of Jack Frost. Paul's big worry was the arrival of his friends and the possibility that they might have to use the yard facilities. In the end Colin solved the problem by taking Paul sixty kilometres to buy a new state-of-the-art toilet.

There were other reluctant residents in the yard waiting for the King to bestow his favour and move them up the work list. Very often our list did not match Jo's. One such couple was Heinz and Gudrun, Germans by nationality. Heinz was a Professor of Comparative Religion at Heidelberg University, a tall, gentle but accident-prone man. Gudrun always reminded me of Marianne Faithfull in appearance and demeanour; she was very resourceful and artistic. While Gudrun and Heinz waited for the bottom of their boat, The Pelican, to be plated they busied themselves painting and making alterations. Gudrun even painted a pelican on the side of the boat, but in the heat the paint ran off the beak and feet, which gave the bird a very surreal look.

Eventually Gudrun thought they were top of Jo's list, only to find him in full welding gear working on the Dutchman's boat. Furious, Gudrun said to me, "I will show you how it is done. Jo will stick to the list, you watch."

I watched. Gudren, her chiffon dress floating, sped down the yard to where Jo, all masked up, was wielding a fiery welding gun. I saw Gudrun sit down in the dust in a froth of gossamer at his side. After a while I saw him lift his shield and turn to her.

It was later Gudrun told me what had transpired:

Jo "Yes?"
Gudrun "Jo! I am not moving until you plate my bottom."
Jo "I will do it tomorrow."
Gudrun "No you won't, you vill escape."
Jo "No I won't, I will be here in the yard all day. I will do your plating."
Gudrun "I do not trust you, you vill escape in your car."
Jo "No I won't, I will give you my car keys."
Gudrun "Yes, you do that."

And Jo gave her the keys. He did start the next day . . . just till he got his car keys back.

A group of people who had been sharing a boat for over twenty years were also spending their waiting time doing the maintenance on their boat. When we finally went into the water they were moored next to us. The boat looked battered and old before they arrived, but soon the covers were off and several Velux windows with bright blue and white striped shades appeared, altering the whole character of the boat. There were several partners in the boat-share, which was of many years standing, but only four or five were present at this time. The leader was very tall and bent, with a flowing beard. In character he was very much like Magnus Pyke; consequently we always referred to him as Magnus. He had two male colleagues, one of whom did the cooking while the other helped him with the construction. The construction, we later found out, was a wooden platform for the back of the boat upon which the pilot could stand, or postprandial drinks be taken. We called the platform the ballroom floor. Magnus was very serious and spent long periods bent over with his beard flowing down, measuring and shouting the measurements into the bowels of the boat. A moment later a disembodied voice would be heard shouting, "Bloody rubbish, do it again!" Magnus *would* do it again, and again shout the measurements to Dave; there would be sounds of frantic sawing and then Dave would appear with a piece of wood that wouldn't fit. The whole thing took days. In the evening, while waiting for a meal to appear, Magnus and Dave would sit amid their work and share a glass or three. As time went on we would here various plops and "Buggers!" as, we assumed, various tools ended in the River Yonne.

After many adaptations the floor was thought to be finished; unfortunately, though, due to the many incorrect measurements, it bounced, making it ideal for a quick-step. More adaptations and varnish, and eventually the floor was finished to everyone's satisfaction. The boat was covered in tarpaulins and Magnus and friends departed before Jo could start the repairs. After their departure, the sun did his cruel work: the floor faded and curled up; the quick-step would now have to be done uphill.

Not all the residents of the yard were reluctant residents. One such was a small Frenchman with thick bottle bottom glasses who wore faded red shorts. Despite his short stature and general weedy appearance, Jo claimed he was a bully so that's what we called him: "Bully". Bully had a short-legged dog with powerful jaws, which he carried under his arm wherever he went. He lived in a small boat so far out that he was virtually in the middle of the river; he was moored there against Jo's wishes, and the first we knew of him was when Jo's son Herbie insisted that, under pain of expulsion from the yard, no one was to help him obtain electricity. Where Bully was moored, only a very long cable would reach the socket and he needed assistance from someone nearer the socket. For days he approached first one and then another of us; Jo had given no reason for the ban on helping him so we all felt sorry for the poor Frenchman but we did not want to lose our place on the list, so feeling sorry was all we did. Then Bully disappeared. Relief all round. No need for our conscience to bother us now – until he suddenly reappeared. Colin and I watched, fascinated, as Bully, with his fierce dog under his arm, jumped across five boats with a long cable and pushed a plug into a socket. Five minutes later a thunderous Jo pulled the socket out and threw it on the floor before stalking off. Bully must have been waiting because he hopped back and replaced it. This time, Herbie did the honours. The sequence of the hopping over boats and plugging in and pulling out of sockets happened five times before Bully gave up and sailed away. Two days later a furious Jo told us the *gendarmes* had been, and said that Bully had complained to them under the Race Relations Act that he was being discriminated against. As Jo described the event I thought of an Englishman and his castle. The *gendarmes* had departed in disarray after Jo had informed them forcefully that Bully owed years in back rent. That information relieved my conscience. I also thought to myself, people should think carefully before crossing the King.

Another resident in the yard was a large man who arrived in a very untidy lopsided small boat. This gentleman was part of the "Cling-on" group of boater. Cling-ons were usually very vociferous in their grumbling about hanging around in Jo's yard but they came back for more time after time. Even I could see that unless their nuisance value became extreme, they languished at the bottom of the list. The large man was a unique Cling-on, and the sight of him coming down the yard in a pair of long faded red shorts and a battered straw boater, with his feet splayed at a quarter to three, was enough for most of the other residents to head for their engine rooms at speed. If you were too slow to make an escape there was a set sequence that most people, because of their innate kindness, were unable to halt. A small gift would be accepted, followed by two hours of conversation during which you would be told how well travelled and educated "large man" was. According to the story, large man was the youngest son of an Anglo Irish peer; he was a Harley Street specialist, a GP, and had spent a lifetime sailing the seven seas, crossing the Atlantic single handed seven times. After two hours, listeners would be expiring from thirst and would be obliged to invite large man onto the boat for a drink. Large man would then sorrowfully inform his hosts that he only drank water with whisky. At least a bottle of whisky later, he would stagger back to his living quarters, which he had obligingly parked right in front of Jo's kitchen. Under the tree by the river, large man had moored his boat, parked his camper van, his battered old van, and an equally dangerous-looking motorbike. He moved all this stuff from place to place cadging lifts whenever he could. I could not understand why Jo put up with him – and then I found out. Large man was ill and on large doses of Warfarin. He should not have been drinking the large amounts he did. The year before we met him he had nearly died and Jo, according to gossip, had been his saviour, visiting him regularly in the hospital. I think Jo now feared that if he confronted large man he might die suddenly and then Jo would have a mass of paperwork to add to his list. It did not mean he did not drive Jo to distraction though: one morning as Jo got up for breakfast, he found large man in his kitchen with a piece of metal in his hand, a frying-pan handle he wanted welding. Jo was still in a bad mood as he partook of his morning cuppa in the café. Not seeing the signs, I mentioned some job on our list.

"I am sick of running an activity centre for geriatrics. This is a bloody boatyard," he told me. "I'll do it when I do it, meanwhile, Arkwright, start it yourself."

In the end I believe it was my fault that large man moved on. I saw him coming down the yard with a bundle of rags and an antique grill pan in his hand.

"Don't bother," I said, "I have got enough junk here to last me a lifetime, I don't need yours."

"Well, I thought Colin could use these shirts." Large man showed me three bits of thin stretched cloth that, with a bit of imagination, could be viewed as shirts.

"I know your game," I said, "I am not going to hide in my boat to save my whisky," (I didn't have any). "Colin's not having your rubbish either, he has too much of his own. Clear off."

"You are a bad mannered South Yorkshire bitch," shouted large man, red in the face.

He turned and sped, flip-flops slapping back to his boat. I was very proud of myself: it takes a Yorkshire woman from Arthur Scargill's kingdom to sort out the aristocracy; my standing among the polite southerners was very high.

Shortly after this, large man left in his boat. It was a long time before the rest of his encampment caught up with him.

We had a celebration meal on the roly-poly Dutchman's boat: he was a fantastic chef, and rather too much wine was imbibed. Colin began banging on a large oil drum. From the other side of the yard came a response, then another and another. It was a magical moment: soon we were all banging away. We weren't celebrating large man's departure, honest! The next morning we took Rene – that was the Dutchman's name – and his wife Fleur to a *brocante* and a *vide grenier*. Colin had put the back seats of the car down for Bob, and it did not occur to him to make Rene more comfortable. We travelled 40 odd kilometres, me, Rene and Bob the dog rolling around in the back of the baking car. We parted at the event and agreed to meet up later. When we met up some two hours later, it was with horror that we realised we had both bought tables, and on the way back to the boatyard the passengers in the back of the car, instead of rolling off each other, which was quite enjoyable, rolled around table legs, which wasn't.

Rene enjoyed himself so much that year he became a temporary and very useful Cling-on, helping Colin cut a hole in the roof to give the boat some much-needed ventilation. Three other residents of the yard were important to us too: Alison and Satch were a couple who were at the end of a very long stay in the yard themselves. Alison called Satch "the ancient mariner" – and he looked like one. An energetic man, quick of movement and thought, with a grizzled grey beard, before his retirement Satch had been a Master Mariner and a pilot in Mombasa harbour. Satch was always the first to answer the call of the praying mantis; all the shouting that Jo directed at his volunteer helpers didn't seem to matter to him.

Mind you, the shouting and the leaping around volunteering to look after the yard while Jo had a day off mattered to Alison: she felt that Satch was being taken advantage of. The previous year Jo had caught me looking at Satch and Alison's boat, a wide-beam English boat, narrow-boat in style, known in France as a *Belle Anglaise*. I was really taken with the pretty boat called Aries, but Jo informed me that plans were afoot to put in a new engine. It had already arrived and was in the workshop awaiting installation. Over a year later the boat was still in the yard, due in part to Jo's slowness in installing the engine.

Alison and I had a lot in common; initially it was anger about not being able to get the work moving in the yard (which was mainly a woman problem: the men, as long as they were kept busy, were happy in Tonka Land). Since then, over the years, when we have offered mutual support to each other over the tribulations of combining family life and gardening with boating, we have found we have even more in common even though Alison and Satch have all girls and I have too many males in the family. I know Alison is at the end of a phone and I will always be grateful for the way Satch tactfully told Colin he should let the wind do the work when turning a bigger boat. Alison and I were such partners, that one day Jo told us he could feel our "evil eyes" on him.

Herbie, one of Jo's two sons, was working for his dad in the yard. Herbie is very different to his dad in his looks: very fair, with blue eyes and a friendly smile. He is good humoured and always helpful. Colin called him his "other set of muscles": when his wooden leg and crooked arm prevented him getting into dark and small places with a big hammer, Herbie was always willing to lend a bit of muscle. Poor Herbie was only 22 years old, a chip off the old block as far as things boaty were concerned, and, as the heir apparent, in the invidious position of being propositioned by most of Jo's clients anxious to get off the list.

Herbie handled all the propositions with tact beyond his years, neither taking the one side or the other; although I think he did have his own issues with his father, as all sons do. Once, when we were in the water behind a big boat, we heard an argument between them. We could not understand what it was about, but suddenly we heard a big clang, what sounded like a hammer hitting the boat sides, and then silence.

"God, someone's killed someone," said Colin.

"I think Jo's probably the better shot," I replied.

"Ah, but Herbie's quicker," came the response.

Sometime later, Herbie and Jo appeared, intact, with Jo shouting "Gladys!" for his cup of afternoon tea. Nothing was said, although they knew we knew.

Herbie spent most of that summer working in the yard dressed in long, lightweight trousers with the crotch down at about the level of his knees. Those trousers defied gravity, and many of the ladies of the yard waited with bated breath for the seemingly inevitable exposure. Herbie, I think, pretended to be unaware of the waves his mode of dress was causing; but I also believe he knew he was quite an Adonis. It is pity the only people in the yard to appreciate his physique were old ladies and men who were after his skill as a mechanic. In appreciation of his appearance, Paul and I labelled him Sir Lancelot to Jo's King Jo.

By the end of August I had had enough, and went home for a month to see the kids and buy some essential supplies. Every time I rang Colin in the evening our conversations were accompanied by sounds of great hilarity, most of the ladies having decided Colin needed looking after and that our wheelhouse was the best place to feed him, since the table seated at least six. Even Jo offered to feed him.

This was not part of my plan: Colin was supposed to miss me. After a month, and having spent another fortune on a new diesel heater, curtains and wood flooring, I returned on the train with our son Iain. His friend and our grandchild Lucy arranged to follow in a transit van, planning to reopen the Café de Gladys, which had been run by various ladies while I was away. I had learned my lesson: I couldn't beat the siren call of the "praying mantis"; I would have to learn to live with it.

No sooner had I opened the café than we decided to move round the corner into the Port of Migennes while we waited for our visitors. I was lucky: the handyman approved all my purchases, and was amazed that, despite my being a woman, I had managed to get all the parts for the stove – not even a screw was missing.

After Lucy had threaded herself through the very small spaces in the boat, dragging pipes, I decided it was time I introduced her to real French food shopping. I saw an advert in *Atac* for *steak haché* at a bargain price; in France they mince the beef in front of you so you know what you are getting, although you are then committed to buy. Too late: only now did I see the rest of the sign: *cheval steak haché*. I made the decision to say nothing, as I had bought a lot. We also bought Iain a treat of ten snails in garlic butter (it's fair to say all the snails ended in the canal). I had more success with the cottage pie made of horsemeat: Iain and his friend declared it the best ever, and only then did I reveal that it was horse meat. Appalled faces all round; only Lucy, ever contrary, found the episode hilarious.

I returned to Paris with Iain and co. to entertain Lucy while Iain and his friend went to the Arc de Triomphe races. After a huge row on the *périphérique* we ended up in a car park under one of the most expensive hotels in Paris. Lucy and I did the usual tourist things and we met up later with Iain, who had won enough on the race to pay for all of them to stay the night in the expensive hotel – a great end to a short break.

With the installation of the heater done in double quick time, it was time for us to leave the yard officially – an event I had often doubted would ever happen.

Chapter 3

Another new beginning

Eventually the day I thought would never arrive *did* arrive. We were off. The plan was to meet our friends Helen and George in Auxerre, two days' sailing from the boatyard.

After spending the morning stocking up with essentials like Allen keys for the bikes, we set sail with an elegant turn against the current, towards the bridge. Colin was blowing on his hunting horn, Bob the dog was howling, and I, ever the lady, was sedately waving to Jo, Herbie and assorted boatyard residents. Smooth as silk, we sailed under the road bridge and out of sight.

A further couple of hundred yards ahead stood the lock and weir. Colin turned to me and said, "The steering's gone."

"Don't be bloody stupid," I replied. Colin is a great wind-up merchant, and he did not look as he should if the steering had really gone.

"It has."

As his face was now white and seemed shrunken, this time I believed him. And at that moment Koopman was heading at speed for the lock gates – which were closed. We had forgotten to inform the lock man that we were setting off.

From that moment the whole thing became like a bad dream from which I was convinced I would wake up. I grabbed my mobile phone and tried to ring Jo. It took several attempts to get his number, and when I did he seemed to react very slowly; I think he found it difficult to believe my garbled message – after all, it was only two minutes since we had waved goodbye.

By this time Colin was trying to control the boat using forward and reverse gears. By the time I had finished the call, he had decided there were alternatives to death. Very calmly he said, "Take off the manual steering cover."

"What cover? Where is it?" I screamed.

The noise from the water coming over the weir was horrendous; sometimes the noise of a waterfall is far from relaxing, more akin to loud white noise. Colin pointed, and under instructions I removed a plate I had not noticed before.

"There's all wet stuff down the back!" I screamed.

"You'll have to fix up the manual steering," Colin replied; but by this time I was in a world of panic, incapable of coherent thought. I just stood there, while Colin said, "Here. I'll do it, just keep the boat moving backwards and forwards."

We swapped places and I grabbed hold of the throttle.

"Push the throttle forward."

I pushed as far as it would go; we shot forward and mounted the bank. I watched in horror as my beautiful new cream curtains I had spent hours making wrapped themselves round a bush.

Bloody hell, I thought to myself, I'm going to have to wash those before they've even been used.

"Back! Back!" a disembodied voice yelled from behind me.

I pushed the throttle into reverse as far as it would go. We dismounted the bank and went back at speed into a circle in the middle of the river, ending up going backwards towards the pouring water of the weir.

"Thank God we bought those Allen keys for the bikes," shouted Colin as he began to assemble the manual steering. "Go slower with that throttle and put it in forward again."

As I looked up, I saw Herbie get off his motorbike and stand with his hands on his hips (posing) as we shuttled back and forth. Where's the bloody lifeboat? I thought, you would have thought they would rescue me after all those free cups of tea.

"Here, you steer with this and I'll drive the engine and tell you which way to steer," Colin instructed; but I was not strong enough to hold the tiller down and steer against the push of the water coming over the weir. The river, eager to be on its way, was frothing and bubbling, making Koopman buck in all directions. Again we swapped places, Colin heading to the back to fit another length of tiller on the steering mechanism. I pushed the throttle forward and back, slowly and bit by bit: I had got the message not to attempt self-rescue by chucking the boat at the bank.

All the while, Herbie watched, seemingly unconcerned. Gradually Colin got control of the steering, but because of the height of the wheelhouse he could not see where he was going. He called out, "Tell me which way to go."

Panic ensued again, owing to my geographical dyslexia. I am told the left and intuitive side of my brain is well developed at the expense of the right and spatially aware side. I concentrated hard and managed the "left hand down a bit" stuff very well – all those years of listening to Leslie Philips in The Navy Lark were paying off. Colin managed to get us into the lock by hopping at speed from the tiller to look through the window and thus check that "right hand down" was not really "left hand down". The Captain would then hop back to the tiller. At the same time, Colin kept a close eye on my throttle hand.

When at last we got into the lock, Herbie diagnosed the problem almost immediately. As with Humph and the grub screws, it was a job that had been started a long time ago and not completed. We were underway again in two hours. A more subdued embarkation this time. With three people installing the hydraulics, it was a case of too many cooks – or mechanics – and no one was owning up that a pipe had been put in the wrong way.

Throughout all this commotion, Bob sat like a statue in the middle of the wheelhouse; for once she was not going to lose the plot as we had.

We spent the night moored to a pontoon in a place that seemed at the end of the world but in fact was only two miles from the yard. The rain came down in buckets and the chimney spun dementedly, but we were warm and dry, with enough food to withstand a siege. It was a pity that for me the world was still whirling like a roundabout; I lived in a state of constant reminder of bushes and curtains.

Next morning, we set off, and by two thirty we were moored in Auxerre, a very beautiful city with three massive churches on separate hills overlooking the river port. On one side of the river are the public moorings and a long promenade lined with restaurants. On the other bank stand the port, boatyard, and moorings for a lot of very expensive and cherished boats, some of them plastic and therefore crushable. Many of the boats were moored three deep – "breasted up", as we call it.

The weather had changed again, and in the sunshine I chatted to our new boating neighbours. Our immediate neighbour was a German who was in the middle of working on an engine refit. Just before tea, the *Capitainerie* asked us if we would mind moving up the moorings a couple of places, as a *péniche* was requesting moorings and more room was needed. *Péniches* are the older workboats of France; to us they seemed, at 350 tons, to be huge – until we saw the newer container-carrying barges of 3,000 tons.

We cast off and started to circle with the current in the middle of the river. "Yvonne," Colin shouted, "the bloody steering has gone again! Get to the front and fend us off those boats!"

I ran to the bow, grabbing the boat hook off the roof as I passed. Those boats we were heading for looked expensive. I knew the German was somewhere about, and I desperately tried to remember the German for help.

Colin had decided that, as he couldn't see what he was doing, the best plan was to try and steer in circles. But that was difficult because of the current. I dropped the boat hook, picked up the rope and shouted to the German boat as we passed: "Alpen! Alpen!" No answer. We did another circuit and I screamed, "Alpen! Alpen! Grab ze rope!"

Slowly a head appeared out of the conning tower or engine hatch, staring but giving no answer. Stupid bloody Germans, I thought, why don't they understand their own language? It also went through my mind that he did look a bit like a U2 captain surveying our torpedo damage.

Round we went again – "Alpen! Alpen!" At last he got the message, and after another two circuits he managed to *grab ze rope* and we were pulled into the side and to safety.

I did not have time to indulge in post-traumatic stress syndrome: our friends Helen and George were due to arrive at the station for the start of our inaugural cruise. We walked the dog up to the railway station; Bob loved Helen to death, and sensing something good was about happen she walked at a fair old lick. We arrived at the station to find that the train I had told them to catch did not run as far as Auxerre that day but stopped 20kms away at Joigny. Where *were* they? Helen's French was as schoolgirl as mine was; I was very worried, and worse, felt it was my fault.

A moment after I had realised what I had done, I heard Helen's voice behind me. The young lady in the ticket office at Joigny lived in Auxerre and had offered them a lift to the station. It was hard to discover who was the most pleased, me or the dog, who was squeaking and whining in pleasure.

Helen and I have been friends for a long time, having met when we worked in the same department. Helen is very different to me, a very elegant size 12 lady who never seems to have a bad hair day; she is also very organised, which I appreciate. Helen is a baby boomer, while I was born at the beginning of the war, but we seem to have had mothers with matching strengths and weaknesses as well as a similar education. I think Helen enjoys the scrapes my chaotic behaviour has got us into. We both enjoyed walking, and one afternoon in the Cotswolds we climbed a very muddy hill. I slipped and rolled a long way to the bottom. Helen cruelly and helplessly laughed until the tree she was hanging on broke and she followed me down the quagmire. I dragged her, filthy and wet, through the village of Stowe and into the charity shop to be kitted out. Charity shop-buying was something that, elegant lady that she was, Helen would never have dreamed of doing, even if it was in a posh area. My friend's horror at how low she had stooped was so amusing to me that it made me ill with laughing. To make her feel even worse I deliberately made a big fuss in the shop. My amusement was increased further when we tried to scrape up and dispose of the mud left in the starred hotel's bath. I finally had a brilliant idea and we scraped the mud into the charity-shop carrier bag. I thought we were being very considerate and resourceful but Helen behaved as if we were criminals.

George, Helen's husband, and Colin had become friends through a mutual interest in the Lions charity organisation. George is an accountant, very tall, serious-looking, and prone to falling off things; he is also witty in a slow, thoughtful way. George thinks long and hard before he decides to act, unlike Colin, who dives into things convinced that however it turns out, in the end he will fly. George always seemed a bit in awe of Colin's mechanical skills; but he could come up with some good ideas too, as the following incident shows.

After croissants and coffee the next morning, George said to Colin, "I have been thinking about car brakes. What you have to do is 'bleed' them. Maybe that's what we need to do."

"You're right," Colin said, and in no time at all they were setting about bleeding the system. Task completed in no time at all, and thankfully all has continued to be well in that department since.

Another great attribute of George's is that he keeps his cool when Colin "goes off on one": he is the ideal First Lieutenant. As a result of experiencing the loss of steering, I insist that the manual tiller always be assembled and ready to go, even though a number of people have nearly knocked themselves out when leaning back in the chair and hitting their head on it.

Sitting and chatting to Helen the following night, I wondered if we would ever be able to call ourselves expert boaters, or were we forever doomed to lurch from disaster to disaster. Helen, ever the pragmatist, told me not to be so histrionic.

"You're still here aren't you?" she said.

"You should have my dreams," I muttered.

Chapter 4

Voies Navigables & Koopman Welvaren V

We set off from Auxerre with our friends, looking forward to the journey south on the Bourgogne. It was quite late in the season and the canal was very quiet. We did not know it at the time but we had been the last off the canal the previous year and were now the first on the newly repaired canal. We hoped that with a taller boat we would be able to manage the locks much better, with blissful marital harmony and a happy dog. How wrong we were: Koopman responded to the Captain very differently to Mr Bean, and while we managed not to have as many maritals when our friends were with us, we certainly had big ones after they left. My job at the pointy bit was to handle the ropes; the bollards were still difficult to lasso despite our increased height, as very often I was aiming blind. Also, Colin was travelling into the first lock miles too fast, which made my task even harder. In fact everything the Captain did seemed to be much too fast for me. The Captain liked his boat to lie neatly along the wall of the lock, but the water poured in, went under the boat, hit the back wall, and drove us forward and sideways. And going down, the water drained out at speed, pulling the boat to the front and sideways. The answer for the Captain in those early days was to rely on my power and dexterity with the ropes. I had to pull in a much bigger boat than Mr Bean, or finely judge how much rope to let out as we went down. Half the time I was really struggling with the weight of the boat and the force of the water. I did not appreciate this arrogant voice yelling at me from the protection of the wheelhouse. Fortunately the noise of the water meant I very often couldn't hear the Captain even if I had wanted to.

We seemed to have forgotten a lot of Tam and Di's training. I was absolutely terrified as Colin charged into locks, seemingly going straight into the gates. I would be on the point shouting, "Stop, stop, you bloody maniac!" while the figure in the wheelhouse would be making frantic hand signals miming catching or winding ropes around bollard. If I managed a "quick catch", it would stop the boat dead, and more than once Bob and I thought we were about to take off. Another obstacle that the Captain resolutely refused to recognise were the rails that ran around the boat and over the bollard.

"Captain Know All" knew before I did when the rope was going to end up the wrong side of the rails. "It's cos you have got no idea about left and right and where things fit," he would say after another "knitting" event.

"*You* try thinking where the bloody rope and rails are when you are about to be impaled on the sodding door," I said. "And that bloody pole's too heavy. I can't hold it up to put the rope on the top bollard."

It was all my fault for being a weak woman with no spatial awareness, not that the driver was going too fast or there was a design fault in the positioning of the rails on the boat. Poor old Bob was caught in the middle of a long-running war of words, with no other boaters to seek comfort from.

We finally arrived in Saint-Jean-de-Losne to meet Alison and Satch off the Aries, and John the eccentric tea planter, accompanied by his lovely wife Sue. For me it was like an oasis in a desert. From the pointy bit of the boat I waved frantically with my pole (which was not too heavy for this purpose). The Captain for some reason decided to do a full circle in the middle of the port before mooring up. It was a complete nightmare for me. I shouted to the Captain from the point, "you're going too fast." But the captain was in his own world, and continued. With my pole supporting me I jumped up and down. "Stop, you bloody fool! Stop, it's too fast."

By now the boat was on the turn so the bank was safe, but other boats were not.

"Get your pole ready to ward off them boats."

"Well, you slow down. Oh God! Oh God!" I covered my eyes and hung my head, bracing my legs for the inevitable crash. Bob, all excitement, evaporated, sitting beside me in a cloud of vibrating blonde hair. At last Colin put the reverse on and behind my hands I could feel us glide past a boat by a whisker. Our friend came forward to grab our ropes and there were hugs and kisses all round; no mention was made of our lack of marital harmony. (Ignoring maritals is an unspoken rule among the boating fraternity.)

After the usual catch-up, the gossip settled into the usual routine: women on the boat drinking wine and talking children, men on the bank drinking beer and talking boats and war.

After John and Sue had returned to their mooring, Alison said, "Come on, let's take the dogs for a walk, it's a lovely evening."

Tilly and Bob were good friends, and as they went off and had a good rummage around, Alison, not looking directly at me, said, "What's the matter?"

My eyes filled with tears. "I think Colin drives this boat too fast and it frightens me to death."

"Would you like me to have a word with Satch? He's used to big boats."

"Oh, I don't want to make things worse."

"No, he won't, he can be very tactful, and I agree, you did seem to come in too fast today."

"Oh! Then yes, please ask him."

It was with a much lighter heart I went to bed that night.

The following morning I went into Blanquart's, the chandlers in the port. Blanquart's is a family-run business with a boatyard and a large shop. Although I could have spent a fortune I thought I was very restrained: I bought smart new black rope to match the black fenders I had bought off Jo, a piece of blue plastic woven mat for the sundeck, and, shock horror from Colin, a new toilet much reduced in the sale. I thought the toilet compartment – its dark wood walls, antique Formica surrounding an unnecessarily large sink and evil looking cupboard, and the ancient toilet itself, which, as well as smelling dirty, looked dirty – was beyond living with. I could not believe it: the story of the toilet continued with a repeat performance of the new damn thing not working. In the hot sun, after installing the toilet, Colin tried every possible way to make the contraption empty. In the end he fetched M Blanquart who, as with Jo, was up to his neck in work – a faulty toilet was not going to be one of his priorities.

To be fair, we did not have to wait long before he arrived and diagnosed the problem as perished rubbers in the pump mechanism. My spirits sank when it became clear that M Blanquart did not have the spare parts. "Bloody hell, Colin, I'm sick of not even having the basics. I hate boating. I want to go home to my nice clean non-smelling bathroom with a proper flush toilet. Another thing I am sick of is you thinking you are Stirling Moss, like yesterday."

I was so angry that all thoughts of tact went out of my head. Poor Colin (as many of my friends say): he was already feeling guilty for buying an old boat and not the ex-hire with two en-suites that I wanted, and there I was criticising his driving as well his taste in boats. I don't know how he did it, but desperation must have showed in his face because he somehow persuaded M Blanquart to spare the time to cannibalise another toilet pump for replacement rubber. Triumphant, the handy man returned and fixed the pump, but the toilet still did not empty. By now Bob had left home and was sitting with Tilly on Alison's boat. Satch and M Blanquart both came round, and the verdict of the committee was that the toilet was mended but the outlet valve was faulty.

"What's that mean?" I asked Satch.

"Well, the outlet is under the boat, so the boat will have to be craned out."

"What! Is that right?" I turned angrily towards Colin.

"Yes."

"*More* money; and we will be stuck here forever, I know it. And with no toilet no one will be daft enough to buy the bloody thing." If our friend had not been a witness I would have stamped my feet in temper.

Trying to lighten the atmosphere, Satch made a jokey suggestion. "Well, you could put a plank out on the opposite side and we'll all sit on it to tilt the boat while Colin shoves a bung in the outlet hole. Then we can change the valve from the inside."

It was meant as a joke but Colin took it on board. "I think I have some wooden bungs that were left by the previous owner. They are in a plastic bag."

We waited with bated breath while the Captain disappeared into the engine room. He returned with a plastic bag containing what looked like wine corks.

"Yes, that's what you want," said Satch.

"Are we really going to have to sit on a plank over the side of the boat?" I asked.

"If that's what we have to do, we'll do it, Yvonne."

I could tell by the tone of the Captain's voice there was no arguing: I had made a fuss about the cost and now I was going to have to pay for it. To paraphrase Jo's saying, "A splash could save us cash." It was just that I doubted my ability to rescue the Captain if he fell in.

The first task was to undo yesterday's dramatics and turn the boat round so that the outlet valve was port side. My heart sank: it was windy, making precise steering difficult.

"Would you like me to come with you?" asked Satch, his voice neutral; there was no hint that this might have been planned.

Alison and I let the ropes off. "Did you ask the Ancient Mariner?" I asked.

"Yes."

"Great, so there is some light on the horizon" I replied.

The two men did a little tour around the port and finally came in slowly for a perfect mooring. Later the Captain told me that he had learned a lot off the Ancient Mariner; driving a taller, heavier boat was totally different from manoeuvring a low, light narrow boat. "You were right, I was going too fast, and Satch has told me about using the wind."

Things were looking up. Alison was right: Satch had been tactful. Our friends went for their dinner but Colin felt that this was a "eureka" moment and was too excited to eat. He took the selection of bungs and lay full length on the quay. "I think I can do this, hold my legs Yvonne."

I grabbed hold of both legs.

"Now hold on tight; with my luck I will probably float upside down," the Captain instructed. The diver's head disappeared underwater and emerged dripping.

"I can see the valve hole. Get me the big hammer and a piece of string."

Puzzled, I did as I was told. "What do you want string for?"

"To tie the hammer to my wrist in case I drop it; we don't

want to lose it. Now, when my hand comes up pass it to me."

Suddenly I was flooded with admiration for the handyman's resourcefulness, and to my surprise (it was either a case of beginner's luck or extreme skill) the hole was quickly bunged. Now we could get on with the valve repair from the inside.

Before our friends had finished their meal we had a fully functioning toilet and Colin's confidence was sky-high – which meant trouble for me in the long run. For the moment, though, marital harmony was restored – all too quickly for Bob, who took until bedtime before she decided to return home. Totally relieved that Koopman's sanitary arrangements were in good working condition, we spent a convivial evening with our friends, the women in the wheelhouse talking children and families, the men outside talking engines and national service. Who was it who said men are from Mars and women from Venus?

We left our friends and continued on our way to Roanne. Roanne is at the end of an *embranchement*, and it took us two days to get there. As we came through the lock I was impressed by the view of the port. To our right behind a promenade of trees was a road lined with shops and flats; at the bottom of the port was a car park behind which was a roundabout with roads leading off to the south. At the car park end of the left side was another lock, which led onto the Loire River. Originally the port at Roanne had been the link between the trading boats of the Loire and the main canal system. The Loire is the last untamed river in France and is prone to flooding; it cannot be seen from the port as it is contained behind a high bank with an avenue of trees on the top. Between the bank protecting the port and the port on the left side is an area where old boats are stored. Situated at the port's top left side as we came through the canal lock was the community centre, port office and toilet block. Immediately to our left was shallow water, a haven for wild life.

I thought Roanne was the nicest canal port I had been to up until then, and even now I think only Coupure in Brugge can rival it. We booked in for a fortnight, moored up on the right in front of the flats and settled to wait for more visitors from home. The *Capitainerie* spoke no English but we quickly made friends; his appointment was only temporary, and the man who was the caretaker for the community centre had high hopes of getting the job. The two men went everywhere together; both were heavy smokers, and visits to the office were definitely a risk to your health. Every day both men would do a circuit of the port, making sure all the litter was cleared and that generally everything was ship-shape. Both men were very Gallic: shrugs were their speciality; they enjoyed life and were definitely not going to die of overwork. The Handyman and I suffer from the Anglo-Saxon work ethic: neither of us can just sit about, so in no time at all we had decided to revamp the toilet compartment, getting rid of the big cupboard and antique Formica and installing a folding sink, white plastic tongue-and groove-lining, and a shower. Luckily for us, further down on our side was another toilet and shower, coin operated and of the self-cleaning variety. Once again Colin was getting hot and dirty, so one morning he took his stool and wandered down for a shower. It was a long time before he returned. As Colin approached me I could see he had blood trickling down his face from his forehead; he always wears a shirt, but here he was minus a shirt, and his trousers were wet through and sticking to his legs. As he got closer I could hear a squelching sound from his shoes.

"What the hell's happened to you – are you all right?"

Colin, looking very shamefaced, replied, "Yes, but what a time I've had. When I got to the shower, a lady was just coming out and she left the door for me, so I went in, leaving the door open a bit, and had a good shower." When Colin has a shower he has to take his leg off and rest his stump on the stool. "I had just finished, and I bent down to pick my clothes up when I saw the *Capitainerie*."

"'Oh, Monsieur, pardon, pardon,' he said, "and then," Colin continued, "he shut the bloody door."

"It was pitch black and the water came in from all over. I couldn't see a thing. I was shouting, 'Mon Capitain, I have problem.' Then I shouted, 'You daft bugger. All me clothes are sopping wet!' and when it stopped I could hear him laughing his head off. Me clothes were that wet I couldn't get them on. The *Capitainerie* shouted, 'Vous OK?' and I said, 'Yes, OK,' but I could hear him on the grass laughing."

"But you've got blood pouring down your face."

"Have I? It must be the scab from where I banged my head yesterday."

Then I was cross. "How much money did you save?"

"50 *centimes*."

"So you nearly killed yourself for 50 *centimes*? Serves you right, said the *Captainerie* shutting the door. For God's sake, we are not that poor that we have to fiddle a bloody toilet."

In no time at all we were notorious around the port, but the incident did introduce us to a lot of very nice people.

By the time Sally and Peter came out for a visit, the pristine new shower and toilet were fully operational. I would have liked to stay in Roanne but the family had come out for a cruise so off we went back along the *embranchement* and onto the Canal du Centre. Colin and I had become more of a team when operating the boat, and Pete and Sally were real chips off the old blocks: before long Koopman was a war zone for short periods.

I must confess I feel gleeful when Sally and Pete complain to their Dad that his instructions don't make sense. I once, in glee, said to the Captain in front of them, "See, I told you that and you wouldn't have it." The result of this crow of triumph was that all three turned on me, saying it was a one-off incident. Now I keep my thoughts to myself, but I do take note.

Like me, Sally loves to chat to people; we were on the river Saône when she jumped off the boat with the rope and began chatting to people on the pontoon. We could see the securing rope in her hand, but the end was not attached to the boat. Sally was too busy gossiping to hear our cries as we drifted downstream; as we journeyed, Peter in his baseball cap and long shorts was jumping up and down shouting in rage; without knowing it they were recreating events from their parents' boating careers. When we finally got ourselves tied up Peter continued to rage at Sally, the cap on his head looking just like the beak of a woodpecker. Sally couldn't see what all the fuss was about, which made Peter worse (but they are evenly balanced, both being small, blonde, and very verbal and opinionated). After the kids left us at Digoin we continued on the Saône, stopping at the town of Auxonne where we went to another son et lumière. Auxonne was where Napoleon served in the early part of his career. The story was that Napoleon brought peace and tranquility, and more important, food, to France. No mention of Russia; but war was alluded to with the fact that French prisoners were treated like dogs by the English. The history continued on a lighter note, featuring the coming of trains. The track was laid and a huge steaming cardboard train emerged from the side. Then there was the coming of gaslight, motor cars and bikes (here a real show of vintage machines), café society, and finally an exuberant can-can. The first half of the show ended with the 1870 war where the action was girls' ballet dancing and men signing a treaty before returning home to the tune of Land and Hope and Glory (again).

The second half started with the First World War and included an episode in which a gentle French nurse is ministering to wounded French and German soldiers. The Second World War started with a stream of refugees being bombed and carrying all their stuff. Then the pièce de résistance: an aeroplane on wires zooms in, dropping parachutists who are rescued by a handsome moustachioed Marquis riding in a lorry. The light switches to a house where a pretty young girl is hiding an airman; boys dressed in German uniforms search everywhere, hampered by the dashingly brave Marquis. Needless to say, the airman escapes. The grand finale is the arrival of the Americans in tanks, lorries and scout cars as the orchestra plays the 1812 overture; the fireworks bang and the crowd rise and applaud in appreciation. (Funny: I thought the 1812 was all about the relief of Moscow. Have I been brainwashed?)

Nevertheless, it was a wonderful night's entertainment and the following night we were treated to a different spectacle. We were in a restaurant when the chef fell out with everyone and began chucking plates about. The food had come out to the customers all wrong, some halves of couples being served while others were forgotten. A man complained, and the owner and chef, an Algerian, got hold of the complainant and chucked him out, followed by manhandling the man's wife. The man, getting his second wind, came back and involved the bar opposite; the result was a lot of arm-waving and shouting but no one actually hitting anyone. The second chef – I suppose he felt he was left doing all the work or was being blamed for the mix-ups – came out and chucked a load of pizzas in a bin. A final crash of glasses in the back brought the issue to an end. We were so entertained we left a 6-euro tip.

That's what I like about the French, they puff themselves up and act aggressive but then remember that the wine's waiting and so pack up and go home – Vive la France!

We had planned to meet our friends on their boat Albert further north, but decided as it was getting lonely this late in the season we would end our maiden voyage in Koopmans, turn around, and head for our winter moorings in Roanne.

Chapter 5

Oh, what a birthday!

We stayed in Roanne until the arrival of the first Christmas card; we used the time to convert the bedroom in the pointy bit, which was designed for a midget, into a comfortable bedroom for two normal-size adults. A masterpiece of design, the head of the bunks were separate and the feet joined. I was really pleased with the result: a lot of space had previously been wasted by the box-like shape of the lining while the cupboard at the foot of the bed had meant that Colin could not stretch out – although perhaps one of the few advantages to having one leg is that it halved the episodes of cramp. Our new design involved Colin reducing the height of the cupboard and constructing the new insulated hardboard lining in such a way that it followed the shape of the boat. Hey presto! We were no longer having to sleep in a foreshortened coffin, but now reposed in comfy, spacious bunks in a peach-coloured room. While in Roanne we had noticed that many of the residents had access to the UK TV system; after enquiring from our new friends, I paid a visit to the "man who knew", and lo and behold, we could get Coronation Street. My cup runneth over!

At home over the winter season we discussed the fact that Koopman would be a hundred years old in 2006 and we felt we ought to mark the event by taking the boat to the place of his birth. As we were in the middle of France at the furthest point south before the River Rhône, we felt it would take two seasons to get to Amsterdam. We planned to journey towards Paris via the Briare Canal, and stay a month in the Arsenal in Paris before wintering somewhere in the north.

We returned to Roanne in late March 2005 to get ready for the boat's epic return to the land of his birth. We were welcomed back like returning children; Hans, the very large Dutchman with a small dog, assured us we would enjoy the canals in Holland: there were so many more pleasure boats there and they had more facilities for boaters. We did wonder why, if the canals in Holland were so great, he had taken up almost permanent residence in France. What we weren't told is that although there are more pleasure craft in Holland there are also far more commercial craft bigger and faster than anything I could have imagined.

Before our adventure could start there were essential man-things to be done – I have learnt that there is nothing a man likes more than worrying about his engine. Finally, after minor repairs and a new battery, we were ready for off. Our first port of call was Briennon, where we came across a couple we had first met in Jo's yard. Over a cup of tea they told us how lonely and homesick they were. The euro was beginning its rise against the pound and they had moored for the winter in a cheaper port; consequently they had been on their own. I could empathise with the couple: I too thought the French countryside a very lonely place, especially for someone whose French will always be spoken with a Yorkshire accent. I found it difficult to understand the mad rush happening in England to buy a restoration project in the middle of the France. I was told by another Englishman that the French government is so worried about the depopulation of the countryside that there are special grants available for anyone opening a shop in certain villages. I was sad as we left our friends: they had come off the UK housing ladder, could not sell their boat, and were unhappy in France, a cautionary tale.

The weather deteriorated and, despite being very snug in Koopman, our spirits were affected by our friends' difficulties. We thought we would cheer ourselves by making a detour to Dompierre-sur-Besbre, a town which, in the map-book, is shown to have the port with everything.

After a journey down a shallow, narrow canal we arrived at . . . nothing. All the facilities were at the hire-boat base, which was deserted, but it was too late to turn round, so we spent the night moored alongside a VNF workshop. We had a walk round the town, which was surprisingly cheerful: the girl in the supermarket was very friendly and tried out her English on us. We felt lifted for a while. On the boat we were warm, snug and had enough to eat, but morale was very low and the trip to Amsterdam seemed hardly worth the effort, especially as I felt that Colin was turning into an engine neurotic, having installed two temperature gauges, which of course gave different readings (one 71 degrees, the other 82). In the end, "do it yourself man" resorted to boiling the thermostats in one of my pans to check the readings. Both readings were correct! My attitude was not helpful. "Put one on, Colin, if the engine blows up we can go home – and sell the bloody boat." In the end Colin put the old one back on, and lo and behold it worked: the engine ran at its normal 92 degrees. I decided not to say if the thing was recording wrong when in a pan of boiling water how does "do it yourself man" know it is giving the correct reading now? Suffice to say, five years on, the temperature gauge has fallen off the scale of things to worry about.

The next morning we rejoined the main canal, the sun came out and we decided to test the generator by doing the laundry. The man who knows about women has a theory that if a woman has sorted her laundry out then all will be right for the men in her life. This time Colin was wrong: my phone went on the blink, which for me, in foreign parts, is a tragedy: I have to know I am being missed. Worse was to come, though, as at Nevers we ran aground on a big rock. The canal was too shallow, and worse, the wind was blowing at gale force, insisting we stayed marooned.

Our timing was appalling, as the lock man had gone for his *mange*. The Captain's brain went into overdrive: before the lock man had returned he had imagined us sinking at speed. I thought, well at least it takes his mind off the temperature gauge.

The city of Nevers is at the end of a beautiful tree-lined branch of the Canal lateral à la Loire, and to get us off the rock, water had to be sent down via the two locks to raise the water level. Although it was now trying to snow, the city and moorings at Nevers more than made up for the bad weather. Like Roanne, Nevers had been a large commercial port but had been converted to leisure use, there being a huge outdoor swimming pool made out of a converted lock at the end of the port. Over the path and up the bank and there again was the mighty Loire, as in Roanne. Bob and I spent a good few hours walking along the bank, chatting to other mostly French dog walkers. There are shops and cafés in the city, and, best of all for the car boot addict of the family, the next best thing, a flea market, where Colin spent what was for him a fortune. The day at the flea market ended in the usual style: French sausage sandwiches, and a special one for Bob, of course. Bob had become used to the boat, and as she was so sociable it usual took us only a few minutes to get talking to any passers-by. She also had another invaluable function: some days we did not see anybody at all and Bob was often the conduit by which we communicated when the marital situation was strained.

Our stop at Marseilles-lès-Aubigny marked the beginning of big-boat country – although a lot of boats seemed either "live aboards" or in the process of being repaired. At that moment the boats presented no threat to us; we were just interested in seeing other canal users after being so long out on our own.

We now had a more or less regular TV signal, and all the news was on the question of "How would the French vote in the referendum on the European Constitution?" We were made aware how important the vote was to the French at a later stop on our journey: Menetreol-sous-Sancerre. Once again we had seen no other boats all day when we pulled up at the village in snow. The port office was a house on the opposite side of the road, and the *Capitainerie*, a man who because of a stroke struggled to walk, came across the road to turn on the electric and water. Turning out for one boat at that late hour and in such weather, I could have forgiven the *Capitainerie* for being grumpy; but not a bit of it: I have never met such a lovely gentleman, and in no time at all I had my arms around him, offering to share my coat. The welcome from the village continued as we had a meal in the café alongside the moorings, and we felt much more cheerful as we cosied down for the night.

Next morning, the sun was out and it was warm, so we set off on our bikes with the chariot to the next village for the supermarket. On our return we realised something was happening: there was a group of young men sat outside the restaurant shouting "Oui, Oui!" to passers-by.

"Let's go and have some fun," I said to the Captain.

After being greeted like long-lost friends by the *patron*, we sat ourselves outside in the sun shouting, "Non!" to the passers-by. Soon a heated debate began in broken English and French. One bit of French I did understand and felt embarrassed about was this statement from one of the young men: "It's alright for you English, you are rich and you come and buy all our houses so we can't afford to live where we were born." And it was true: as a result of our housing boom many people were buying cheap French properties and I had noticed they were no longer as cheap as they were.

Another reason for the "Oui" is the belief that the European community means there will be no more war – very important to a country that has been invaded so many times. I felt ashamed of being so light-hearted about such an important topic.

Our next stop was Saint-Satur, another port alongside the Loire and a beauty spot in the summer, judging by the campsite and log cabins strung out along the banks of the river. At Saint-Satur we planned to meet up with our friends the Ancient Mariner, his wife, Alison, and their dog, Tilly. As usual, much tea and wine was consumed and a good time had by all – especially the dogs. Before we went our separate ways we agreed that we would book in for winter moorings at Arques with them. The Ancient Mariner departed, and we left Saint-Satur in the *Capitainerie's* taxi to catch the train home.

While we were at home, "Do It Yourself Man" embarked on a project to put a canopy over the sundeck. As usual, in my opinion, the idea would have put Heath Robinson to shame. A visit to the local bus scrapyard, and several redundant passenger support poles were brought home, along with attachments that enabled the vertical pole to be attached to a horizontal half circle so that once again Colin's alterations would follow the "line" of the old boat.

On our return to France we found that some adjustments to the poles had to be made, and Colin cycled up through the vineyards to Sancerre, where once again a French welder made good the error *gratuit*, and in gratitude "Do It Yourself man" contributed to the coffee fund. The Sancerre region produces a very fine white wine; Colin and I are no connoisseurs so I cannot describe the taste, save to say it is best with something savoury, and well worth a try. Neither of us could believe that from the black gnarled stumps something so delightful could grow; it proved to

Colin something we always argued about: that mutilation or pruning is very good for vines and roses.

Our next big stop was at Briare. On most of the maps of the waterways of France, the bridge that carries the canal over the Loire just before the Briare *embranchement* is shown. This canal bridge is often attributed to Eiffel, but was in fact the work of a waterways service engineer, Mazoyer. Mild steel was used for the first time in France as it was the only material light and strong enough for a structure of this size. Daydé et Pillé made the steel, while Eiffel was responsible for the stonework. At the entrance to the aqueduct are two stone pillars covered with ornate ironwork and supporting electric wrought iron lights. The building of the Lateral Canal brought to an end boat transport on the Loire, and looking at the river today it is hard to imagine that boat transport could ever have been viable.

Before the port of Briare there are tree-lined linear moorings and we decided to spend some time here. Colin had another project on the go: from the back of a scrapped articulated lorry he had obtained the big rubber bumper, and he intend to fix it to the prow of the boat. Narrow-boaters turn their boats using the bank as a fulcrum; with a rubber bumper, Colin intended to do the same with Koopman.

Fitting the bumper was a nerve-racking job. Colin would lie down on a plank with me holding onto his legs while he drilled, screwed and hammered. All was well until a boat passed and the boat joggled around; sometimes the poor man was left spluttering on the end of the plank while his head pounded with the wash. All these renovations were carried out in full view of the passing tourist train, and in no time at all the two show offs, Bob and "plank man", were playing up to the mostly geriatric passing tourists, who often had their hands in front of their mouths as the man on the plank appeared to meet his end. Other times, Colin would leap out of the wheelhouse in his "Eric Morecambe's", blowing a very old and battered horn and closely followed by the dog, who would raise a paw to the passing train; both would be rewarded by a toot from the jolly, moustachioed driver and waves from his passengers. While we were in Briare we arranged for the bus pole canopy to have a canvas roof. A very intense Frenchman came and measured and, until we gave him the job, assured us that the canopy would be ready in a week. At the end of the conversation he was equally adamant that the canopy would be ready in six weeks. As we were due to meet family in Paris, we could not wait, so decided to come back for the finished product.

Briare was a wonderful time but as our friends Helen and George had arrived it was time for us to go. We were now on the Canal de Briare, and our first stop with our friends was Rogny-les – Sept-Écluses, or Rogny of the Seven Locks, a wonder of engineering science. The staircase was extended in the 1830s from 27 metres to 32 metres, and later in the 19th century it was replaced by six 38-metre non-staircase locks. In case you have forgotten, the Bingley five-rise staircase locks mean that if you are going down, the water in the lock you are in empties into the one you are dropping down to. If you are going up, no 2 lock must be full, so that it can empty into the lock you wish to rise in; therefore the preceding lock must be full when you start the sequence: quite complicated unless you are a master of physics.

We moored alongside the quay at Rogny and enjoyed an evening on the bank drinking wine, chatting and watching the activity. It seemed that tomorrow was a big day in the Rogny calendar: it was fête day. Colin was over the moon, and next morning he was up bright and early, dashing around the car boot in search of unmissable bargains while Helen and George lazed around and ate croissants. Colin spent a lot of time circling a stall with a gas burner on display; he wanted it for his other project, restoring his car boot purchase from Doncaster, a three-wheeled ice-cream bike which he intended to convert to sell German sausage soup around the village. His patience was rewarded and he eventually got the burner for 25 euros. As part of the ritual we had French sausages cooked on the barbeque with very thin frites and tomato sauce, the only British export the French appreciate. The afternoon was spent sleeping off the feast before the start of the evening activities, the dance. My father, who was in the First World War in France, always said the smell of wood smoke reminded him of the country that, despite the mud and pain, he came to love. And when *I* think of France I will always remember those warm summer evenings on a makeshift dance floor under canvas, dancing to the accordion. For me, that day in Rogny was what boating in France was all about: a huge number of French passed the time of day with us; they love dogs, and Bob as usual played her part, milking an enthusiastic audience for all it was worth.

We continued on our way next day, journeying along a very attractive canal and meeting the occasional big boat, but nothing that caused me any problems.

No matter how much you enjoy company, a boat is a confined space, so it was a relief when Colin, Helen and George decided to leave me with the dog and go for a walk into Nemours. As we moored up before the lock, Colin and I had a heated debate about the wisdom of mooring on a water point so near the lock. As usual, Mr Know It All won the argument, and we moored English style, using pins. On my own in the boat, I decided to have a shower; I did not have to close the door, but could spread myself about. I had just got mid-shower when I heard a mighty bump. What the hell's that? I thought, and looked through the shower porthole just in time to see the front mooring pin pull out of the ground and be dragged along by the freed rope until – *plop!* into the canal. I quote from a letter I sent after the event:

. . . I dashed out to see the cause of the bump, pausing only to half put my knickers on. As I was wet through I had difficulty pulling them up. Just as I reached the wheelhouse I saw the back mooring pin gracefully fall into the canal. I could also see the back of a large péniche as he disappeared behind the closing lock gates. I could not remember the words for help, so yelled "Assistez moi" at the same time as desperately clanging the big bell on top of the boat. No one took any notice. Meanwhile, the back end was drifting out and it seemed after we had crushed several moored plastic boats we would turn and head back to Briare. It seems ridiculous, but at the time I really feared I would drift back to Briare and no one would know where I was; they would see the wreckage and assume all was lost. Oh, I am cursed with an overactive imagination! I realised I was going to have to help myself, and I remembered that Colin had once said that in order to steer a boat you had to have engine power. The information had been given after we had cruised on the Chesterfield with Helen and George in our old boat. The boat had broken down and Helen and I in searing heat had pulled the thing a mile to the moorings with George "steering" and singing "Just One Cornetto". Colin had gone on the bike to fetch the car and when we met at the moorings I casually dropped the news that Helen and I had done the all the work. Needless to say we made George pay; his excuses that he thought he was steering by occasionally wielding the pole as a punt were disregarded as we harangued him at every opportunity.
Armed with this bit of prior knowledge, I started the engine and managed to make the boat turn, narrowly missing the parked

plastic boats. The next problem was how to stop. As I looked around a jogger hove into view; he was loping along on thin spindly legs covered in short satin red shorts.

"Assistez moi – grabbe ze rope!" I shouted, waving the rope about. The jogger continued without a pause. Stupid bloody French, can't they understand anything, I thought, and did what all the English do with stupid foreigners: I shouted louder and slower. "Assistez...moi...grabbe...ze...rope!" I also waved the rope frantically.

Success! The jogger stopped and after a moments' hesitation he indicated I could throw the rope. Another hesitation and he fastened it to the road roller parked behind him. The jogger, his good deed done, made to move off, but I needed him to continue. "Moment: mon derrière," I yelled, dashing to the back down the gangway. The jogger, now in the swing of things, understood immediately. I threw the rope and his thin legs, showing surprising strength, pulled me to the bank. As the boat reached the bank I bent to pick up the rope. I was going to say that I could manage now, but as I bent down my naked boobs came into view.

I looked up in horror. I could see by jogger's face he knew I had forgotten my lack of clothes and he was worried about what I thought he might do. I decided in a flash to act normal. "Merci beaucoup, Monsieur."

"Bon soir, Madame," he graciously responded.

"Bon soir," I replied as he resumed his jogging. I tied the boat to the ring on the water point as Mr Know It All had desired.

When I recounted my experiences, the Captain's immediate response was, "Do you remember at which point the pins went in the canal? Maybe I can fish them out." As usual, not one word of sympathy.

Colin spent the next two hours fishing with the magnet with 50 per cent success. Helen, more intuitive and caring, got the wine out.

Helen and George left us after a glorious few days in the sun at Moret-sur-Loing, and we continued down the Seine. We were now with the really big boys, blocks of flats on the water and huge push-tows full of sand were passing us. I had read that the drivers of the big boats could not see obstacles for five hundred feet in front of them, and I became obsessed with making sure we were seen. My French requests for passage through the locks were responded to by torrents of words. I hadn't a clue what they were saying, so we had to rely on the lights and common sense. But common sense was to cause us to get a telling off big style.

We were waiting along the quay when the lights changed to green. "We're off, and I am going to give that big boat coming out of the lock more room," said Colin as he headed off mid-river. I was at the front, and as the *péniche* passed us on our right an obviously angry driver mimed throat-cutting and shouted, "Merde!" I dashed back to the wheelhouse. Colin appeared unconcerned; he was too busy coping with the *péniche*'s wash and negotiating us into the lock.

As we passed the entrance, the lock man descended from his eyrie, crossing himself. After an exchange of pidgin French I learned that we should have stayed where we were on the quayside: the *péniches* are so large that they exit from locks at an angle and pass on the left. I was in an absolute panic, while Colin kept saying he had used his common sense. In a rage, I said, "Well, from now on *stop* using common sense."

So now we were totally reliant on the lights. Twice we set off on the green light, and it was only when I looked up from winding the front rope that I saw the green light was meant for a *péniche* speeding up behind and not us. As if we hadn't enough problems, we had to do an emergency stop. In another letter I wrote:

Approaching Melun the weather changed: the skies became very dark and the rain came down in buckets. Our windscreen wipers could not cope. Péniches were coming up behind us at amazing speeds. I was absolutely petrified and the dog was shaking in every hair. We saw a large building with steps coming down to the water's edge. On the lower steps were some bollards. We thanked god for deliverance and decided to moor up. The minute we stopped, me and the dog were off the boat and onto the safety of very wet concrete. Then came a clap of thunder and Bob was back on the boat in a flash, scrabbling to get in the wardrobe. I followed and settled her down between the beds, covered in a quilt as she felt safer in the dark. As I settled her, there was the biggest bang I have ever heard, followed by screams and Colin shouting for me to come and have a look. The sight that greeted me was amazing: a huge plane tree at least eight feet across the trunk had been struck by lightning. Colin, who had witnessed the strike, said the tree had risen in the air and fallen straight back down within the width of its canopy. The trunk was in shards no longer than four feet. Colin had been witness to the amazing power of nature and I thought that some good spirit was looking after us.

It was late when we arrived in Paris after the storm. We were the last boat admitted to the Arsenal: once more our Good Spirit was looking after us, I felt: another night moored on the Seine would have been too much for me and Bob.

The next morning we explored our new and very welcome resting place. The Port de l'Arsenal is a large rectangle of water and along the side we moored there was a grassy area with shrubs and flowerbeds. The far side was a smaller paved walkway. The long sides of the port are enclosed by a high wall. At one of the shorter ends is the lock to the Seine; at the other, the entrance to the canal system of Paris.

We were moored near the Bastille monument in the centre of Paris, with all facilities for 25 euros a night. Things were definitely looking up. In the guidebook, I read a brief history of the Port de l'Arsenal. In the fifteenth century, the Arsenal was a dead arm of the Seine noted for its frog population. The modern usage of the port dates from when, as an adjunct to Napoleon's plans for developing a clean water system for Paris, Pierre Simon Girard was asked to construct a port in the Arsenal basin. The work was completed after the fall of Napoleon in 1815. Between 1920 and 1973, H.P.L.M., a major inland waterway company, set up shops in the Arsenal Basin. In 1973 the H.P.L.M. buildings were sold to Sani Central Co. The company kept its sanitary ceramic objects, leading to its nickname, the "bidet port". In 1983 the City of Paris and industry decided to join together to build a true yachting port. The port is now managed by the Port de Plaisance de Paris Arsenal.

We spent a week in the Arsenal before returning home, leaving Koopman to act as a B&B for various family members. We were so happy to be there. I quote from a letter home:

The weather here in the Arsenal Paris is fantastic, and we find the French visitors to the boats so laid-back and friendly that we have not bothered to do any of the touristy things that people expect of visitors to capital cities. The side we are moored on seems to be part of the gay promenade. The first weekend here was the Gay Pride Parade: men in full Shirley Bassey-sequinned frocks with bushy beards sat on the grass enjoying the sun. Local Parisiennes bring picnics, stop by, and have a chat with us in pidgin English we reply in pidgin French. The Port is full of promenaders and picnickers until 11 p.m. when everyone goes home and the port is quiet. As usual Bob has got her ports of call, especially a lady who lives in the port and who has several cats and insists on giving Bob treats. One of her white cats comes to call on us every day.

As expected, all our "tenants" thoroughly enjoyed their time on the boat, Peter having planned the holiday with three friends like a military campaign.

While we were at home there was a horrendous terrorist attack in London, which saddened and frightened me. Bob had always been very frightened of tunnels and subways, so another consideration when we were planning cruises was to avoid returning to base via the metro or underground. Our last few days in Paris were spent with our son Iain and his family *en route* to Disneyland. Iain and two of our grandchildren had stayed on the boat in the early days, and as a result were quite impressed with our restoration so far. A highlight of their stay was a trip on the bus to see Paris by night, a trip made extra special by a wonderful bus driver. Colin has to be very interested in what he is doing to forget the pain of walking; car boots are interesting, cities are not, so he was coming with us under pressure. At the end of the port there was a bus, and we thought our luck was in. In pidgin French we told the driver we wanted to go on the city tour. The driver told us where to buy the tickets and catch the right bus. It was miles away, and we retreated to discuss whether Colin could manage the walk. The bus driver waved me forward and told me to get the others on the bus: he would take us to the terminus as he was going that way. From disappointment to happiness in five minutes was fantastic.

En route, the driver told me he would be the driver on our excursion. When we got to the ticket station we disembarked from the bus and were about to head for the long queue when the driver put his hand on my shoulder.

"Arretez," he said, and walked off, to return shortly with tickets for all of us. I paid him, and he showed us where we could sit and wait for the bus to open its doors.

We were first on the bus and therefore on top in the front seat, a fantastic viewing place. We were in the middle of the trip in the busiest part of Paris when Lucy decided she was desperate for a wee. Expecting a Gallic shrug, we went downstairs to tell our friend the driver, who said, "Ah. Moment," and stopped the bus outside a very elegant restaurant. Lucy and I shot in, Lucy used the toilet, and we dashed out, shouting, "Merci beaucoup," over our shoulders.

At the end of a sparkling journey we looked around for a taxi or inspiration. There was a call from the driver of the bus, indicating we should get back on. He then told me that he would have to put the lights out but he would take us back to the Port de l'Arsenal.

It was a happy band that sat in the bus as we journeyed through a brightly lit Paris back to the boat. Iain declared that the lights of Paris were very much second best to the kindness of the driver, a sentiment we all shared. The next day he, Julie and the kids departed for the fairytale land of Disney, and we embarked on the unpredictable nightmare of the Canals du Nord, Saint-Quentin and the Grand Gabarit. First, though, there was a trip back to Trézée via the Seine, to pick up the "Surrey with a fringe on top".

The canopy was all we expected: the supplier was an artist and a perfectionist, and it was only after many adjustments that we finally turned round to head back north along the canals Briare and Loing, and then along a stretch of the Seine, turning before Paris onto the Marne. It was on the Briare that I had another accident. I quote from a letter I sent to my friends:

One lovely day, I stepped off the boat straight into the canal. I was up to my neck in the water, which was so warm it felt like a bath. At the time we were travelling in convoy and were the last to moor. Immediately three Frenchmen leapt into action. I am up to my neck in water; three feet above me is a metal bar four inches square, and then a steep bank. I am wet through and thirteen stone. All three men ran down the bank and pulled my hands off the metal bar; they then began pulling and shouting encouragement to me. I began to rise in the water, but only as far as my chest on the metal bar. I was screaming with pain and could not remember the French for stop. My rescuers thought I was panicking because I was drowning, and redoubled their efforts. My screaming reached epic proportions as I shouted in English, "Stop! Stop!"

Eventually one of the men got the message and went to fetch a ladder. I managed to climb up onto the bank with a very painful chest, I suspect a broken rib.

Our troubles continued as we overtook a stationary péniche to go into a lock.

"Bloody hell," I yelled to the Captain, "Look at that monster waiting to come out." We had no way of securing ourselves properly; I managed to get the rope onto the corner of a fence but we were obviously going to get knocked about. And suddenly it was an even worse scenario: another péniche appeared behind us. Péniches get priority, so we would have to wait – but how. I shouted at a passing lady cyclist (I am becoming expert at the "Assistez Moi" scenario). The lady cyclist managed to get the rope further over the post and then Colin shouted at her to catch the

mooring pin in order to hammer it in so we could attach the rope at the back. Colin was in sergeant-major mood, and fumed at her "hopelessness". I shouted at him to shut up, and a marital ensued.

The ropes held on. Just. As we approached the lock I tried to shout our thanks to the lady on the bike. There was not a lot of response: I think she was in shock. An hour later, all is forgotten as we sit down for tea in the local town. Colin has this facility for wiping disasters from his mind – and moving with a clear mind to the next one . . . As a narrow boater, he has great faith in his mooring pins, but I have put my foot down: along with common sense, the pins are now banned. We use bollards from now on. Also we now always have the manual steering at the ready, and spare parts for the toilet. And if our vision is obscured we stop and think. Is there no end to being prepared?

There is a sequel to this story: months later, to my horror, I found that my right boob had gone completely numb. All sorts of weird and dramatic diagnoses went through my mind, but a careful history taken by my GP revealed that while hoovering I had opened up the broken rib and trapped a nerve. I was mightily relieved, and in no time at all was fully recovered.

We had an uneventful journey back on the Seine towards Paris; we knew now where we could moor safely overnight, and I almost enjoyed the trip. We turned right at the "Pagoda", onto the Marne. There were fewer big boats than I had expected, though there were still more than I would have liked, and of course Bob picked up and magnified my fear. What a pathetic pair we made, the dog silently shaking in clouds of hair, and me alternately screaming instructions or berating the Captain for his risk-taking or tardiness in getting out of the way. I tried very hard to master my fear but I shocked Colin when I asserted that I felt I would die on the waterways of France.

After I had made this statement, I began to feel better and we settled down into a boating routine, a highlight being a visit to Reims. At Abbecourt we had a big debate as to which way to go north. To me it seemed a choice between the devil and the deep blue sea: to the left was the Canal du Nord, a very busy waterway; ahead was the Canal Saint-Quentin also a busy canal with the additional hazard of a very long tunnel.

From the *péniche* drivers we learned that our map-book was out of date: the Saint- Quentin was very quiet and we would manage the tunnel easily, as we would be towed through. Colin preferred big boats to being towed through tunnels; I preferred a quieter canal. I won the day, and very pleased we were with our final choice. We hardly saw any big boats and were the only boat to be towed through tunnel. Because we were the only boat we were allowed to keep the engine, even though we were attached by ropes to the towing machine; that meant Colin could steer. Unusually for France, the tunnel was dark, and the towing machine almost filled the place with its lights glowing and the horrendous noise of clanking as it pulled its way along the underwater chain.

We were in there for an hour and our concentration was intense – too intense for any fear to manifest itself. Even Bob lay on my feet and forgot to shake. We were euphoric as we moored in Cambrai; I jumped off the boat to go and find Tam and Di Morrel and let them know what their pupils had achieved; sadly, they were in England at the time.

It was getting late in the year for painting, but we decided to do some anyway and stay a while in a lovely port before heading north towards our winter mooring. It is so easy to become port-bound: in no time at all we had made friends with the boaters and fishermen. As usual, I had set up the table and umbrella, and a constant stream of visitors monitored our painting progress. When

248

it was time for us to leave, a lovely *éclusier* organised the locks so that we were on our own to start with. We now had no choice but to join the big boys on the Canal du Nord.

On the big rivers and commercial waterways in Europe, the difficulty for small boats is finding moorings away from the wash of their big brothers and sisters. Another problem is the increased traffic at certain places, caused by the locking system. On the modern waterways the locks are fewer and the distance between them longer: the later in the day a commercial boat can get through the last lock, the further the distance he can travel in a day. These boats moor in front of the first lock of the next day.

Because we travelled slower, it would often be midday before we encountered commercial traffic. Then there would probably be several, the encounter usually coming just before a lock, where we would have to cope with the wash of several boats entering before us. Until we had further training from Jo, I insisted we wait until the commercials had tied up before going in ourselves. Jo had told us that we needed to tuck in behind them as soon as possible: the *péniche* drivers expected us to do this, as time was money to them.

Our first experience of coping with the wash of the commercials while moored came on the Canal du Nord. We had passed what I called a "bleb" (a small area off the canal where small boats can moor up for the night) and I refused to allow Colin to turn round in the canal, expecting a big boat to appear at any moment and crush us. In the Captain's opinion I was being completely irrational, but he went along with my opinion and we continued.

Too late – we realised the only place to moor now was along an old quay. By the time we were secure it was getting late; boats were still passing, and the time had come to put the navigation lights on. It was then we learned that the mast-light was faulty and all the navigation lights' fuses kept blowing. As each boat passed, the wash hit us, went underneath Koopman's hull, hit the quay wall, and rocked us the other way. The rocking reached epic proportions when several boats passed us in both directions at once. We were also without navigation lights.

I had two bags of tealight candles "in store", so I got them out and spread the contents of one bag around the wheelhouse. I still did not feel safe, so I got the deckchair and sat on the bank with the gibbering dog at my side. By eleven p.m., Colin had had enough and he went to bed; I insisted he keep his false leg on in case he had to make an emergency exit. Even so, I sat until 11.45, wondering how I was going to rescue him in the event of a capsize.

At last there seemed to be no more boats and I risked going to bed myself – but not before lighting the remaining fifty candles. Colin muttered something about "We ought to go to bed with the fire extinguishers". We were underway at first light, not a big boat in sight. It was a lovely misty morning and we had a serene morning's cruise.

From that day on, we made sure we had agreed on the night's mooring before we began the day's cruising; even so, finding safe moorings on the commercial system remained a problem. I likened our being on the commercial waterways to being a milk float on the M25: we were treated with consideration by the commercials, but they had timetables to keep to. The locks are incredibly big, and on the odd occasion we were the only boat in there; I should have been jumping about with glee, but then the global warming stuff would kick in and I would feel guilty about all the water being wasted in moving a pleasure boat from A to B.

Eventually we reached our winter moorings at Arques, a very different place from Jo's boatyard. It was almost clinical in its tidiness, but a friendly base nonetheless.

Chapter 6

Goodbye to a very dear friend

I was glad to get home and back to normal. I had a new job with some great people who had a lot to put up with in those first few weeks, as I talked the fear out of my system. Before we had left Jo's we had noticed that Bob's breath smelled awful and we diagnosed a bad tooth. The result of a visit to the vet on our return was a total shock: Bob had chronic renal failure, and apart from a special diet there was nothing that could be done. When we asked the vet about the future he said we would know when it was time for Bob to leave us.

Even as I write these words five years later, my heart aches. Bob was my mirror: many of her neuroses were mine; we comforted each other, sat on the roof of the saloon at the front of the boat; the feel of her fur soothed and comforted me. Bob was very sociable; in no time at all she would make new friends for us; and she had a memory like an elephant: years later, she would always investigate any blue boat, looking for June of Slocomotion fame.

We once forgot her and set off down the M1 for France leaving her locked in the house. We had gone a couple of junctions before we realised. Thereafter, as soon as Colin began packing the car, usually a couple of days before departure, Bob would take up residence in there, only leaving to answer the call of nature. She was not going to be left behind again.

It was Helen who was her particular favourite and I swear she had conversations with her – no doubt telling her about all the terrible adventures she was having. Bob was such a gentle dog that when I worked with the elderly I would take her to work with me. She would extend her paw and then put her head on the knee of a patient in the advanced stages of dementia; they always responded with a smile and a pat.

But gradually Bob got weaker. Walks now consisted of once around the churchyard. After Christmas we noticed her knees buckling as she crossed over the step. The time had come.

The night before the visit to the vet I lay on the floor with my face in her fur and told her I loved her. The next day she lay in my arms; her great head went down on her paws, and she fell asleep for the last time. It was a dignified end to a life of mutual devotion.

We were sad but not devastated. Bob's last weeks had been managed well and she died at the right time. As Colin said, "Sometimes it's better to be a dog."

BOOK FIVE – BELGIUM AND HOLLAND

Chapter 1

Koopman nearly goes home

Over the winter I tried not to think of the time when we would have to return to the boat. The panic I felt when we were around the commercial boats was out of all proportion and, for some reason, I believed that we would be alright once we were out of France and the routes to Calais and Dunkirk. Our friend George took this on board and offered to travel with Colin from our winter mooring at Arques, along the canal behind Calais, Dunkirk and Ostend to Brugge. I was to follow in the car. As it happened, the pair of them hardly saw a commercial boat, and the biggest problem was with me and the car.

The first Port de Plaisance was Watten. All was going well: I could see the canal and the boat as they went under a bridge and . . . disappeared. I waited in the car on the other side . . . No boat. I did a three point turn and went back to the entrance of the tunnel, but still nothing. By now my imagination was in overdrive: where were they? Again I turned round and drove a couple of miles further than before. Still no boat. Yet another three point turn, and back to the entrance.

By now I was convinced they had sunk without trace under the bridge. I needed help fast. Again I reversed, and this time I heard a loud bang.

I stopped dead and got out of the car. Oh, God, I thought. Trust me. Now I'm not only a widow but the bloody car is impaled on a gatepost.

I jumped back in the car and headed off (on the left-hand

side of the road) to look for the gendarmes. As I went up the bridge I glanced to my left; and I could swear I saw George sitting on the back of our boat, reading. I got to the other side of the bridge and turned yet again back over the bridge. I turned right, and then sharp left down a lane, and there they were. They were both sitting in chairs on the back deck supping tea.

I was furious. "Where the hell have you been? I've looked everywhere. I thought you had sunk . . . and I have crashed the car!"

With that I burst into tears, although I am not sure whether it was out of relief that I was not a widow or anger that I wasn't, because they were unimpressed by my outburst.

"Why would we sink?" asked Colin.

"Well, I saw you go under the bridge but I never saw you come out."

"Oh, there are two bridges close together and the turn is in the middle," explained George.

From the road I could not see the canal approach to the port; in fact I couldn't see the port at all. By this time we had realised how humorous the situation was and had a good laugh over another cup of tea. No mention was made of the huge dent in the back of the car.

The rest of the trip to Brugge was uneventful: Colin and George met a few cargo boats and had to wait for the swing bridges, but they enjoyed the trip to the Coupure. Because of the one-way system, I had a more difficult time, but eventually we were safely moored in the small port in the centre of Brugge. I immediately fell in love with the city and the port. Brugge is known as the Venice of the North; the city is criss-crossed with small canals now used for tourist traffic only. Around the outside of the old city is the large commercial canal known as the Gent–Zeebrugge canal. We came off this canal under a pedestrian lift bridge into the port of the old canal system. The old city canal system is now only used for small tourist boats; the towpath is mostly cobbled and lined by steep-roofed three-storey terraced brick houses of an infinite number of designs. There are enticing restaurants everywhere with umbrellas and tables outside. All motorised vehicles go slowly and their tyres make a lot of noise as they travel over the cobbles, so it is easy to avoid them. The biggest danger to pedestrians in Brugge is the bicycle, of which there are hundreds. The cycles are mainly of a comfortable old-fashioned large-wheeled design; you can sit up and converse as you travel along – and travel they do, often faster than the cars and usually in pairs. Colin and I have two similar bikes, so we were at home immediately. Everywhere else we have ever been on bikes we have felt very much second-class citizens but here we were kings. Pedestrians and vehicles had to give way to *us*.

The Coupure is just off the main canal, and the boats were affected by the wash from passing commercial traffic. For me it was great to be able to see the big boats passing the end of the port and to feel their wash and know I was safe.

In no time at all, other residents of the port had made themselves known to us and we spent a pleasant evening with a couple who had bought a boat from just down the road from us on the South Yorkshire Navigation Canal.

George stayed a couple more days with us and then we took him to Amsterdam to catch the plane home, taking the opportunity while we were there to find our next winter mooring in the city. We were very excited about the prospect of staying in Amsterdam and envisaged actually living on the boat for the winter. A new air route to Amsterdam had started up from Robin Hood airport, six miles down the road from where we lived and, now that we no longer had Bob, we envisaged going home for holidays more often but having a longer cruising season.

After George had left us we decided to get to grips with the toilet situation. A malfunctioning toilet had been an issue ever since we bought the boat, and I think the reason Helen had not come with George this time was her concern there would be another "bucket and chuck it" situation. I have since found out that we are not the only ones to have problems with a toilet. Canal boat toilets have either a manual or electric flush, and both systems are extremely temperamental. Discharge is either into a container or tank, or, on the Continent, directly into the canal (which is now no longer legal). When we first boated in France there were only a few sanitary pump-out stations servicing a very large canal area. All the stations we had seen were there purely for effect, as they were not connected to either a sewer or to electricity.

Our toilet was of the manual flush variety, and very few of our visitors understood how delicate an instrument the pump was. A visit to a marina in Ostend resulted not only in another new toilet, but a spare pump, just in case. We had a visit from our son Iain and his family, who thoroughly enjoyed cycling round the city on hired bikes; but by the time they left us Colin had all the jobs done and was anxious to be off. After consultations with various other boaters, we had decided to journey to Holland via the Westerschelde, Oosterschelde, Volkerak and the Dordrecht Kil. We had no idea what this journey would be like; all we knew was that we would need charts and I had it in my head that crossing the Schelde would be something like travelling on the Trent, which I had really enjoyed. We went to Rotterdam and spent a fortune on maps and charts and on Sunday 4th June, along with five other boats, we emerged from our lovely Coupure onto the main canal, on our way to Amsterdam to celebrate Koopman's centenary.

We thought we were well prepared. We had spoken to people in the know, who said our boat should cope with the journey fine as long as we travelled when the wind was under four on the Beaufort scale. The Beaufort scale measures wind speed, and, in layman's terms, four is a breeze. We had maps aplenty and advice from experienced boaters when to deviate from the route, as we were able to sail in much shallower water than the commercials and therefore able to get out of their way.

What we were *not* prepared for was the ability of my imagination to exaggerate a scary moment into a near-death experience. Nor had we realised that many of the boaters we spoke to were taking Colin's experience into account and not the shape of the boat – and we neglected to take into account the "roll effect". The boat would roll nearly horizontal; I would be looking at the roof of the wheelhouse before it stopped and rolled equally as far the other way. (A few weeks later, a lovely Dutchman travelling in choppy water in front of us declared to Colin, "Your boat is a swan: it is designed to roll. It has been rolling for a hundred years without sinking." But by then my nerves were beyond redemption.) In the following letter, the events I describe happened as I wrote; but, as before, my interpretation of them is influenced by my imagination. Apparently, at no time were we really in serious danger, but at the time we believed we were.

We left the Coupure at 10 a.m. in a convoy of five. It was great to be part of a fleet because we did not have to wait for the bridge-keeper to acknowledge our presence. As the boats approached the bridge, it simply went up. The morning rush-hour was over but there were enough cyclists waiting at the bridges and observing our progress for us to feel very important. I know now how Francis Chichester felt when the little boats escorted him into harbour after his epic voyage around the world. We turned left before Gent onto the canal ringway, went through one lock and moored up for the night at the Royal Belgian Yacht Club. We had covered 47.5kms in 5 hours: a good time. Despite a huge ferryboat doing a sharp three-point turn in front of us to get into the dock, completely blocking our way and necessitating some dancing about, we were in good spirits and spent the evening planning how to decorate the boat when we got to Amsterdam. The following day we travelled 25km to Turneuzen, passing loads of big boats. With each passing my confidence grew, despite the maniacal rocking of the boat. After lunch we got on the bikes to go and have a look at the water. I could not believe how beautiful the view before us was. The water was slate-grey and still as glass. There were myriads of small yachts tacking in the slight breeze, tiny dots in the distance. There were no commercial boats on the misty horizon. We could not believe our luck: we were going to sail on that in our beautiful boat with the surrey on top.

I will take a break from the letters here because I think it is time for a few facts about the water we were about to cross:

The headwaters of the Schelde are in the Aisne department of France. The river flows north through Cambrai and Valenciennes and enters Belgium near Tournai. After being joined by the River Lys near Gent, it turns east. Near Antwerp, the second largest port in Europe, the river turns west into the Netherlands and comes out in the North Sea. Along its route the river's name changes from the Escaut to the Schelde. (It took me a while to adjust to the name changes of rivers across Europe; it was a long time before I realised the Rhine became the Maas in the Netherlands).

In total, the river is 217 miles long. The basin is nearly eight and half square miles. The river is navigable from its mouth to

Cambrai. Originally there were two branches, but in the nineteenth century the river was cut off from its eastern/northern branch by a dyke that connects Zuid-Beveland with the mainland in the region of North Brabant. The river connects with the basins of the Rhine, Meuse, Seine and the major industrial areas of France and Belgium. It is one of the major waterways of Europe.

I should have read up on the river before we set off: I would then have been able to make a more realistic assessment of the problems we would face. But being used to the Trent, we were more worried about getting the wind, tide and water depth right. The name of the Schelde in Old English means shallow, and the changing depth of its waters means that the charts have to be renewed frequently and depth-soundings constantly taken. (I now realise its shallowness means that the big commercial boats have little room for manoeuvre; hence the very good advice from the lock-keeper, to take a different route from the big boys into shallower and calmer waters.) But back to the circular letter:

The Westerschelde is the western exit of the river Schelde into the North Sea. As a result, it has a huge tidal change. The next morning we checked the wind scale: it was between two and three: perfect. Because of the tide, we asked the lock man what the best time to set off in the morning was; he also advised us to turn off the marked route at a buoy before the indicated turning. The water would be too shallow for the commercials but deep enough for us.

At 8 a.m. on a lovely, slightly misty morning, we set off onto a virtually deserted Westerschelde. Wearing the lifejackets seemed a bit over-the-top and we relaxed and enjoyed the journey. It was so easy that we began to debate whether it was worth following the lock-keeper's advice and veer off the marked route. We were bent over the charts in concentration when suddenly I was on the floor with the bike on top of me, quickly followed by the table, and finally Colin. From my vantage point on the floor, looking at the wheelhouse ceiling, it seemed the boat was about to tip over any minute. The rocking was different to how it had been with Mr Bean: with that boat, I anticipated a head-first death; here, I was convinced I was going to roll into the deep.

we need to make a turn soon keep a lookout ahead for the marker buoy

Colin got to his feet long before me. I lay there in shock, waiting for the inevitable inrush of water. Colin had got up in time to see the rear of the ship that had overtaken us, a tanker from Bahrain. Lying at Colin's feet and looking up, I could see him wrestling with the violently swinging wheel.

"Have you got control"? I said.

"No, but trying to steer the wheel makes me feel better," was his stupid reply.

There was no decision to be made. If we were to survive, we had to turn off the main route. And immediately we turned, we were back to beauty and peace, as the big boats passed us ever farther away. But we were still in a state of high alert as we entered the lock at Hansweert. We stopped at the first yachthaven and tied up for the day.

are you in control?
NO   but it makes me feel better
will we turn over?
probably

That evening, we spent a very convivial time with the Dutch laughing at our adventure; it all seemed quite surreal. In the safety of the clubhouse, mellow from the wine and the company, I did wonder if my memory was a bit like my father's memories of the first war: surreal. How difficult, when in safety, to make sense of terror, even if only a few hours before.

Before going to bed we spent the rest of the daylight hours redistributing stuff to improve the stability of the boat. The generator was taken off the prow and put in the engine room, the table in the wheelhouse went on the lower back deck, and the huge

261

toolbox went in the front bedroom. After all that effort on top of a few beers, I had a good night's sleep and forgot about big boats until the middle of the next day, when the terror returned with a vengeance. The Oosterschelde is an enclosed part of the estuary, an area famous for its oyster beds. We, in our innocence, thought that, as the tide was minimal and the wind a gentle breeze, we were in for an enjoyable sail. Our new friends in the clubhouse thought it would be better for us if we took the longer route around Tholen; that way we would be out of reach of the big boats, as they tended to use the canal Schelde-Rijjnverbinding, which reduced the sea mileage to the Rhine. We set off very early around 7 a.m. The morning held the promise of a hot day: the water was calm, even glacial in appearance, the sky was blue, with no sun yet to disperse the slight mist. As we emerged from the small Kanaal door Zuid-Beveland, which is the canal connection between the two mouths, I felt that I had never been so moved in my life. As a true Yorkshire woman, I think there is no beauty as great as the view from the top of Malham Cove over Wensleydale, but this sea with its misty humps of land in the distance rivalled anything I had seen before. For two hours we sailed alone on this beautiful sea until we turned north and saw the first of the dreaded "slugs".

It was 11 a.m. precisely, when we sighted the first "slug". (I think that instead of the number thirteen being almost abolished, the number eleven should definitely be: just think of all the dreadful things that have happened at 11 a.m.!) Well, Colin knew how to handle the wash of a boat passing us from the front: he turned the boat at right-angles and faced the bow wave. Our friends in the clubhouse had advised us to turn and face boats approaching from behind and, as before, turn into the bow wave. By 1 p.m. we were spending more time going the opposite way to what we wanted, and I was in a place beyond fear, bracing myself against the boat as we frantically rocked from side to side. To our right, in the few moments of calm we were granted, we could see small work-boats sailing between poles that had been placed in a grid.

"I bet they're doing depth soundings," said Colin, "I think we will be better sailing the wrong side of the buoys."

Sometimes Colin has brilliant ideas, and for a while we were safe and were able to sail in the right direction. Then came the point when we had to turn right again, coming to the T-junction with the short-cut. Oh dear! There were slugs to our right, coming out of the canal to turn right directly in front of us. There were slugs overtaking us from behind and slugs coming towards us; we had no idea which direction they would take. All the ships we could see seemed to be travelling at a 100 miles an hour. We had lost the depth-sounding grid and were in the middle of this maelstrom.

It was then that I noticed a small exit off the main body of water.

"Get down there!" I shouted.

"Why?" said Colin in his slow way.

"For once, Colin, do as you are told. Go! Go!"

We turned into the exit and ground to a halt in the mud of a seemingly abandoned ditch. As I looked round I saw three ships passing. We were safe, but it seemed like we were in the middle of a bog. African Queen sprang to mind.

"We can't stop here, just look at it: no one will ever find us and we can't get off the boat," said Colin.

"Well, we'll get off the mud. Turn round and peep out; if there is nothing coming we will make a dash for it."

I compromised, preferring to be marooned to being drowned. After much sweat polling the boat, we were off the mud. We turned round and I peeped out of the exit until we felt it was safe to make a quick exit. The lock that changes the water from sea *to canal was huge, but – wonders of wonders – we were the only boat in the lock, and in the late afternoon sunshine we entered the port of Dintelsas.*

The port was huge, and it took some time to pass the commercial moorings and get to where the leisure boats were moored at the back. We booked for three nights and again spent a very convivial night in the pub. After a heated debate, several couples came out to look at the boat. The men were saying they felt we should continue, while the women argued that no way would they travel on such a small boat . . .

The following two days were spent asking advice from everyone – i.e. trying to avoid a decision that had in fact already been made in our subconscious minds. The next part of our journey was through the very aptly named Dordrecht Kil. Kil means something different in Dutch, but I was convinced we would indeed be killed. We had heard the canal was narrow, with concrete sides, so that, in addition to the wash of passing boats, there would be the problem of "rebound" as the water returned from the walls. Thus, a truly fairground-style ride was in prospect. On a positive note I had reasoned that there was maybe a "window of opportunity" if we travelled on a Sunday. In a religious country like Holland, Sunday is a day of rest and still largely observed as such. Also, Holland was playing in the World Cup, and so, surely, I thought, there would be no big boats on the move that day. But I could find no one who would agree with me, although I was later to discover that I had been right: not one boat sailed on the Dordrecht Kil that Sunday afternoon.

Not willing to take the risk, though, we decided that we were going home on a lorry.

Chapter 2

Running for home

It is a good job that all the Dutch we met spoke English really well and, as long as there was no chance of you scratching their boats, were really kind and helpful. Then again, if there was a prospect of your causing even the slightest damage to their pride and joy they underwent a complete character change and could rival Hannibal in their ferociousness. I have even seen tanker captains dusting their boats. Despite their prowess at our language, certain words could sometimes be taken differently by a Dutchman, and it was because we attached a different meaning to the word "small canal" that our next adventure happened.

On the third day at Dintelsas we both agreed we were taking the boat to a broker on a lorry to sell him. There appeared to be plenty of cranes about; we just needed help in organising the lorry; so off we went to the Yachthaven master's office to ask for assistance. The lady in the office was rightly astonished as, before we had even begun our tale, I burst into unstoppable sobs. It was Colin, therefore, over the noise of my snuffling and grunting, who had to tell our sorry tale and ask for assistance in finding a lorry and a crane.

"Why don't you take the small canal at the back? You can get to Amsterdam that way," the young lady said

The comment was like a dash of cold water on my face. Suddenly, I hadn't the breath to sob anymore: there was a way out, all was not lost, Koopman would get to Amsterdam.

We decided to stay at Dintelsas for a few more days to explore the country, shift the stuff we had moved back again, and generally rest and recover. Colin's idea of rest and recreation is designing, sawing and hammering, and in no time he had cadged some wood and borrowed a jig saw off a very helpful German. DIY-Man began building a floor and shelves alongside the engine: so much easier at night to lay alongside and whisper sweet nothings to it. The German seemed a kind man who excused Colin when, despite my dire warnings, he had 'mentioned the war'.

It was also pleasant to get the bikes out and bowl along the flat country lanes. On one expedition we visited a 'bring and buy' at a church, and it was here that we bought an engraved tile in a frame engraved "De Koopman". The tile showed a merchant doing his accounts at a high desk while his customers waited; we bought the tile for four euros, a gift for our own stout-hearted but mercurial Koopman.

A week later we set off on the next part of our voyage.

With high hopes we steamed out of the back of the port; the weather was 30 degrees Celsius and we were glad to be underway at last. After two hours we moored up at Roosendaal for tea, showers and the usual chat with the engine. The weather was cooler, we had seen no big boats and we were content.

Contentment reigned for the next day as well – and then our luck ran out. After a two-hour wait in humid conditions for a broken railway bridge to be repaired, we tried to moor at Breda. The moorings were so awful, we decided to move on to the next moorings at Oosterhout. But somehow we missed the moorings and went through a lock onto the Julianakanaal.

Big mistake. Without realising it, we were in big-boat country again. And it seemed as though they were passing in droves. Unbeknown to us at the time, we had joined one of the canals that connected all the big shipping lanes in Holland. The only consolation was that the boats were not coming from the side, as on the Oosterschelde. No sooner had we stopped rocking from the wash of one boat, than we started again from another. The weather was also deteriorating, the clouds being almost black.

Suddenly, there appeared some stanchions to the right, and after a short debate we decided to moor to them. Stanchions are really for the big boats; pleasure boats are not supposed to moor to them, but we reasoned that if a big boat wanted to moor we would move and ask to moor alongside that boat. But mooring to a stanchion is difficult for a boat our size, as the mooring post and cleats are positioned for the bigger boats. Hence we were unable to make ourselves secure front and back: it was one or the other. And in order to get off the boat we would have to climb up a vertical ladder to the platform and gangway.

For once we were glad to be without Bob. We tried our best to knit ourselves securely to the posts using the long rope to tie us the length of the boat, secured by a cleat at both ends, while the front and back were attached individually with shorter ropes. For the entire time we were we doing the fixing big boats were passing by, and their wash was causing us to bang into the stanchions and then float out again. The noise reminded me of a fast-approaching machine gun, front, middle, back: bang, bang, bang. I looked at the rocking roof of the wheelhouse and it seemed that only the ropes were stopping us from rolling right over.

But it was about to get worse.

I have never in England experienced the violence of storms such as the ones we experienced on the Continent, always preceded by a small hurricane. The hurricane came from behind, down the canal, the wind getting under the Surrey with the Fringe on Top and almost, it seemed to me, lifting the boat.

"Come on, we will have to put extra straps on!" the Captain ordered. So out we went in the sheeting rain and howling wind, trying to balance on the narrow side of the dementedly rocking boat while throwing "bungee bands" over the Surrey.

Having completed the task, I spotted a woman on the bank with an umbrella, walking a small dog. The woman was trying to shout some pleasantry to me, so I forced a friendly gesture. I had no chance of hearing what she was saying; in any case, I hated her with a hate that was as big as my body. How dare she? I thought, walk her bloody dog in the rain as though it was nothing when I am having a near-death (I hope) experience?

Around midnight the storm subsided; the boats went to bed and calm descended. I learned later that there was a big tanker base nearby and the boats were engaged in short but frequent fuel and gas delivery runs. The next morning I had a more civilised shouted conversation with the very pleasant dog walker.

The entrance to our next stop was not auspicious. The area looked abandoned, vegetation taking over in parts, and the banks crumbling in other parts. At the back there was an old bridge and we were debating whether to attempt to moor when the rain came down in sheets.

"I don't want stop here, it's derelict," I shouted, "and there is no way I can get off."

The Captain barked, "Jump *now*!"

I jumped – straight into a crumbling bit disguised by nettles.

I was now stung and wet through, and full of hatred for the world; there was no way I could get back on the boat – and did I care? No. I would get a train home. The bloody Captain could stuff his boat. Just then, I noticed a man on a bike. He seemed to be opening the bridge. It is surprising, the power of the mind. I leapt six foot back on to the boat and we moved towards the bridge.

What a surprise awaited us: the port was large, with few boats; and it was surrounded by flats and shops. Excitedly, we moored opposite a bar with outside seating. There were baskets of flowers on the lamp-posts, and all in all it was a very attractive place. At the moment of mooring, the clouds parted and the sun came out.

We were out pottering with the flowers that grew in the window-boxes on top of the boat when a slight man with a beard came along on a very old, sit-up-and-beg-type bike. He greeted us in perfect English as he got off his bike, taking off his cycle clips. He had stopped to admire Koopman who was looking very handsome, the flowers having survived the storm without any ill effects. We explained as much of Koopman's history as we knew; we also took the opportunity for some post-traumatic stress offloading.

The man told us he was a journalist from the *Brabant News*, in search of a story. And boy, had we given him one! As he listened, he translated our papers and told us about some of the cargoes of milk, cheese and calves that Koopman had carried from the farms around Amsterdam to the market in the city. He asked if he could come back with a photographer and we readily agreed. Later, the reporter returned on his old bike with a very modern young lady photographer who arrived in her car. They were fascinated to hear we had crossed the mighty Westerschelde with tomatoes growing in tubs on the prow.

Colin wanted a stern "master mariner"-like picture of himself holding the wheel while peering knowledgeably towards the horizon. But our interviewers had other ideas: the photograph that finally appeared in the paper was of a grey-haired couple in a pair of silly hats, sitting on the ship's rail – and yes, you've guessed it: admiring their tomatoes. We did not see a copy of the paper until very late in the day, but became aware of being the centre of a tourist phenomenon when I slipped out in my pyjamas before breakfast to water the flowers and tomatoes.

A few days later we were inundated with very helpful Dutch people bearing maps, all intent on making sure that brave Koopman reached his birthplace. A very old gentleman who came and told us his father had worked on one of the other boats in the Koopman fleet (sixteen in all) was able to confirm that the translations of our papers were correct. For all of us it was a very emotional moment: he had not seen a similar boat for years. The journalist also called to translate his article for us, which, far from being *factual*, had us down as typical English eccentrics, brave but foolish – and of course gardening enthusiasts.

The weather had turned very hot, but we were lucky we were moored under a tree and the pub opposite sold sixty-five different kinds of beer. When it was cool we did the painting, which seemed never ending; when it was hot we sat outside the pub, working our way through a variety of beers. At the weekend we went on our bikes to a giant Caribbean festival – very colourful and noisy. There were four bands, all playing at the same time: a veritable cacophony of sound. What most attracted us was the "takeaway African food": rice, onions, peppers and chicken. We felt the fears of the last weeks fall away.

We went home for a fortnight's holiday. We left the boat on our bikes parked them in safety at the station for twenty euros and caught the train for Amsterdam. At 7.30 a.m. we caught a flight to Robin Hood Airport, Doncaster. We were home and sitting in the garden in the early afternoon. Getting home easily was one plan that had worked spectacularly well.

On our return we found that numerous caring Dutch had watered the flowers, which, in desperation, were about to swim off the roof. The final plan – agreed by too many Dutchmen to be ignored – was to head for 's-Hertogenbosch and make a mad dash over the Maas (Rhine) to the other side, travel a short distance, then turn into the narrower, quieter canals which would take us through very beautiful country along the Vecht to Amsterdam. I had real trouble understanding the maps, which were small, and my brain found it impossible to retain the Dutch place names; but it would be up to me to ensure we did not deviate from the quiet route again.

Along the route towards 's-Hertogenbosch, I became more and more worried. As far as I was concerned, all the so-called quiet canals in Holland linked at some point to a big-boat canal. Also, Koopman was mechanically incapable of anything remotely like "a quick peep to see if all was clear and then a mad dash" across a canal the equivalent of the M25. I had been there before, and I no longer trusted the experts.

Our first stop was Helmond, where we got on the bikes to cycle into town to watch France versus Portugal with the Dutch in a bar. I had the longest night's sleep I had had in a long time (it must have been the beer, which I tended to drink like water!)

Next morning we set off and came to a T-junction on the Zuid-Willemsvaart canal. Turn right and you head towards the Meuse and France; left, the Maas and Holland. Reluctantly, we turned right to spend the night in 's-Hertogenbosch yacht haven. The following is an extract from a letter I sent home:

The harbour was full of very expensive, pristine yachty boats. There were not many people about and we were glad to see a convoy of boats come in off the river at speed. At the back of the convoy by some way came a narrow boat. To me it seemed as though all the boats were glad to be in the safety of the harbour, especially the narrow boat. After some tea we went in search of the narrow boat's captain, who, to our surprise, turned out to be a very chatty middle-aged woman. Sue travelled the European canals on her own, although at this point she had her brother with her; he had been concerned about her safety and had come for a while to offer moral and physical support. From these two I got a more realistic picture of the way ahead.

Like us, Sue had a slow boat and had at times been very frightened, but it seemed to me her powers of recovery were quicker than mine. Sue's brother told us a story of being grounded in the Biesbosch, which is apparently a bit like our fens: a haven for wildlife, or a deserted bog, depending on how you look at things. Just as in <u>African Queen</u>, they had spent a great deal of effort trying to get off the bottom, but to no avail, and were feeling quite desperate when the tide suddenly lifted them off.

After meeting Sue I was even more reluctant to continue being marooned. She could cope with running the gauntlet of the big ships – I couldn't. Leisure boats didn't travel in convoy unless there was a very real danger of not being seen before it was too late.

It was 2 a.m. when the phone rang. I was too late to answer it, having fallen out of bed with shock, and had to ring Peter back.

"Mam! Mam! Ted's dead."

Ted was the kitten Peter had rescued earlier in the year. He was quite a character and regularly sat at the gate awaiting Peter's return from work. Peter was totally besotted with the creature, and although he is now forty years old his distress was like a child's on the phone.

I could hardly get a coherent sentence out of him. I rang Sally, but unfortunately there was no reply, so in desperation I rang our neighbour who eventually rang back to say he had found Peter in the road nursing Ted in a towel and crying.

Peter blamed himself: Ted had got fed up of waiting for his return from the pub and seemed to have gone looking for him. He had been run over. Sally visited Peter the next morning to sort things out and together they buried Ted in her garden.

After the phone call, I lay in the dark, and as well as grieving for our beloved Ted I thought, what the hell are we doing here? We should be at home where we're needed. Well, after forty-eight years of what was, as you know, a very volatile marriage, we do sometimes think alike. In the darkness I said, "Colin?"

"I know," he said. "We'll turn round and head back to France."

And so it was decided. Koopman was willing, but we had had enough. Boating was no longer fun.

"We've never been big on birthdays anyway," I said before going to sleep.

The next morning over breakfast we decided we were definitely selling the boat, and the only place to sell a boat from was Jo's: we needed the comfort of someone we could trust, even though, as I have said before, I want to kill him at times. We now had another destination: Migennes. I know: after all I have said about that bloody yard! Even a hole in the floor-toilet pales into insignificance in the face of the big boats that are waiting at the end of every "small" canal.

It was with relief we said goodbye to Sue, who thought we were making a mistake turning round, though her brother, who had been really frightened in the Biesbosch, thought we were making the right choice. Having turned round, we were crowded into the first lock with several other boats. The lock was very strange: there were stanchions in the middle; I suppose it was designed to take more than one big boat. We were in the middle and, as I have said, the stanchions were not designed for smaller boats to tie up to. As the water began to rise, we began to wobble uncontrollably, banging into the Dutchman's small cruiser to our left.

"Pardon, Monsieur. Je suis désolée,' I said, trying unsuccessfully to fend us off his boat with our boat-hook. I was in a panic: I knew what these Dutchmen were like if you touched their boat.

"It is OK, you are on *vacances*." The man waved at me with calming gestures.

At that moment I knew I had met "The Man".

At the next lock it was their turn to bump into us when their rope snapped in the melee. "It's OK, you are on *vacances*," I laughed.

I encouraged an exchange of information, telling him and his wife of my traumas and of how we were intending to sell the boat.

"Oh! You can't do that!" he replied as he hung onto the new rope. "You have the most beautiful boat. If I could afford it I would buy it. All the Dutch want to buy boats like yours."

"Why don't they?" I asked – quite aggressively.

"Because the English buy them," he said.

I felt chastened. "The Man" told me he was meeting friends at Namur and more importantly, that he had served in the Dutch Navy.

We are going with you, I thought: after all, the Dutch discovered the new world, even if they did polish their boats, and The Man did like our boat, if not us.

"Yet!" When we came to the canal's T-junction again, Colin and I had intended to turn back a short way – the way we had come to moor at Eindhoven for the night. My husband, unaware that I had met The Man, made to wave goodbye and turn right. But I ran back to the wheelhouse.

"Keep going. Keep going!" I yelled.

"Why?"

"Because we are going with that boat: he was in the Dutch navy."

"Have they said we can travel with them?"

"No, but they will."

We moored that night with our unwitting guides at the side of a very quiet canal where the biggest enemy was the nettles, which we attacked with relieved gusto.

The next morning, we decided to come clean to our neighbours and tell them we were going to accompany them to Namur. I could sense their reluctance, but they were too kind to say no, as my desperation was very apparent and I was equally determined. For our part, we resolved to be of as little a problem as possible, and from this unpromising start a mutually rewarding friendship was begun. (I learned later that Peter and Gemma were meeting friends on a certain date, so time for them was limited. But as we travelled along and our new companions realised we were more than happy to fit in with their schedule, they relaxed and our friendship began.)

Looking back, the time we spent with Peter and Gemma on the canal to Maastricht seems long. In truth it was only three days before we were back in big-boat country; but during those three days Colin and I totally relaxed and enjoyed boating at its best. The weather was hot. Peter was the captain and knew all the best places to stop. Gemma and I got along very well, and I can only describe the journey as idyllic.

On the fourth day we turned onto the main Julianakanaal, another of Europe's main boat highways to Maastricht. I had always associated the city with John Major and the kerfuffle over the country becoming more politically united with Europe. The river was getting larger and there were many big boats thrumming along to and from the largest inland port in the world, Antwerp. Peter led the way, and judging by the way his white baseball cap sat on his head, he seemed unconcerned by the violent swaying of his boat. Peter guided us into a yachthaven off the main canal and we moored up for the night.

Our friends had no sooner moored up than they were off sightseeing, so we decided to follow them on our bikes. Maastricht, I am told, is a lovely city, but all my terrors had come back and I can remember hardly anything of our visit. We watched about twenty boats pass the wall alongside which we had been recommended to moor by many "experts" – thank goodness we were in a safe harbour, as we could feel the boats were moving long into the night.

I think many British citizens find it difficult to imagine the importance of water transport in Europe. Economically, Europe appears to be so connected that it is unimaginable that it should ever break up into independent states again; if only the British could forget that we are an island fortress we could have a bright new future. There is always a danger of war for us. But not so in Europe: they have had enough of that game.

Frightened as I was of the big boats, I also saw that their size, presence and internationalism on the canals and rivers represented the future, not the past.

The next morning we set off for Liège, going up in the largest lock in Europe with no drama. Our dramas were not over, however; here is an extract from a letter home:

As we approached Liège the river was very wide and choppy. Moored to the left was a large tanker from which diesel could be bought. We hung about rocking in the swell while Peter filled up, and as he moved off we made towards the boat to tie up to receive our diesel. The choppy water made steering alongside difficult and we went in pointy-bit first. Finally I managed to grab a hanging rope, with the idea of pulling the boat up the side of the diesel boat until we got to the dispensing position. We had only moved a few yards when a small pleasure boat nipped in, threw a rope over the bollards and shouted to the men on the big boat. The cheek of it! Both Colin and I yelled, "Hey, we are first!" but we had enough work to do stopping ourselves turning round in the swell. The small boat's occupants pretended not to have heard us, but the tanker crew had, and refused to serve them.

For what seemed ages it was stalemate as a big boat passed, increasing the chop on the water.

"Come on, let's go!" I yelled at the Captain.

"Not bloody likely, they've pushed in," was the angry reply as Colin revved the engine and we smashed into the side of the tanker.

"Colin, for god's sake, all this bloody stress to save fourpence. Go! Go!"

"No!" the stubborn captain shouted back, "they've pushed in. I'm not having it."

I could not believe the Captain could be so bloody stupid.

Then something happened which, had I not seen it, I would not have believed. The woman on the pleasure boat was holding a small dog aloft; the tanker crew appeared to be not only refusing to fill them with diesel but they would not accept the dog either. Finally, in desperation, the woman jumped up and chucked the dog onto the tanker, where it scampered off. I think being boarded by a soppy-looking pooch was the last straw for the tanker crew: they gave in and began filling the pleasure boat with diesel, handing the dog back to the woman when it had finished its business. I too gave up: there is no point in arguing with Colin when saving money is involved. I consoled myself by imagining my revenge, for I was sure we were going to roll over and sink. I was also sure that at my funeral my kids would point out to everyone that I had died as a result of their dad trying to save fourpence.

When we moored up that night, Peter said to Colin, "I was watching your boat, it sails like a swan. It is designed to roll, and it will always roll back. It really is a beautiful little ship".

I will try and remember that comment.

The trouble with rivers is that there are not many mooring places, and we are right in the middle of the Dutch holiday season. The

Dutch do not follow the British custom of "breasting up"; in fact, for the most part they actively discourage it. The following day Peter was well in front of us and as we approached the yacht moorings at Huy he picked a mooring among the beautiful Dutch boats and high-rise yachts. There was 46ft of mooring space, and we were 45ft. Peter beckoned us in, semaphoring the measurements. Suddenly almost every boat was heaving with crew armed with poles and bobbles, several of them yelling, "Go away, Englishman, we don't want you, go away." The crews were pushing our boat away with anything to hand, including their feet. This was war: there was nowhere else for us to moor for miles and it was late.

"Bugger you lot, I'm coming in," yelled an irate Colin as he revved the engine. Come in he did, just like a fighter pilot, missing all obstacles by inches. Peter caught the rope first time and we stopped dead and in position. Some wars are just worth fighting.

The Dutch boaters retreated to their BBQs in stunned silence. Let them bloody sulk, I thought. We had supper on our friends' boat, finishing off with a bottle of champagne we had been keeping for a memorable event. I think winning a war could be classified as that. Peter explained that many of his compatriots had mortgaged their houses to buy their boats and were boating on a shoestring; the bigger and more pristine the boat, the higher the status of the captain. Again I marvelled at our good luck in meeting Gemma and Peter, so relaxed about their boat and boating. They were the antithesis of their countrymen – and for that matter me and Colin.

On Friday we arrived at Namur where we had to moor in a high wind, but Peter's influence has made us much calmer, and so, despite the difficulties, there were no maritals. Peter and Gemma met up with their friends and it looked like our time together was running out; but he has brought to us to safe waters and we have *only nature to worry about from here. We were sad this period was coming to an end, but confident and excited about "proper" boating.*

As if our cup wasn't full, there was a further treat in store: a quayside car-boot. Colin was in his element. I bought a plastic tablecloth and Colin bought a replacement penknife.

I don't think I told you what happened at Robin Hood airport on our way back to the boat in Tilburg, so here is the tale. Colin's prosthesis set off the alarms as usual, and he had to be searched. The result was they found his penknife. Colin was given the choice, either to pay to send it home or have it confiscated. Colin chose to argue: "Old men all over the world have penknives. We are not bloody terrorists, you can't take it off me, how am I going to cut string? I am damn well not paying to post it home."

I told them to take it off him and the "old man" stormed off without the knife. Security shouted after him, and he responded, not by not turning round but by waving his stick and shouting, "Bugger off!"

It wasn't until we got to the boat at Tilburg that we realised he had left credit cards, money, etc. in the tray at the airport – which was presumably why security shouted him.

Once again there were frantic calls to the kids for them to rescue their parents. Peter, as usual, wanted the whys and wherefores answered before he declared he couldn't help as he was playing cricket. Sally responded positively and rescued the wallet on her way to work.

Colin now had a new knife in his pocket; once more he is a man among men – albeit an old one.

We waved goodbye to Peter and Gemma at Dinant, going through one more lock before mooring up on our own for the last time outside France. At the next lock, we bought a licence for France. Hurrah! We were on our way home. The weather was very hot, the Ardennes seeming much more attractive than when we travelled on the Meuse with Mr Bean. The extra engine power of Koopman made such a difference; I think if we had had even more engine power, our time among the big boats could have been much more comfortable. As it was, I wrote home to friends:

"It was like being on the M25 in a milk float!"

We arrived once again at the big port of Charleville-Mézières. Colin had hoped to do boaty things, but the weather was too hot, so we spent the time relaxing under a tree.

It was a largely uneventful journey towards the Seine, first through the Ardenne canal in beautiful weather and countryside. We enjoyed the freedom; in fact, there was even time for me to declare that I was getting bored. Here is an extract from another letter home:

We set off after lunch from Le Chesne to complete the remainder of a 26-lock sequence. At lock 22 we met a gang of eight girl guides thumbing a lift. The Captain decided to brighten his life by giving them one. What an excitable bunch they were, and Colin lost twenty years as he showed them how to drive the boat. The girls' spoken English was brilliant, but their concept of personal safety on a boat left much to be desired, and I averted my eyes when they decided Koopman was the Titanic and one of the girls leant over the point, her arms outstretched, her friends holding her ankles while singing the theme song from the film. It was when we got to their destination that they told us they were supposed to be on a very long hike and had just managed to cover most of it on the boat. I thought, well done, girls! I have always had an aversion to exercise; I just hope they managed to keep Titanic a secret – although they were so excited, I doubted it.

Further along the route we spent a convivial evening with some Americans who, it seems, had broken many boating rules with seeming unconcern. Coming downstream on the Seine before you turn into the Arsenal Port, there is a red light, and the Americans had sailed through it on red. The river police had caught up with them just as they were about to enter the Port. The captain had genuinely not seen the red light, but once aboard the boat the police espied the radio.

"Where is your licence?" they asked the captain.

The captain pretended not to understand and kept saying he was American, but they indicated that if he did not produce the licence they would remove the radio, which was part of the fixtures of the boat and so its removal would bring down the ceiling of the wheelhouse. The captain, with a burst of understanding, said he hadn't got a licence but would get one.

"You have to go on a course," they said.

"I will. I will go immediately." He grovelled, fearful of his wheelhouse being wrecked. "It's a two-year waiting list," they said.

Finally, after intense and heated negotiation, it was agreed that the radio would be disabled, and the captain was allowed to go on his way. As the police sped away, the captain ran up the Stars and Stripes on his mast – a lucky man that he was not caught. Quaffing his wine, I reflected how police and Americans are the same the world over.

After such a run of fine weather a storm was inevitable, I suppose; but it couldn't have happened at a worse moment. We were between moorings on the Marne when the heavens opened and visibility went down to almost zero. We were going to have to moor on the pontoon reserved for users of the lock. I jumped off the boat with the rope in hand when Colin suddenly "took off".

"What the hell are you doing, you stupid bugger?" I yelled as the rope shot from my hands into the water. Colin was away and couldn't hear me over the roar of the weir; he seemed to be turning round. I was furious: what a stupid time to start positioning the boat correctly. We always argue about him "faffing about" positioning the boat, and here he was in pouring rain and wind, at a tiny mooring, with no warning, positioning the boat. Jumping up and down in panic, I hurled further abuse at him. He had completed his "turn" and was now presumably yelling at me not to drop the next rope he threw at me. Fortunately I caught it and quickly tied the boat up at the front; getting the back in, though, took all the combined strength of me and the engine. It wasn't until we were finally secured that I learned that a surge of rainwater into the river had whipped the boat around like a cork, and the reason Colin had not paid attention to my shouts was that he was too busy trying to control the boat. Well, I had said I was getting bored.

After we had settled down for tea, another boater in distress breasted up to us, which, what with the flow of the river, put a lot of strain on the pontoon and ropes. The constant squeaking – and my imagination – kept me awake most of the night.

We have finally arrived at Poincy and I am getting more and more nervous about going on the Seine with the big boats. Poincy is a small boat club and we were only just small enough for the moorings. The Capitainerie spoke good English and lived on site with his wife and daughter in a small cabin on stilts. A slight and amusing worry was negotiating our way to the toilets past a mad and aggressive goose. I should be enjoying myself; it is a perfect

*place for us . . . maybe we could winter here and then I wouldn't
have to go on the Seine.*

The fear of the big boats on the Seine finally overcame me
and I ended up crying and shaking, saying no way could I sail on that
river. I hadn't eaten since we arrived at Poincy; I had been taken to
the doctor's by the *Capitainerie* with a urinary infection because I
was not drinking enough, so I was on antibiotics as well. Colin was
so concerned for my mental health that, unbeknown to me, he rang
Jo Parfitt. I was surprised when Jo rang one afternoon and said he
fancied a trip up the Seine and would be with us the following
week. A wave of relief washed over me; I could not believe it – how
did he know? After the phone call Colin confessed he had rung Jo,
telling him, "Our lass has lost the plot through fear," and that Jo
had responded by saying he would see what he could do.

The afternoon phone call was to confirm he could do
something. Sometimes Colin does get it right: I slept properly that
night.

In the morning, I started the spring cleaning – it's
something I always do when a decision has been made and I am
getting ready for what's coming; and on the Saturday we set off for
our rendezvous with Jo at Nogent-sur-Marne. Jo texted to say Jeff
was bringing him down on the Tuesday afternoon. I could not
believe it: Jo was coming at the promised hour. Colin *must* have
been concerned for my mental stability.

Jo arrived at 2.30 p.m., and after a cup of tea we set off for
the locks and the tunnel before turning onto the Seine. Jo was so
tactful with both of us: he treated Colin as Captain, and between
them they managed our journey through the tunnel and locks. We
entered the Seine at half past four, Jo advising Colin to tuck himself

in behind the big boats as soon as their prow passed the lock gates. That advice directly contradicted what I had allowed Colin to do: I had always wanted the big boat tied up before we set off for the lock. Jo told me, "they have a living to earn, Yvonne, they don't want you hanging about. They expect you to follow close behind."

As we sailed along, Jo told me what the big boats' captains expected of us; he also gave Colin tips on controlling the boat while waiting for lock lights – "dancing about", I always called it. But Jo's instructions were more precise: "Put the boat in tick-over," he said.

At 7.30p.m. it was time to call it a day. We had intended to moor on the lock wall at Évry, something I would NEVER have allowed, believing it to be illegal. In the event, there were too many protrusions that could pierce the boat, and we had to lash ourselves to some pontoons, Jo leaping about as he plaited the ropes. I was reassured: even Jo could get it wrong at times, and it was no big deal. We had our supper and were in bed quite early, as Jo was falling asleep as we chatted. We had an early start next morning, stopping at Melun for lunch and reaching a mooring in front of the first lock on the River Yonne at 7.30 p.m. Colin and I did not expect any big boats on the Yonne and, although the locks on the river have peculiar steep sloping sides, we felt we could manage.

Jo left us after we had fed him. We felt so grateful for his help. The next morning, the first thing we noticed was that it was very misty; the second was a huge sand-barge nosing its way past us to get into the lock. We had no time to think; we quickly cast off and followed him in, and he indicated we were to tie up to him. For once I was not only comfortable with a big boat, I was glad to tie up to it. We were treated by its captain as though we were experienced and reliable boaters. I basked in the euphoria of my new-found skills: thanks to Jo, I was able to trust the captain of

Koopman Welvaren V.

After a steady sail we arrived at the yard and moored up. We were due to go on our fiftieth anniversary trip across Canada by train in the middle of September, so we decided to come back and winterize the boat in October. I had booked the trip the year before, and it wasn't until a friend remarked that she thought we were married in 1958 that I realised I had been a bit previous and booked the trip too early. As I said before, we have never been very good with dates – hence the six children.

The idea of the holiday was that we would not be in control of any new experiences, and I must say the trip lived up to expectations. I loved Canada. The group who accompanied us were also great company, and added to our enjoyment, although I know Colin missed being in charge of his own destiny – and of course talking to the engine.

We had two weeks back in England before we returned to France. I could stand it no longer: we had grieved for Bob long enough; it was time to find a new four-legged companion. We paid two visits to the local RSPCA where we were made to feel very unwelcome, being lectured for wanting a replacement dog by some officious woman. I know they have to be careful, but this was ridiculous, and Colin vowed never to darken their doorstep again. We had promised our young grandson a visit to the dogs' home, but Colin refused to go, and a tantrum from our son, the lad's dad, threatened.

I found the web page for the Springer Spaniel Rescue near Barnsley and, as a compromise, I suggested we pay them a visit with young Tom, who was eight at the time. We were greeted at the rescue by a jolly and very enthusiastic manager called Alison, who clearly loved the dogs to bits. Slowly, we walked past the kennels. I looked straight into the yellow eyes of the ugliest dog I have ever seen. This dog had the head, ears and short fur of a terrier atop the stocky body of a spaniel; he also had the colouring of a liver spaniel. We had always had bitches; I regarded them as gentler and more amenable to discipline.

None of the available dogs were what we were looking for, and Tom was disappointed. Alison said to me, "You are not supposed to bring young children round, but Tom has been so well behaved, would he like to take a dog for a walk?"

Of course Tom would like to, so Alison went to the kennels and came back with the ugly dog. My heart sank.

Immediately, the dog jumped up and fussed Tom. And that was it: I fell love with it (and later found that Colin had the same reaction). Did Alison know we would fall for this dog, or was it just fate? I will never know.

The dog's name was Mole. Mole had come into the rescue from the RSPCA, who had named him Benjamin. Because of his condition, they had thought he was a spaniel and had passed him on to the Spaniel Rescue, who had rechristened him Mole.

Mole had been found with another pup, buried alive, and at the time of rescue had no fur. His breed had been identified by his skin markings. Alison had spent hours medicating him, and consequently Mole was very socialised and gentle. Thus it was that Mr Benjamin Mole joined our family and became known as Moley; and now he is known throughout France, Belgium and Yorkshire for his gentleness, playfulness, obedience and sociability. Wherever we go in no time at all Moley has a circle of friends that he will visit regularly while we are there. When Colin is asked what breed he is, Colin will say he's a cross between a spaniel, a terrier and a meerkat, because of Moley's habit of sitting back on his bottom and surveying the petting opportunities.

Although it was the following year before Jo met Moley, he and Jeff quickly fell under his spell, as he followed them from boat to boat, jumping fearlessly from one to the other. And I often feel quite panicky when I think how we nearly missed getting him. Moley is not a replacement for Bob, he's a different character; the only similarity is that we love/loved them unreservedly and have been and still are rewarded in spades by their devotion to us.

We were due to return to France for a week to winterize the boat, leaving Moley with Alison at the kennels; but after five days we came back. I couldn't bear to be parted from our new companion.

Chapter 3

Calmer waters for Koopman Welvaren V

While we were at home for the winter, we contacted Jo and enrolled on the Rally of the Amis du Nivernais, which was to be held the following year at Châtilon-en-Bazois. After our arrival and before we could be craned into the water, Colin was taken ill with vertigo; he had insisted on doing all the driving from Calais, and this was the result of sitting, hardly moving his head for hours. The symptoms are very distressing: everything around the Captain was on the move except him, the result being that every time he tried to move, he vomited.

Jo was having a barbeque in the yard, and when Colin did not join in and I only stayed for a short time, he came to have a look at the patient. Colin has had the condition several times, and I know from past experience that in three days he will have recovered. But I don't think Jo was as confident as I was, and in the morning he came to say he really thought Colin should go to hospital. I agreed (although privately I thought they would never get him off the boat, as we were at least six foot up in the air).

But the King had other ideas, and soon we heard the sound of the fork-lift truck. On the forks was a pallet, and on the pallet was a plastic chair. Colin groaned as he moved gingerly from the wheelhouse step to the pallet. Still groaning and protesting, he sat in the chair. The Captain's protests were cut short as the truck moved and he vomited violently into the hastily passed bucket.

In France, *pompiers* combine fire and ambulance duties, and Colin was moved into their vehicle. With blue lights flashing, patient and crew were off to the hospital in Joigny. I followed behind in the car, leaving Moley with Jo. When I got to the hospital, there was Colin sitting up in bed, wired up to monitoring machines, but looking as healthy as a pink pig. I could tell from the read-outs that the Captain was as healthy as he looked; in fact he had the pulse-rhythm of a young man, not a seventy-year-old.

The vertigo disappeared and Colin was never sick again.

The doctors insisted on keeping their patient in overnight, and we were able to see that the much vaunted French health service was in fact no better than ours: they too are struggling to cope with all the old people needing their services. While "in recovery", Colin was able to tell me how he had looked up from the bucket to see three women spectators running in panic to hide round the back of the workshop.

We had a planning meeting and decided to stay for the winter in Roanne, as I fancied visiting the boat when the weather was awful in the UK, and escaping the hype of the British run-up to Christmas. On the way to book the mooring, we visited the Millau

Bridge, a true wonder of French engineering, although I was more impressed with the journey into the gorge and the aerial flights from the houses across the river to the road. The road had emulated the erosion of the gorge, leaving the houses perched high above.

In recovered health and full of high hopes of a peaceful boating year, the boat was craned into the Yonne, but as soon as we sailed to the other side of the river we realised we were sinking: water was coming in at an alarming rate. Immediately we had left the bank, Jo had started shifting boats in preparation for other work, so we were unable to get back to the quayside for some while. When, eventually, we managed to moor up some hours later, we were aware that the bilge pump was just managing to keep pace with the leak.

Jo came aboard and surveyed the situation. "Well, I can't do anything for a while, but I'll lend you an automatic pump," he said, seemingly unconcerned.

The honeymoon was over. I thought: he doesn't bloody care if we sink overnight – but we had no alternative but to wait. I set the alarm clock for every two hours to wake us during the night; but then I realised the automatic bit of the pump *did* work after the alarm woke us in the early hours of the morning, just before the clock alarm. We watched the pump doing its job, and were able to relax.

Eventually, we were lifted out to begin the waiting game again. As before, the yard had people waiting their turn for repairs, and the whole cycle – of men lurking around corners to catch Jo in order to casually enquire where they were on the "list" – began again.

My friend and *bête noire* was Roger, whose boat was undergoing major surgery, mainly by himself in Jo's paint shed. We got on well with Roger and his wife Margaret; they had two dogs: a big greyhound and a dainty whippet. We would share a cup of tea and an occasional night out at the restaurant in the port. Another couple also having major work done were Christine and Bob. They had two lively black labradors, and their boat also required major surgery. Moley's best friend was Malcolm, a spaniel that belonged to Jadel and Jack, two Americans on a huge boat. Jack was a kindly man, but he was, in my opinion, having lots cosmetic work done in intermittent spurts between the essential surgery being done on the other boats. Jack was expecting guests from the US, and because the man was in the early stages of Alzheimer's, Jack wanted to give him one last fantastic holiday.

I am ashamed to say I was less than sympathetic: the chances were the man would not remember the holiday by next year, so why rush? At the time, I felt guilty about my feelings; but I had been nursing Alzheimer patients for a few years and had lost faith in memories: only now mattered to me, and we were sinking.

Jadel was a lovely lady who by chance had stumbled on a way to make a living in France. She bought "stuff" from *vide greniers*, and stored it in a barn near Roanne. The "stuff" was then exported as features for American homes and gardens. An example of one of her finds was a metal milk-bottle carrier, bought for fifty centimes and expected to realise ten dollars as a wine holder.

All the dogs were friends and we took it in turns to take the "pack" to a low spot on the riverbank for a swim. I became very emotional when I saw Moley so happy; all the people and dogs in the yard were enamoured of him, he was so sparky, funny and gentle. We humans were all friends too – until there was movement on the list, when we all tried to jockey to come first, even if it meant doing our friends out of an opportunity, and circuits of the yard reached epic proportions. Bob and Christine got so fed up with hanging about they actually built Jo a portable workshop, the bits of which had been lying around the yard for ages. I was truly in awe of Christine: not only was she a fantastic steel erector and painter, but she cooked and baked in any spare time she had. The establishment of an upmarket Gladys's Café was unsettling for me; what was even worse, she gathered the cherries off the only tree in the yard and made jam. Jo was chuffed to bits, but our position on the list looked decidedly dodgy.

We decided to go home for a while, since I knew I was winding myself up again: if the fact that we were sinking failed to move us up the list, there was no hope of us *ever* getting out of the yard. But Colin convinced me that, as Jo had suggested the rally, he would make sure we were ready in time – his time, not ours.

It was while we were at home that we were visited by an elderly gentleman who had built his own yacht-style boat and was intending to take it though the canals of France to Marseilles. We plied him with tea and cakes and regaled him with stories of life in Jo's yard. Neither Colin nor I believed our guest would ever get to France, but old men should be allowed their dreams; and we had warmed to him: he really was a gentleman in his manners. Alistair was our visitor's name; but more about Alistair later.

The Captain was right: on our return to the yard, Koopman was on the bank with two small patches on his bottom, and our rivals had departed. Even so, it was going to be a tight-run thing to get to the rally at Châtillion-en-Bazois in time. Excitedly we set off, worrying that we might not make it.

En route we met and partnered up with two other long-term travelling residents of the yard, "Big Al", an American, and his wife Dorothy. Jo had spent ages adapting his boat when we first arrived with Mr Bean, and again when we were trying to restore Koopman in the early days, so in the past our present partner had been one of my arch-enemies. Big Al was a great conversationalist, and in the very near past Roger I had become a team trying to head Big Al off from finding Jo on his yard circuits. During our two year absence from the yard, Big Al had decided to have a different, and smaller, boat built. Jo had built him a beautiful, small tug, but even though Big Al no longer had any boating problems it did not stop him doing the circuit to find Jo, just to discuss at great length the progress – or lack of it – on other people's boats. Big Al was older than us, and not a well man; but together he and Colin made a staggering effort to get to the rally in time, so much so that we arrived early and chose what we thought was the best spot.

Châtilion-en-Bazois is a large half-oblong-shaped port, widening out from the canal and set below a typical French Château, the garden of which slopes towards the port. The canal bank approach on the port side is lined with pollarded horse chestnut trees, beneath which boats can moor without facilities. At the far short end of the port are small pontoon moorings that carry electricity; they used to be used by a hire company. On the long side of the port opposite canal are linear moorings with facilities that belong to the VNF, and at the other short end there are linear moorings that belong to the town. Behind the town moorings on the same side as the Château is a grassy patch, and then a cliff that makes the port a wind-free sun-trap. At each end of the port on the canal side is a lock.

As we came out of the lock, we saw that, on the far side, the hire-boat pontoon moorings had a lot of spaces the ideal size for the tug and us. We moored next to a very old small cruiser and were met by, I later found out, the volunteer captain. We paid for a fortnight. We then had a busy time putting up flags and helping other boaters to moor. Here is the story I sent home of the rally:

We are moored next to a scruffy old cruiser-type boat. His Small Ship's number is 2000-something, so the owner has been in France a long time. Chris, the owner of the boat, is the volunteer Capitainerie, collecting money on behalf of the hire company to whom the moorings belong. In colouring, Chris is very fair, and consequently, because of the sun, is also very red of face; he also likes a glass of wine or two. He is taking his position very seriously and getting very annoyed that people are mooring up willy-nilly and not paying their dues. He is particularly annoyed that he has some keys for Jo, who has not arrived. I told him Jo has a business to run and would not be here until the last minute. In the meantime Jo has rung me and invited himself for supper, so I said to Chris I would give him the keys. But Chris was having none of it: he wanted to give Jo the keys himself. Later that evening I heard loud shouting and swearing from Chris: Jo was on a big boat visiting friends and Chris was on the bank, the worse for wine, haranguing Jo for being late. As part of his tirade, Chris misquoted what I had said, resulting in Jo shouting, "I don't care what she said, I am running this rally." I was hurt, but there was no point in arguing: Chris was drunk and Jo was very angry, mainly, I think, at being sworn at: even when angry I have never heard Jo swear.

A while later, Jo came for his supper and we tried to have a good evening, but it kept being interrupted by Anglo Saxon expletives directed at "that Jo Parfitt", as well as bumps and crashes from the boat next door. I thought it funny but dared not laugh because Jo was clearly on a short fuse.

According to the programme, the first item was a "Picnic in Fleury Fields with our Friends of the Canal". The event was even more attractive than its title in my opinion; it was magical, and set the tone for the rest of the rally. Fleury lock and weir is a local scenic and picnic spot. The dam is made up of removable wooden slates, the water of the river Nivernais pouring over the weir being controlled by the number of slats removed. By stemming the flow of the river, water could be fed into the canal as and when needed. Above the weir there was an old narrow bridge carrying the road. Spread below the bridge was a large river pool surrounded by the grassy banks of Fleury Field. In an old riverside building which the workmen had used in times past, there was a little souvenir shop. The Amis du Canal de Nivernais had erected a large marquee where, on long tables, there was picnic food: French cheeses and quiches accompanied by fantastic crunchy salad, baguettes and jugs of wine. We sat in the sun on picnic benches with our baguettes and wine, listening to the water and the accordion music – a truly French occasion.

On our return, we found the port had really filled up and almost every boat was dressed overall. Moley, after his initial excitement at our return, disappeared to do his rounds and to make sure Chris, his new friend, had not forgotten him, while we pottered around the boat. In retrospect, perhaps we should have not been so laid back about Moley disappearing for long stretches, but here there seemed no danger and he was enjoying life so much. We did not realise what a risk we were taking in allowing the wandering behaviour to become a habit; but more of that later.

We had asked Chris if he would have Moley for the day while we went on a bus trip organised by the Committee. Chris was more than willing, and Moley jumped aboard his boat. The first stop on the trip was a tool museum, followed by a visit to a pottery and, in the searing heat of midday, a viewing of a Château garden. The old couple who stood under a tree and welcomed us to their home wore straw hats, and the garden was their life's work; but in their enthusiasm they failed to think about the comfort of their visitors as they expounded on the attractions of the garden. I was supporting a very opinionated and vociferous English lady who was even older than the couple and was not backward in coming forward loudly with her opinions, both on the couple themselves and on what she could see of the garden.

I think we were all beginning to feel in danger of expiring as the story went on.   Colin nudged me and said he could see woodpecker holes in the tree above the old couples' heads; and trying to lighten up the lecture, he interrupted the flow and asked after the woodpecker. Oh, he had touched a raw nerve!

"They are pests. A few have got in the wood of the turrets and caused a lot of damage, that is why we have those," the countess responded, pointing to two small cannon. "When we hear the tap, tap, tap of the woodpecker, we go out and fire the cannon – we always have them primed and at the ready."

"Well done, young man!" came a loud voice from one side of me, "at last something interesting! Now, let's get on and have a look round."

I told the old lady off for being rude, as I would my grandchildren; but secretly I thought she had voiced all our thoughts.

The garden was lovely, but it was obvious that the old couple were gradually losing the battle with nature: unlike the natural look of English gardens, French gardens are very formal, with much clipping, pollarding and fanning of trees – a lot of work.

After the tour of the garden, there was another lecture from the chatelaine. This time she had exhibits and frantically waved her pointing stick in the air, narrowly avoiding decapitating me and resulting in more comments from my elderly companion along the lines of telling the countess to keep her stick to herself.

Our final port of call was a farm where we had a very interesting talk on the farm and farming methods, followed by some exquisite homemade nibbles and wine. The farmer's wife told us how lonely life could be, living in villages that had been depopulated by the mechanisation of farming. The lady was a very enthusiastic member of a knitting circle, something I would have associated with the elderly, not a dynamic, forward-looking farmer's wife. But the knitting circle was a good way of maintaining a social life for the women.

The following day saw the start of the rally proper, with events and stalls enough to entertain everyone. We gave the evening dance a miss; as in England the music was far too loud for us. On Sunday there was water jousting, a demonstration of raft building and log floating, but the weather was on the turn and the heavens opened for the firework display. Chris was having a bit of a do himself with his mate, and did not relish having to turn out in the sheeting rain to go up twenty-four steps into the old lock house to turn the electricity back on. After three or four trips followed by rewards of bottles of wine, Chris began falling up the stairs, becoming more and more belligerent as he fell. Jo seemed to have decided to stay in the background, and on the fourth occasion he sent his most mild-mannered lieutenant to pacify the irate Capitainerie.

The lieutenant was used to belligerence, being the son of my elderly friend, and through the eye of the storm we could see figures running about and gesticulating at the other end of the port. We learned the story the next morning. Some of the electricity sockets were not responding to being switched on by Chris, and a Belgian boater, panic-stricken about his powerless freezer, had pulled the plug out of another socket that was being used by an English boater. The Englishman had come out to see why his lights had gone out, and pulled the Belgian plug out and replaced his. This had happened several times to different boaters. Eventually, the

English boaters had stood guard in the pouring rain and a big commotion had resulted. Several dogs, frightened no doubt by the thunder and lightning, had joined in the melee, until the Belgian retreated, powerless, to his boat. When we left the next morning, we had no opportunity to say goodbye to Chris, as he was still fast asleep at lunch time; so, along with about twenty other boaters, we left a bottle of wine on the roof of his boat to warm for him in the sun.

We had decided to travel to Cercy-la-Tour by "leapfrogging" the boat and car. After mooring up for the night, we would get on the bikes and go back to the start for the car. This was because the transport links across country were difficult and time-consuming. We reached Cercy, and were pleased when the very pleasant lock-lady said she would look after the boat while we went to visit our friend Moira and her family, who live in the Vendee for a week each year. The day before we were due to set off, Moley had been bathed twice after rolling in a dead fish. After the baths, we spent the day making the boat secure for while we were away. I called to Moley at tea time and got no response. Colin and I were not worried: he would be somewhere. He was fascinated by a circus on the opposite side of the river, particularly the grazing camels – that was where he would be.

We searched the circus area and campsite where some young lads looked decidedly shifty. I began to have uneasy feelings, as there was no sign of Moley and he usually came back after the first call. We spoke to the lock-lady, who had made a fuss of Moley, but she had not seen him either. Now we were all on high alert. Colin got in the car and went back to the previous lock, the lady in the house next to the mooring got on her bike and went into the town, which meant her cycling up a very steep hill, and I stayed and worried near the boat.

We all met up again half an hour later at the lock house. No luck: Moley had disappeared. The lock-lady phoned the animal rescue, which she told me, with signs, was run by an eccentric English countess. The lock-lady handed me her mobile, and an aristocratic, bossy, plummy voice demanded to know if Moley's name and our phone number was on his collar.

"No it's not, but he has been chipped," I sheepishly replied.

"That's no good!" she exclaimed, "he's gone for good. It's a tragedy. A tragedy, you are a careless woman. He will be found by the French – and they eat dogs, you know."

The lock-lady gave me a sympathetic squeeze of the arm as I hopelessly gave the countess a description and asked her to phone the lock-lady. Colin and I got in the car for another look around the town. Everywhere we called – vets, shop, the tourist office and the police station – all knew about Moley; and there were notices on the lamp-posts asking people to look out for a "marron et blanc spaniel". The lock-lady had been busy, but to no avail. On our return, Colin said he would go and look around the previous lock again, but I had given up and started putting Moley's things away. I tried to convince myself he had gone willingly to someone who wanted him and would look after him, but I knew that inevitably a wave of grief would hit me. I heard the noise of a car, and thinking it was Colin I looked up to see a battered old Peugeot coming towards the boat. In the front of the car were an elderly Frenchman and a younger one, and I saw when they drew closer that both had a roll-up dangling from their lips. When they spoke I could see that their teeth were nicotine-stained. Behind the drivers were four children crowded together, and in the middle . . . was Moley, sitting up straight and looking as alert as a meerkat. I can't remember who said what to whom, I was so overwhelmed; I just understood Moley had been found by the children three kilometres away on a football field. The children had arrived home with him just as the father was listening to an appeal for his return on local radio. At the time I believed the story, but now I think Moley had been playing with the children and they had decided to take him home. I also suspected that the boys on the campsite knew what had happened.

Anyway, he was back. I looked in my purse to give the family a reward. I had ten euros or a fifty, and I gave the men fifty with profuse thanks. Their faces showed their shock, but I was determined they would take the reward.

When Colin returned, he too was overjoyed at Moley's safe return – until he found out I had given the rescuers fifty euros.

"That's it. No meals out for a month, or until we have recovered the money," he declared.

Shortly after the departure of the rescuers, a blonde lady in a very short bouffant skirt and incredibly high heels arrived to interview us for local radio, and as I was feeling defensive about the fifty euros, I let Colin do the talking. Later that night there was a knock on the boat door; the lady with the bike from the house opposite stood there.

"I have made these for you because your heart was broken," she said, her left hand over her heart and her right hand passing me a present. The lady had crocheted two pan holders in white with Moley on one and Cercy-la-Tour and the date on the other, written in blue. I was very touched – I think it's the English aristocracy who eat dogs, probably raw.

The next morning, before leaving, we took some flowers for the lady at the lock. I have made a resolution to make sure Moley's name and our phone number are on his collar and to check more regularly where he is.

We arrived in Nevers just in time to watch the preparations for a triathlon, which are very popular in France. Candidates run, cycle and swim, and I have always been appalled that the candidates swim in ports around boats with toilets that flush into the water. So-called marine toilets are just becoming illegal in France, and more and more pump-out machines are being installed; but at the time we were in Nevers they were still very much used.

After a few days we decided to cruise for a stretch before returning to the port to leave the boat while we came home. As we came to a beautiful little port we saw a boat we recognised; it was our fellow ex-residents in Jo's yard, Jack and Jadel, and their dog Malcolm. Moley's body was hardly big enough to contain his excitement as he and Malcolm chased frantically about. Colin was also excited: Jadel offered to take him in her car to several *Vide Greniers*, and if he could have wagged a tail, he would have.

A couple of days later it was time to go home for a holiday. It had been good to have time with friends when we did not have the spectre of the "list" hanging over the relationship. I even changed my mind about the cosmetic surgery Jo had done on their boat: the result was spectacular.

On our return from England, we were excited about the proposed cruise to Roanne for our winter mooring. Colin set about doing his pre-cruise jobs and noticed water seeping into the bottom of the boat. There were discussions with our neighbours: while the boat leaked we would be unable to sell it, but Colin was reluctant to plug the hole with fast-setting concrete as barge owners had done in the past. He had to have the boat repaired properly, and I could see where this line of reasoning was going: back to the yard and the King's court. A phone call to Jo confirmed my expectations: we would turn round and head back to Migennes and probably spend another year in the kingdom. But I was no longer a rookie: I would be prepared this time.

We had a lovely cruise back; it was just a shame we were concerned about the possible outcome of the consultation with Jo. But we really were in a bind: we had to spend the money on repairs, otherwise the boat was unsaleable. Here is an extract from a letter I sent home on the return journey:

Here we are back at Châtilion-en-Bazois – so different from when we were here before. It is very quiet. Chris, the voluntary captain, had been taken ill and has been in hospital, and although he is on the road to recovery he is not coming out of his boat much. We have been here for a week, mooring up at the other end of the port below the Château; between us and Chris, an old friend, Frank, is moored. Our friend is a tall elderly grey-haired but very fit gentleman; he lives on his own because he has chosen his pipe over his lady-friend. Frank is another person who insists he is a loner, but as soon as he sees the table coming out to signal the opening of Gladys's Café he is on his way to partake of coffee and cakes. He also firmly believes you can live well on fourteen euros a week. A chicken bought cheap at the end of the market, for Frank, makes six meals. He has breast of chicken for two days, wings and leg for two days, and finally soup for two days. Voilà! Meanwhile, he is adding variety to his diet by eating at Gladys's Café. I don't object: he is good company for Colin, who enjoys some man talk with him.

This was followed by a letter I wrote after a brief visit from our son Iain:

The weather is beginning to change and many boaters are now in home ports. One particularly cold day when we had lit the fire, we met up with Roger and Margaret, who were moored on the opposite bank. They too were heading back to their winter moorings. We travelled with them for a few days until we had to hurry off to rendezvous with our son.

Roger's boat still persists in attempting to go sideways into locks; his modifications have made it steer straighter, but he still has to use the "bow thruster" a lot to avoid hitting lock gates and walls. I think seeing our "swan" glide through awkward turns finally convinced him to have another go at making the boat more responsive to the wishes of the captain; he told us he had booked the boat shed in the yard for May next year. Once again we were to be rival customers in the kingdom of King Jo, and I was pleased and put out at the same time.

The final week of our journey has been a nightmare. Iain and his son Tom were due to visit for a week, and we chose a pick up spot with a train station at each end of a cruise, only to be told they were coming for five days and then a long weekend. We had to dash from starting and stopping points, begging lock-keepers to work beyond their hours. But finally, the boat was in position to meet Iain and Tom. To complete the preparations, we needed the car, which we had left at Nevers. With a day to spare, we cycled two miles to a railway stop to catch a train to Paris, leaving the bikes locked to a post. Once in Paris, we had to catch a train to come all the way back down another line to Nevers, where we took a taxi back to the car. The journey to pick up the car took seven hours; the journey home to the boat took an hour and a half.

A further complication was, now that we were in a position to catch a train, was there a train to catch? The strike was supposed to be for one day, but, typical of the French, the organisation of the train strike was totally chaotic. No one seemed to know the start or end date. Some trains were running, but no one at the station could tell us which, or even when. In the time we had allowed for water filling and shopping, we decided the best course was to go to Paris in the car in the hope of meeting Iain at the airport. Iain was not answering our texts, and we were not sure he was receiving them, so we set off totally "in the dark".

I was proud of us two geriatrics: we got to Charles de Gaulle with no problems, just in time to meet our visitors. I wonder how we looked to our son as he emerged from the arrivals gate. We had had no time to get dressed up, and both of us were tired; we had been travelling up and down the country for days, followed by a hair-raising ride in the rain on the Paris périphérique. We all got back to the boat after midnight, to be told that the long weekend was now two days because of Iain's work. More planning required, as even fewer trains were now running.

Exhausted as I was, I could not sleep that night because I was so cold. The next morning, I found out that the back door had been left open and there had been the first real frost of the year. We had run out of water, and I asked Iain to help his dad fill up, as we were moored several boats out from the bank. Colin went to get the water pipe out, but Iain seemed disinclined to follow. Eventually, he told me that on the plane from England there had been loads of rugby fans heading for the world cup game against France.

"It would be awful to come to France and miss the opportunity to see the game here," he told me. "Do you think dad would take us back to Paris?"

I could not believe it, and answered for Colin. "No he bloody wouldn't." I suddenly felt tired and disheartened, and thought to myself that if I could get them back to Paris it would be for the best. I could not cope with Iain and his son's hyperactivity; we could not compete with a world cup, travelling on an old boat at four miles an hour on an almost empty canal.

"I tell you what, we will go in the car to Migennes and see

what trains are running," I told him.

"Can we go now?"

"Tom has had no breakfast. We have to fetch croissants," I replied.

"Oh we will get something on the train," Iain said.

I explained to a bemused Colin why we were going to the railway station as we set off. There was a train in for Paris, the only one expected that day. Iain and Tom went for the train and I ran for the tickets, pushing them into Iain's hands as the doors closed and they sped off.

On the way back to the boat we consoled ourselves with coffee and croissants in a café. We were totally disorientated, our visitors had had no supper because it was so late, and no breakfast because they wanted to be away.

I heard nothing from our departed visitors until late in the evening. I texted Iain to ask where they were and had they found a bed for the night. The only reply I got, obviously from Tom, was, "Good job I was wearing my lucky underpants." I felt disinclined to find out more. The generation gap seemed very wide, and it was a relief to get back to life on the canal. We have returned to the yard and made plans for the repairs to be started next year. Meanwhile I am looking forward to resuming life at home. I think I am ready for a change. I feel I am losing touch with the kids and events at home. Our kids are getting to the stage where their children are grown up; they want to do their own thing, as we did, and while the grandkids are interested in the boat, it's only if we are not there. I miss my garden, which I plant up every spring and then never see; I even have a yearning for an allotment.

Oh dear – is this just end-of-season blues, or the real thing?

There had been gossip on the towpath, that Jo had a new

girlfriend. All we knew was that they had been involved in organising the rally together, and that she was Dutch.

As we pulled the boat in to Jo's, we noticed a very slim, curly-haired, natural-looking young lady sitting on the quay with her legs swinging over the bank. "I bet that's the new girlfriend," I said to the Captain – and indeed she was.

Door, as she is known, helped us tie up, and her English as we chatted was impeccable. I decided there and then that I liked her, but wondered how she would adjust to life in a boatyard. Door assured me she had been around boats all her life and knew what to expect.

Love was certainly in the air in the yard. Jeff, who was Jo's' right-hand man, and Sally, who did all sorts of odd jobs, had in our absence become an item in a big way. Jeff was French, and understood more English than he spoke. He was a bit of a hippy; his skin was very dark and usually covered in oil and muck, his teeth when he laughed, which was often, were very white and strong. His long black ponytail was his pride, and was always shiny and well cared for; Colin frequently grumbled that the shower was left full of long black hairs and rubbish after Jeff had used it.

Jo grumbled about the disgusting state of the small caravan he had provided Jeff with to live in, and Jeff just laughed, and did nothing to clean up. Another trait of his was that he left all the tools about, driving Jo to distraction; but Jeff was a hard worker, and jumped from boat to boat like a gazelle. Watching Jo and Jeff move boats about, like pieces of a puzzle, was fascinating. Jo had the know-how, and Jeff had the agility.

Sally, Jeff's girlfriend, was English, and had in the past been an occupational therapist in the NHS. She had short, wild, curly hair and was naturally very slim. One of Sally's joys was to roll herself an extremely thin roll-up, sit with her long legs crossed, and give herself up to the delights of tobacco. She was so in love, she did not seem to mind the hovel, and whenever she could, she and Jeff ate the meal she cooked outside the van. In the morning they would emerge from the hovel, beaming. Jeff and Sally certainly had the *Aaah* factor; with Jo and Door, the demands of the work in the yard made things more complicated.

We winterised the boat after Jo had lifted us out, and returned home. That winter, every penny I earned went into the Jo Fund, to pay for the plating that we knew we would have to do the following year.

Our first visitor when we got home was our new friend and pupil, Alistair. We were, in the Yorkshire phrase, gob-smacked to learn that Alistair's boat was now moored at Douai in France. How had he done it? Here is the amazing story.

Alistair is not a well man; he is in his late 70s and has had heart surgery. The building of the boat had taken him years, but it wasn't until his wife died that he felt able to contemplate realising his ambition to sail to Marseille via the canals of France. After our chat earlier in the year, Alistair once more advertised for a pilot to take him and the boat from Hull down the coast and across the channel to Calais. In a very short time he found a candidate, but the man had only the following weekend to spare. Alistair dashed – as far as you *can* dash on the canals – to be at Hull, ready for the pilot; he was in so much hurry that he had no time to drop the keel – important, if you want to keep your boat steady.

The pilot arrived and they all left Hull with the tide – the Humber estuary has a big tidal range, is wide and very bleak. Once out at sea, the boat began rolling in a heavy swell, and the mast and tool box were swept over the side. Finally, Alistair fell and injured himself, so a decision was made to put into Folkestone, where the pilot left, as his time had run out.

I wondered if the boat was up to crossing the channel, and asked Alistair if he was scared when the boat rolled.

"No," he said, "I built the boat; I know every weld and screw in her. I was not afraid."

I looked at this slight old man with a different eye: was he brave or mad?

The story did not get any better. At Folkestone, Alistair was hospitalised for a few days, and then, on his return, he began looking around for another pilot. Somehow, the coastguards became involved and had a trial steer of the boat, running it into the harbour wall and causing non-fatal damage. Eventually two coastguards volunteered to get Alistair and his boat to Calais.

I do not know how our friend managed to get himself out of Calais through the locks and on to the Grand Gabarit; he has no understanding of the language, no experience of canals, and had never met anything like the big cargo boats that infest the northern canals of Europe. I am amazed and sympathetic, but my sympathy is wasted, as Alistair seems unconcerned about the danger I perceive him to be in. All that a lone sailor wants is a companion to share the long boring stretches with, and he is now looking out for such a person.

Alistair had come a fair way on the main canal when tragedy struck.

"It's difficult to hold my boat in the wind," he said, "and I had decided to stop for the night in front of the lock. I was on the bank with the rope, and the next thing I know I am on the floor and the lock-man is slapping my face."

It seems Alistair collapsed. The VNF towed the boat to a spot off the main canal while Alistair was carted off to hospital by the *pompiers*.

I said, "if the boat is difficult to hold in the wind, how do you manage when you have to wait for the red light to change at the lock?"

"What red light? I have never seen a red light."

Colin and I gave each other a knowing look; I could imagine the French *éclusiers* radioing each other, saying, "Get this mad Englishman out of our patch or we will be up to our necks in paperwork!"

While in hospital, Alistair had visitors – the VNF – who said he shouldn't be on the main canals on his own. The police also came and said the same thing; and so did the French Social Services, who booked him on the bus home.

"I don't suppose you are going back," commented Colin.

"Oh yes I am!" our intrepid sailor replied. "I am going to find winter moorings after I have seen the heart specialists, and then I am going to head for Jo's."

Oh dear, what had we done?

I gave Alistair a list of useful French phrases and advised that going to Jo's was a mistake, since his boat was too high for the Bourgogne and Nivernais bridges. But he was not to be deterred.

"Oh, I need some repairs, so I will see you in Jo's yard," he insisted.

It is the way Alistair talks to me sometimes that makes me feel maternal towards him somehow.

I consoled myself with the thought that he was not well enough to go back.

I was wrong again. But more of that later.

Chapter 4

An unexpectedly long journey

We set off for the gathering at Clamecy. We were very proud of ourselves: the boat was watertight, and the paint pristine in white and Cambridge blue. Inside, the new kitchen sparkled, and due to the dog kennel on top of the bedroom in the prow, we were now able to stand upright to get undressed for bed. The atmosphere in the bedroom was cooler and less coffin-like.

We were obviously not taking the shortest route to Brugge, but we did not expect our journey to be as long as it was. From the Nivernais, we travelled along the centre in the company of a couple we met in the Arsenal in Paris who actually lived less than four miles from us in England. We travelled with Brian and Liz for six enjoyable weeks. Brian was an ex-fisherman, and familiar with old boats, and I was glad of his advice to Colin, who, with nothing to worry about had begun imagining oil leaks and funny noises. The engine of Koopman was old and it did leak a bit of oil, but nothing to worry about, Brian the senior Fred Dibnah, assured Fred Dibnah junior.

After travelling along the Canal du Centre, Brian and Liz turned back and we turned north up the Saône à la Marne, a very lovely rural canal. We were now a team, and enjoyed the days boating along the canal. We stopped under the apple trees at Viéville, where Moley was adopted by a couple from Paris who used their boat as a holiday home; Moley insisted on sitting on a chair at their table, perching upright and once again looking all for the world like the meerkat which the Captain claims was his father. We had canal-side moorings in a lovely port with all facilities, and we were happy to sit a few days under the apple trees. Soon, though, a couple loading their car to go home informed us that the locks further up were closed for repairs after being damaged by a *péniche*; the expected time for the repairs to be completed was fourteen days, which usually meant three weeks.

We decided to go home, and the lovely French couple gave us a lift to the nearest train station twenty kilometres away so we could pick up the car. Instead of going to Zeebrugge via the *autoroutes*, I elected to go on the red roads through Belgium, passing through the battle areas around northern France and near Mons, where my father was in the First World War. Just before the border there was a road diversion due to a bridge repair; the French seem to use minimal diversion signs and we found ourselves travelling miles on the green roads in the dark and the pouring rain, passing ghostly cemeteries. It was awful, like the end of the world. I thought of all those poor souls, including my dad, in the trenches in rain and cold similar to this, and marvelled that more of them hadn't said, "bugger it, I would rather be shot at dawn than live in this!" I cannot bear the cold; I remember a childhood where my parents had to ration coal and my brother and I used to pull the frozen net curtains off the windows – the result of another bloody conflict.

On our return, we were finally able to get underway. We hoped to turn left and head up north past Reims onto the Canal de Saint-Quentin, and finally sail along the river Lys; but we hit another problem, one I was quite happy to work round. Five locks on the approach to Reims were to be closed for repairs. We were made aware of this information by one of the organised boaters we had met, who also informed us that we were so late in the year that we had run into the "*chômages* season". The *chômages* were planned lock closures for repairs and maintenance; the VNF put out information on the internet at the beginning of the season to warn boaters of the closures, the winter and just after the French summer holidays in August being the prime time. After eight years' boating in France, we had never heard of *chômages*, but we were soon to learn that closures were like dominoes: once one fell, the others followed suit in quick succession.

I was quite happy to go the long way into Belgium because it meant we would avoid many of the big-boat routes; so we elected to turn right and head for the Meuse. It wasn't until we had spent a day on the Canal de la Marne that we learned from a chap who looked like Jesus that the VNF were closing the last five locks on the Meuse in just under three weeks. For the following two weeks, then, we travelled twelve hours a day when we were using the zapper, and we persuaded the lock-keepers to push us through fast where the locks were manned. One lovely lady even worked her colleague's shift in the pouring rain to speed us along. I pored over the maps and estimated new times every night; it was touch and go whether we would get out of France before the closures.

We did it with three days to spare, and had a celebratory meal at a Vietnamese restaurant in Dinant. We had made it into Belgium. Next, we had to travel down the Canal de la Sambre, a canal that is thought so horrendous that pleasure boaters avoid it at all costs. We had met a Dutchman in Namur who gave us a written guide to all the hazards and mooring points, and in thick fog we set off. We had not travelled far when we had to moor up on an old quay in a factory yard because we could not see anything beyond the prow of our boat. In the gloom, a silent shape came up behind us and stopped. Somehow, this was reassuring: it was obvious, I thought, that we were showing up on their radar. From then on, despite big boats passing from in front or behind, I enjoyed the trip – through what I imagine is the reclamation centre of Europe. Huge piles of scrap metal and wood awaited treatment. The canal travelled through the heart of factories; the smoke and flames from furnaces were clearly visible from the wheelhouse. We found sailing through the smoky orange inferno absolutely fascinating; had my early travels on the bus to Sheffield been a preparation for this moment?

The only moorings in this part of the canal were at a lock, so that is where we spent the night. Further on, the only moorings we saw were on the other side of the canal. As we crossed the canal to moor, the wind started pushing us round; two attempts, and we were still dancing – and now a big boat was approaching. I kept my panic down as I screamed at the Captain to forget it. With relief we made it back to the right side.

We thought we were okay to proceed now, and it was almost too late when I noticed we had passed a red light. Another mad scramble, and I tied us to a ring in the wall to await the changing light. We were becoming better boaters, yes; I was still panicking, but I was able to do something about our situation. I felt quite proud of myself.

Our next big test, which we passed with flying colours, was the boat-lift at Strépy-Thieu near Mons. Even the Captain was nervous, navigating our way onto the lift. We had been to the opening of the lift and as spectators we had been amazed at the size of the works; from the top of the amphitheatre we could just see little midgets running around. The size of the landscaping and structure was awesome. I quote some extracts from Wikipedia:

History

The boat-lift was designed during the Canal du Centre's modernisation programme in order to replace a system of two locks and four 16-metre lifts dating from 1888 to 1919. The canal itself began operations in 1879 and its locks and lifts were able to accommodate vessels of up 300 tonnes. By the 1960s, this was no longer adequate for the new European standard of 1,350 tonnes for barge traffic, and a replacement was sought.

Construction of the lift commenced in 1982 and was not completed until 2002 at an estimated cost of 160 million euros (then 6.4 billion BEF), but once operational permitted river traffic of up to the new 1,350 tonne standard to pass between the waterways of the Meuse and Scheldt rivers. The lift increased river traffic from 256kT in 2001 to 2,295kT in 2006.

The four older lifts, now bypassed on the original line of the Canal du Centre to the south, are still in use, but are limited to recreational traffic only. Their architectural and historical value has led them to be placed on the UNESCO World Heritage list.

We were to use the lift Strépy-Thieu in 2008 and 2009, and during that time the old lifts were undergoing renovations. For those readers interested in how the lift works, I will quote again directly from Wikipedia (with very little understanding of the contents!).

Design

The structure at Strépy-Thieu consists of two independent counterweighted caissons which travel vertically between the upstream and downstream sections. Due to Archimedes' Principle, the caissons weigh the same whether they are laden with a boat or simply contain water. In practice, variations in the water level mean that the mass of each caisson varies between 7200 and 8400 tonnes. The caissons have useful dimensions of 112m by 12m and a water depth of between 3.35m and 4.15m. Each caisson is supported by 112 suspension cables (for counterbalance) and 32 control cables (for lifting/lowering), each of 85mm diameter. The mass of the counterbalance was to keep the tension in each of the control cables below 100kN at all times. The suspension cables pass over idler pulleys with a diameter of 4.8m. Four electric motors power *eight winches per caisson via speed-reduction gear boxes and the 73.15-metre lift is completed in seven minutes. The structure is massively reinforced to provide rigidity against torsional forces during operation and has a mass of approximately 200,000 tonnes. The vertically moving watertight gates are designed to withstand 5km/h impact from a 2000-tonne vessel.*

In my opinion as a lay person, the approach and departure earthworks were far more impressive than the lift itself, and travelling in the caisson resembled riding in a lift. All the same, we were pleased with ourselves as we negotiated our entrance via the radio, our calls being responded to by the lights changing to green almost at once. We were elated.

We cruised to Kortrigk to spend a few days with the friends we first met in Brugge, Dave and Lil. Dave and Lil were moored on the canal near a high wall; they had heard that permanent moorings were to be put in place and wanted to be the first in the queue. To me it seemed a lonely place, but Lil is a great walker so she is able to get out and about in the town. We decided we wanted the comforts of civilisation, and moored in the port, which is situated on a tributary of the river Lys, a very pretty mooring.

We were having a leisurely morning breakfast when a near disaster struck. Colin faffs around with his tablets in the morning, counting and sorting them out, and it annoys me no end. I believe we are persuaded to take too many unnecessary tablets. For months after his accident, Colin took antibiotics in the hospital; it did not prevent him from losing his leg. I have worked in old people's homes and no one questions why so many old people die six weeks after having the flu jab. Colin has one risk factor for heart disease, has never had flu, and is expected to take all these heart-disease prevention tablets *and* have a flu injection every year. The only year Colin defied my advice and had a flu jab, he got a chest infection and was ill, when, apart from diabetes and vertigo, he is never normally ill. He has lost various bits of his body but he is healthy.

Well, this morning, having sorted his tablets out and left them on the settee, Colin was having a shave when Moley decided to hoover up the tablets. They were gone in a flash. Colin would not believe it, and wasted ten minutes looking for the tablets while my anxiety went through the roof. I ranted on about bloody doctors, and threatened that if anything happened to Moley I would ram the lot down his throat.

I rang the vet help line in the UK at a £1 a minute. The conversation was as follows:

Me "I am ringing from Belgium: my dog has swallowed a load of my husband's tablets and I don't know what to do."

Phone "Oh, you must see a vet."

Me "We are in Belgium on a boat. I do not speak the language and have no car; it is Sunday. I do not know where there is a vet on call."

Phone "You must see a vet."

[I go through the sentence again.]

Phone "Well, I will get in touch with the poisons unit. What has he taken?"

Me "1000mcg of Metformin, 75mg of Aspirin."

Phone "I'll get back to you."

For the next thirty minutes I worried while Moley sat waiting expectantly for breakfast and his walk. Colin finished his shave and got himself a bowl of Cornflakes. Neither of them seemed to appreciate the horrible death that awaited Moley. After the thirty minutes I rang Vet Help in the UK again, and got another operator, who immediately suggested I administer salt water via a syringe to make Moley sick. Why had I not thought of that?

Hastily, we washed out the diesel additive-measuring syringe, grabbed Moley, and pumped the salt water down his throat. As soon as we had finished, he rushed out and vomited all along the pontoon. We followed, inspecting the vomit. I was relieved to see that among the froth of vomit there looked to be the remains of the tablets; and sense was coming back into my head: I knew what to do next. If Moley had ingested Metformin, his blood sugar would go low, so for breakfast instead of dog food he had a feast of cornflakes and sugar. I swear Moley's yellow eyes sparkled with pleasure: he loves man-food and tablets, it seems.

Now, with our boating experience, the rest of the journey to Brugge was uneventful. The two frightening episodes that followed could have happened to anyone and both happened on the swift-flowing tidal Scheldt. The first incident was when Moley just walked off the boat. Colin missed him almost immediately and shouted me. I had learned with Bob that I must remain calm, and I thought of that as I made eye contact with the little figure swimming frantically in the water. Colin's swimming lessons in our local marina were paying off: Moley's eyes pleaded with me as I speared his harness with the boat hook. My first lift resulted in a large splash as the hook slipped out of the ring; I was not going to be strong enough to lift the wet dog. Colin put the boat into tick-over as I threaded the hook again, and together we managed to lift the sodden little body. As soon as Moley landed on deck, all fear was gone, and he was jumping up and down wagging his tail – it was the Captain and I who were shaking.

318

The second episode was very dangerous, and all due to a water skier. Water skiers are generally oblivious of their effect on other river-users and, in my opinion, should be confined to the sea. The wash from a water skier is worse than that of a big boat and, as they travel backward and forward, the water becomes horrendously churned and fragile river banks are washed into the water. It was late in the evening when we were mooring up on a pontoon; it had taken some while to find a mooring on the river. I jumped off the boat with the rope and threaded it through a cleat when a skier passed us; the wash jostled the boat all over the place, trapping the slack rope between the prow and the pontoon. The water was pushing the boat forward and sideways, the foreshortened rope was preventing the boat going where it was being pushed, and the result was that the boat began to tilt to at least thirty degrees.

As the rope was threaded through the cleat, I could not slacken it off, and the boat was in danger of tipping right over as the stupid skier headed back on another run. Frantic signalling from me to stop had no effect as he shot past, intent on keeping upright. Colin had to run out and axe the rope, hanging on for dear life to the tilted gangway. Oh, how I hate water skiers.

The pontoon, we found out later, belonged to a water skier who came later to ask us to move on, as the pontoon was his private moorings. With difficulty I controlled my temper and offered him ten euros for the night. He accepted with alacrity and departed. Never have I resented paying a mooring fee so much, and I did wonder if he was the stupid skier who nearly killed us. I content myself with the thought that what goes around comes around – I hope.

We continued cruising the next day, arriving a couple of days later two bridges away from our winter moorings in the Coupure in Brugge. We missed the opening times of the bridges by a few minutes, Colin did not want to spend the money mooring in the Brugge yacht club, and in high winds we therefore attempted to moor alongside what turned out to be a very busy road. As soon as the boat slowed down Moley made a leap for freedom and ran across the road, but it was clear to me that where we were was no place to stop, as we had nowhere to exercise Moley. Unfortunately, the Captain was obsessed with saving money and mooring where the wind was blowing. We had a huge marital after I had caught Moley and eventually managed to get the boat in at the yacht club. We were both upset, as we had travelled all that way and were so near to our destination. We had spoilt the triumph of our arrival. We arrived in the Coupure the next day, left the boat and headed for home.

We returned to Brugge for Christmas and the coldest winter there for years. We lay in bed at night, all cosy, listening to the ice scraping up and down the boat with the wash from the big boats out on the main waterway. Christmas in Brugge was magic: no hype, no false, commercially-led goodwill. We put a Christmas tree on the prow, walked around the city on Christmas Day buying our bread, and having a coffee in a bar. Then we had a simple but tasty Christmas dinner, just the two of us on the boat.

Between Christmas and New Year, Peter and his girlfriend came and stayed opposite us in a hotel and, together with another visitor, our Dutch saviour, Peter, we had a fantastic meal in a port restaurant. It was a shame that, in the time since we had last seen Peter, Gemma had died. The news made Colin review what he and I wanted to do in the future: we must not waste our time: it was finite.

On New Year's Eve we went to our Lancashire friends Lenny and his wife Suzy's, for "lobby" and wine. Lenny knew Fred Dibnah; he talks just like him and has a similar interest in old engines; he promised Colin he would give our engine "a coat of looking at".

It was about this time that the residents in the port became concerned about the water supply. The pipes from the main tap had frozen, and it looked like it would be some time before the water would get through. Eddie the *Capitainerie* put a call though to the local fire brigade who came one morning and filled up several boats from their tender. I found the whole morning very enjoyable: uniforms do make men more interesting! It was also very satisfying to feel that once again we were safe.

By the time it was time to go home, Colin and Lenny were satisfied that the engine was as good as it could be, given its age – after all it had done over 1,000 kilometres that year with no problems, except for requiring a new fan belt. I thought, what's the big deal about a bit of oil leakage? All old ladies leak! But we knew the time had come for us to get serious about selling Koopman. Colin needs a challenge, and he fancied building a steamboat; and I wanted to be at home for the summers.

Before we left Brugge for home, I spoke to Jo's partner, Door, and we agreed that she would put the boat on the internet in several languages and handle any enquiries. We hoped but did not know whether the next cruising season would be our last; in the meantime we intended to enjoy ourselves, now that my fear had somewhat abated, and we enrolled as part of a small convoy heading to Strépy-Thieu for the rally to celebrate the grand reopening of the old locks that the huge boat-lift had replaced.

Chapter 5

An Indian summer for Koopman Welvaren V

In early 2009, the credit crunch was deepening and houses were leaping towards negative equity. The pound had fallen to very nearly equal value to the euro and as a result English boats on the Continent were not selling. Many people had funded the boating life by letting their houses in the UK and living off the income, but with the exchange rate so low, everyone was cutting their expenditure, and the whereabouts of "free moorings" was something you kept a deadly secret known only to you and your friends. Colin and I decided to drastically reduce the price of the boat and meanwhile enjoy the benefit of having a boat ready to weather the next hundred years.

We returned to Brugge in April, looking forward to being part of the convoy heading to the Rally at Strépy-Thieu to celebrate the opening of the four now-repaired boat-lifts. The lifts had been replaced by the giant new single lift described in a previous chapter. The hydraulic lifts were built in the late half of the 19th century and are an illustration of the highest quality of engineering of that era. Of the eight hydraulic boat-lifts built at that time, only the four at Strépy on the Belgian Canal du Centre remain in their original state. They were designated a World Heritage feature in 1998.

Although I was not so panicked by the big boats any more, I was still not comfortable in their vicinity, so we decided to take a slower route via the river Dender. Slower being the operative word . . . it was really very shallow, so required constant vigilance to stop us running aground. One lock-keeper on the Dender spoke very good English and it emerged that he was a previous world champion town crier. As our town has a town crier, the father of a nurse I once knew, I mentioned him. The Belgian was not impressed; he said it was true, our crier was once a world champion, and I was informed that he had a huge appetite but left the feasts in time to avoid clearing up. A typical South Yorkshire male, the son was not known for his work-rate.

I thought: like father like son, and said so. We all had a good laugh, and as a reward we were shown a free place to moor.

There were no facilities, but it was a magical spot, very near the centre of a very attractive town. (Of course I shall not say where!) The boat battery was giving us some problems, and the Captain went on his bike to get a new one. The Captain regards himself as a haulage and leverage expert, so with much grumbling and doubting from me we managed to lift the old battery up six foot via a pulley, lever it into the bike trolley, and pull and push the heavy load up the bank to the road before fixing it to the bike.

I was very relieved when a young man from the garage followed Colin back and, quick as a flash, lifted and installed the new battery. It took him ten minutes, where we had taken an hour and a half over the same task. The young man could not believe that two geriatrics had managed to get the old battery out, so we were quite proud of ourselves in the event.

Later that day, as I walked the dog along the old canal that surrounded the town, I received a frantic phone call from our son. In the credit crunch he had lost his job as a hydraulics engineer in the plastics industry, and, desperate to keep a roof over his children's heads, he had decided to go back to his original work as an electrician. Before he could do that, he had had to take a course and an exam to test his fitness to do the work. The test is called an "edition" and on this course there were young men who hadn't been born when Iain had taken his last test. Iain was in a right old flap, and I reassured him, at the rate of a pound a minute for thirty minutes. Worried sick, I returned to the boat to await what Iain had convinced me would be inevitable failure. Three days later, fearing the worst, I rang him, only to be told he had passed the test with flying colours two days earlier. Ah, the joys of parenthood . . .

After a few days we arrived at the rally; below are extracts of letters I sent home after we had left:

When we arrived at the rally we were impressed by the level of organisation: there were over three hundred boats of all sorts in a relatively small yacht-club port, but the harbour master and his assistants had got it all planned. Boats were pushed and shoved, mooring three abreast, wires were plaited and draped all over, and lo! we were all in. The group from Brugge were all moored together. Moley soon learned how to travel from boat to boat, getting a fuss and biscuit at all his ports of call. He would stand on his head, bum in the air, tail windmilling, whenever he saw our friend Lenny. The Belgians have a strict rule that dogs must be on leads at all times, but as long as Moley was on a lead for walks they seemed to bend the rules for him.

An American couple had a blue-eyed collie-cross which they had rescued. Dexter was very fearful and unfriendly, but in no time he and Moley were firm friends and spent hours chasing up and down the grass to an ever-growing audience. It was not long before Dexter was also doing the biscuit run along with Moley. Once again, the only time we saw our dog was when we called him for his tea.

We really enjoyed the rally; it was friendly and well organised; the only problem was that the lift repairs had not been completed and no one seemed to know when they would be. But we celebrated all the same and the Belgian beer flowed.

And here is the second Letter from just after the event:

The Captain and I have had a discussion as to where to sail to next and have decided on Nancy. As you know, it has been an ambition of ours to visit the city again, this time with "me teeth in". I hope we will find that Alice is still there. We then intend travel up the Sarre and look for a winter mooring.

We have had a busy but uneventful sail down the Meuse, DIY-man has kept himself busy painting and varnishing – I am afraid to stand still. We are now at Charleville Mézières, our visit coinciding with the Festival of the Fish. The French are mad keen fishermen. Moley, as usual, was soon involved and has spent the day sitting with the stall-holders.

Just now, one of the exhibitors came across with a huge freshwater fish on an oval foil dish. The fish is dressed with lashings of mayonnaise, tomatoes and salad, the whole lot lukewarm and oily from being in the sun. The fish is really beautiful, with a pinky-white boneless meat; but I am afraid Colin and I are not fish lovers. I tried a bit on a small plate: the warm, oily earthy taste made me gip.

We moved everything in the fridge to get our gift in, and then sat in the evening sun worrying about how we were going to eat it. The Captain and I are war babies and regard wasting food as a "war crime", especially when you have been given it. I can remember when my dad got all excited because he was going to have a boiled egg on Sunday morning, only to be disappointed when the egg was bad. At four years old, I dusted Mrs Smith's house all morning just to get an egg out of the chicken coop.

We had to eat our fish gift, but the old stomach was rebelling at the thought of the impending assault. We could not go to bed knowing the bloody fish was waiting in the fridge, and as darkness approached I dashed into the boat, re-murdered the fish, and wrapped it in newspaper. We shut a disgusted Moley in the boat, biked into town and deposited the body in a rubbish bin.

After the evidence had been disposed of, we had to assuage our guilt by consuming a bottle of wine in a café in the main square. The treatment worked and we slept like logs. Colin's snoring failed to irritate me: for once, I felt I deserved the punishment.

Third letter:

We are continuing our journey onto the Canal de l'Est (Branche Nord), through the First World War battle sites. Verdun was too crowded with leisure boats hogging the free moorings for us to get anywhere near them. I get so angry with live-aboards: the town provides the moorings for tourists who will spend money in the town, not free loaders. It is so different to 1916, when the port would have been busy with boats unloading war materials; mind you, it is only different to a degree, I think: it's all exploitation of the local workers by the rich.

We moored on a pontoon on our own a mile away, and DIY-man converted an old chair we had acquired into a high chair for me to sit on in the wheelhouse as we cruised. Colin needed the legs welding, and he visited a small factory across the towpath who not only welded the legs put painted them as well. Once again the work was done "gratuit". Colin insisted on giving something for the workers' coffee – I get sick of "Little Englanders" slagging off the

French for being bolshie when in reality the English, Dutch and Germans take advantage of their innate good manners and generosity.

A few days later, we were nearing the junction to turn left onto the Canal de la Marne when we heard the locks towards Nancy were closed for at least ten days and a boat jam was building up. Moorings were at a premium. At the time we were at Saint-Michel, mooring in an inaccessible spot, when we saw that someone had moved off. We made a mad dash to get into their spot before anyone else did and as we were jumping about in triumph a big leisure boat drew alongside and asked us to move and then moor alongside them.

All my possessiveness rose in my throat as I began to refuse, and was on the point of telling them to "bugger off" when I spotted a wheelchair.

We moved.

The Captain has not got a mollycoddling bone in his body. I remember him towing a cricket sightscreen behind the car with a madly excited lad with cerebral palsy. The wheelchair had been tied behind the sightscreen, and round and round the cricket field the trio careered, the lad's arms flying all over the place, a mile-wide grin on his face. Balloons attached to the chair handles were flying high, straining to be free as the air. At the time I was surprised at how much the lad's mother was enjoying her son's adventure, not appearing worried about the possible consequences. But she was right, there were none, and I suspect the lad has never forgotten his escapade.

Now, and in no time at all, Colin had this young lad of a similar age off the boat racing around with Moley in our trolley being towed behind the electric bike, doing mad spins and hairpins. It was obvious to me that the lad was going to get too excited – but then I had cautious parents.

All seemed to have ended happily when, as we were having our tea in the boat, we heard a mighty splash, followed by a scream.

We dashed outside; the young lad's brother was shouting and pointing to the water. "The wheelchair's gone in the water!" he was yelling.

For a few moments everyone's heart stopped: the user of the chair was nowhere to be seen. Then a little head popped round a corner grinning from ear to ear.

What a relief! The story the giggling head gave as explanation was that he had got himself out of the chair and had given it a push. In the lad's excitement, he had pushed the chair right off the boat. The explanation was followed by slightly hysterical laughter from the adults, and then, on my part, by a drawing of limits to the excitement with the captain.

We did not fancy staying moored up for an indeterminate number of days followed by a canal jam, so we decided to turn right and head for Paris, looking for winter moorings en route. We found the perfect place to leave the boat for a couple of months: Ligny-en-Barrois, a large port with a campsite alongside. The port also had a very obliging *Capitainerie* who spoke very good English. As we were just leaving the boat and not using any services, we were to be allowed to moor *gratuit*. The local tourist office agreed to store the bikes, so we returned home. I was tired of being on our own; there were hardly any boats about, and with the French leaving for their holidays the area had an abandoned feel. I was desperate for family and friends to whom I could communicate without thinking of which words to use.

We returned to Ligny to find that the Mayor, probably fearing an influx of freeloaders, had decided to charge us for our stay. But the fee was reasonable and we paid without grumbling. The weather was autumnal, warm and sunny, the trees just coming into colour as we sailed out of the port. Eventually, we came into the Champagne region, just as they were getting the grape harvest in. The sun shone and the air was heavy with the smells of fermentation; we seemed to be following the end of harvest parties, a magical time.

It was early one morning when we heard from Door that someone was interested in buying the boat and would like to come the following weekend to look at it. I had had enough of cleaning and decoration, and refused to join Colin in his preparations for the sale. *Que sera sera*, I thought.

In order to meet our visitors, we moored at Chalons-en-Champagne, in the pool at front of the lock under the brightly coloured chestnut trees. Every so often, a thud would indicate that another ripe nut had fallen. The sun was shining, the water sparkled and the air still smelled of grapes when our prospective buyers arrived.

It was two hours before, with encouragement, they actually went on board to look at Koopman. The Captain and I then left them to their own devices.

After the viewing, we all sat in the chairs on the grass and enjoyed the afternoon sun. Later, our buyers treated us to a meal, and after another look round the boat they departed, promising to contact us in a few days. Three days later they rang to say that, subject to survey, they wanted to buy the boat – and guess where the nearest crane was that would lift the boat out? – Jo's.

There followed a magical but also a stressful journey back to Jo's boatyard. Magical, because the weather was perfect; we also met some good company on the moorings, and I was at ease with the big boats on the Seine. If this was to be our last cruise I was proud that I had faced my fears and that we were making the journey together without the crippling anxiety I had experienced for so long.

I had learned to have confidence in the Captain and his boat. But all the time, at the back of our minds was the thought: will the boat pass the survey? Had we been right to rely on Jo's old-fashioned thickness testing?

We spent a week on the pontoon before the boatyard, emptying Colin's stuff from the engine room in order that the surveyor could have an unobstructed view of the engine and body of the boat. Door came to visit, all excited and worried, as we were for her; this could be her first boat sale as an agent.

At the end of the week, we sailed for probably the last time into Jo's yard at Migennes. I decided that we would go away for the day to let Jo lift the boat out and the surveyor get on with the job without us hanging anxiously around biting our nails. The very first friends we made when we came to France were Satch (the Admiral) and Alison, and they were moored at Pont Royale on the Bourgogne, so we invited ourselves to spend the day with them. We had a lovely time: Alison had made a wonderful meal, especially a French-style apple tart. She and I had met in Jo's yard in the hot summer of 2003, when they were at the end of their long residence and we were about to begin ours. Later, we met up in various places along the canal system to enjoy a glass of wine or two and a natter, but the most important thing for both of us, I think, was the mobile phone. In dark and happy times we would share our experiences and feelings; we had so much in common, including strong-willed, eccentric husbands with a penchant for old boats with holes in them, and families we missed like mad when we were away. Alison and Satch were clearly sad that we might not be companions on the water in the future, but glad that for us it was the right time to move on.

At 5 p.m. I could stand it no longer, and texted Jo. The surveyor had just left. He had arrived before lunch and not spoken to Jo, just got on with going all over the boat.

And on leaving, all he had said was, "It's OK."

We had booked to go home in a week's time, and we spent the next five days wondering what to do, as we heard no word. The Captain solved his problem by painting Koopman's bottom; whatever happened, he intended to leave his ship a tidy ship. On the fifth day, I heard Door shouting, "Gladys." She was running towards us waving a champagne bottle. As she got up to us she gasped, "They are buying the boat!"

The three of us jumped up and down in excitement as Jo came up, much more restrained – he had seen it all before.

The next two days were mad, as we completed the emptying of the boat, putting all our stuff in Jo's shed for collection at a later date. Finally, and for the last time, we winterised the boat.

On the last night, we took Jo and Door out for a celebratory and thank-you meal. Our relationship with Jo had travelled a long way since our arrival in the yard with Mr Bean in 2000. In the beginning he was the patron and we were the customers, but through the vicissitudes of all our lives the relationship had changed to friendship. Despite the huge distances we had travelled from the yard, we always thought of Jo as the safety-net at the end of a phone, as well as wanting to know what was going on in his and the yard's life. For us, Migennes and the yard became our home in France. In return, I hope we were able to bring some fun and laughter into Jo's life at times of stress. We tried never to take advantage of him as some did, despite his fierce pride and sometimes bolshie attitude. And now the relationship was changing; we were moving on, and so was Jo. He now had a partner in Door, a new grandchild, and another on the way.

It was the end of an era. We had spent many months as willing and unwilling residents in Jo's yard, good times and bad times – but always interesting and life-enhancing. We did not know at the time but almost on the first anniversary of Koopman's sale Jo, having sold the yard, retired to his home in the Morvan. We wonder how the boating fraternity will cope without the gossip provided by the "complicate" Jo.

Epilogue

It was thirteen years since we had begun our odyssey, and it seemed to be all over. During the winter months of 2009 we reflected on our experiences. I had started our journey with a preconceived notion that life on the canals was all sitting on the pointy bit drinking wine and admiring the view. I did not realise until much later how frightened Colin was in those early days when his mechanical expertise was being challenged; but of course as his skills passed muster his confidence grew. For me, a control freak, the reality of dark tunnels, huge locks and even bigger ships knocked my confidence in my ability to survive. I now realise that when my husband had his accident, without paid work, not only were his physical abilities reduced but the opportunities to express his natural and learned abilities were severely affected as well. As the challenges of the boating life became ever more complex, the Captain found more opportunities to extend and express his talents. My journey was different: for years I had been a mother, nurse, team leader, and always in charge of my own destiny. On the water I had to learn to be a team player and to rely on my partner and others; by the time we sold the boat, although I had not always succeeded, I had learned to accept the need to depend on the Captain and also, at times, other people, with good grace.

We find it interesting that all our memories are related to the people we have met and not the amazing scenery of the countries we have been through. We have found that for us, family, friends and community are what life is all about; I think we were predisposed to think like this, being brought up in the South Yorkshire coalfields. There, there are very few tourists, but a powerful tradition of interdependence and comradeship (encouraged further by various misguided governments). For me and Colin, the French, German, Italian, American and of course the polyglot Dutch boaters became part of our community.

I thought, on our return, it would be inevitable that without a focus we would drift into comfortable old age and decrepitude, but after a short period of rest our minds had other ideas. The Captain began to talk steamboats. I had already enrolled him in the Steamboat Association for his birthday the previous year, but now his interest was getting serious. In February, therefore, we travelled down south to view an old sixteen-foot wooden Scottish fishing boat on a trailer. The lady who was selling it had been a young widow and had spent her summers messing about on the river Thames with her son who was now in his forties. Christine did not see the boat as it is, very rotten in parts and painted with emulsion, but as it was as it was in its heyday on the river, and she took it personally when Colin stuck his knife into the wood to test for rot.

The boat needed a lot of work to make it watertight, but it was a beautiful shape and we decided to buy it.

Colin says he has sold a dream and bought a nightmare – so nothing has changed. We are even back to having a boat in the yard, as when we started. The boat was called Dram; we will call it Arkwright's Dram, as a salute to past glories. Later, we bought a half-constructed steam boiler and engine, which will challenge DIY-man mechanically.

In the summer we went on the steamboat rally in Windermere and had a fantastic time; I think we will have a very different boating experience from now on: less distance and home comforts, but more engineering. Colin will have to up his game again. I am sure he will, and that I am destined to be the fireman.

At least it will keep me fit.

While Colin quickly found his new project, I struggled. I did the family history bit, and baked until the family begged for mercy. I retired from paid and later voluntary work. After a trip on a hired narrow boat with friends on the Chesterfield Canal, I realised I was pining for a boat — not to go on long treks, but just to enjoy the exercise, fresh air and, most of all, the company of the canal community. And finally, after much propaganda on my part, Colin has agreed to buy a boat, as long as it does not need any work (he is too busy raising steam to bother with all that again, although he does miss the social life). For the moment, then, old age and decrepitude have been put on the back burner.

Postscript

Two years after we gave up boating Jo retired to his farm and tractors only to become ill a year after. He died in 2013 and our dream of continuing with a steam boat died with him. Jo's death at a relatively young age was a great loss to the French boating community but for me and Colin he left a large hole in our lives. We miss Jo a lot: his mercurial nature, kindness, humour, humanity and above all his friendship.

Cast of Characters

The Wright Family Tree

Colin and Yvonne Wright – the parents of girl and five boys

Sally - our only daughter and most frequent visitor and *Jennifer* her daughter

Steven - our eldest son

David - our second son who visited us twice with his son Daniel

Iain - number three son who visited us several times with his wife *Julie* and children *Adam, Tom and Lucy*

Andrew - number four son. He was reason we started boating, he visited us in Henley and helped transport stuff to Migennes. Andrew and his wife *Mandy* used the boat on the Shropshire canal and when it rained every day, Mandy decided boating was not for her. Their children *Richard, Jo and Laura* visited us several times with their Aunty Sally or with Uncle Peter

Peter - our youngest son and most enthusiastic visitor

Long Term Friends

On all our journeys *Helen and George* were a constant presence. Helen, a colleague from work, visited us many times with her husband George who would take over first mate duties from me and bear with stoicism the ropes and verbal arrows thrown at him by the Captain.

Meanwhile Helen and I practised our schoolgirl French on the local shopkeepers and cooked fantastic meals from local produce. Bob the dog loved Helen to distraction, even waiting at the bus stop to catch the bus to follow her home after one visit.

Peter and Carol at Strawberry Island

Prof Peter could diagnose a problem from miles away. Peter was hyperactive, fit and very tall but was prone to falling into locks because he would take short cuts. *Carol,* his wife a very elegant lady, loved the rituals of the canal and would produce drinks and cake as soon as the sun was over the yard-arm. Without Peter our boating days would have ended on the first voyage.

George and June

We first met *George and June* on the tow path at Birmingham and they became a secure base for Colin and I but most importantly for Bob the dog. When there was a threat of a 'marital' and we were travelling with them Bob would move onto their boat. *'Slocomotion'* was blue and all her life for Bob the dog blue boats signified safety and peace. It was George who told Colin how to travel through tunnels in a straight line ie: move fast. June was not physically strong but emotionally a rock and I loved her dearly.

In Boatyard France

King Jo and his son Herbie, Jeff and Sally. Sally was the odd job woman, very hard working and merciless with a high pressure hose. Jeff, of the dark flowing hair, his job was all things mechanical but his main role was keeping the peace between Jo and Herbie.

Jo, the patron of the boatyard, loved and hated in equal measure by the canal users of France. Latterly also his girlfriend *Door* who tried and failed to bring some order to the chaos, she stuck by Jo until his death and I know he made that difficult.

Satch and Alison. Satch looked like the sailor he was. He taught Colin how to handle the bigger boat - 'use the wind ' he would say. No matter where we were Alison and I were always in touch one or other of us firmly believing the end was nigh.

John and Sue on their boat *Albert*. John had itchy feet and always wanted to be on the move. For him any time spent in port was time wasted. This was unusual for a man, because in my experience, men buy boats to tinker while women want to travel. Sue his wife was also unusual in that she liked to stay in places and get to know people. As a foursome we got on extremely well with John and I consuming large amounts of 50p a litre red wine in the shade of the trees. I have to be very careful to put a lot of water with, even quality, wine now. I was devastated when relatively quickly Sue died.

Roger and Margaret I always got on with. Margaret and I walked our dogs together but my relationship with Roger depended on where he or I was on 'the list'. Roger was a perfectionist and I resented the time Jo took on what I perceived to be unnecessary 'modifications'. Roger in his turn, whilst happy to visit Gladys 's Café, thought I was using tea and scones to influence Jo and 'the list'.

Robert was an old friend of Jo's and a fellow from Sheffield, South Yorkshire. At our first meeting we fell out over politics and Jo had to intervene. Robert was from a working class background and he loved to sing the old industrial songs of exploitation. He had moved to a stone cottage in the Cotswolds, near Prince Charles, and you can guess the rest. Despite all our differences the three of us became firm friends and he showed he had not forgotten all his industrial skills when we had to put Koopman back together again after having its bottom serviced.

Itinerary on the canals of France, Belgium and Holland

These voyages took place between 2000 and 2012. Some years we were 'at rest' or did not travel far.

On Mr Bean

1st year   Yonne, Bourgogne, Saône, Canal du Centre, Canal du Nivernais Yonne

2nd year   Canal du Rhin and Vosges mountains, Rhine, Strasbourg, Marne, Canal d l'est to Charleville , Canal de Ardennes, home on a lorry

On Koopman Welvaren V

1st year   Bourgogne, Canal du Centre, Canal du Roanne, Digoin, Roanne for the winter

2nd year   Roanne, Lateral a Loire, Canal Briare, Loing, Haute Seine, Arsenal Paris, Oisae Canal du Nord, winter mooring Arque

3rd year   Arques, Canal Saint-Quentin, Canal du Nord, Belgium, Dunquerque, Nieuwpoort, Brugge, Gent, Teneuzen, Westerschelde, Oester Schlede, Port Dintelsas, Tilburg, Eindhoven, 'S- Hertogenbosh.

Next stop the Rhine but we turned and headed for home via Kanaal Juliana, Mass, Meuse Canal des Ardennes, Aisne Marne, rescued by Jo onto the Seine, Yonne to Migennes

4th year   Yonne, Nivernais, Briare, Yonne, Migennes

5th year   Nivernais, Canal du Centre, Marne au Rhin, Canal de l'est (branche nord) Meuse to Namur, Sambre, Dendre, Gent. Brugge for a long winter stay

6th year   Brugge, Gent, Samdre, Meuse, Reims, following the Champagne Harvest along the Marne, Seine, Yonne, Migennes and then goodbye to Koopman

#0036 - 020218 - C0 - 210/148/18 - PB - DID2112176